P9-CIS-326

All About Small-Game Hunting in America

All About Small-Game Hunting in America

---

edited by Russell Tinsley

Winchester Press

Photographs, unless otherwise credited, were taken by individual authors.

Library of Congress Catalog Card Number 75-38768
ISBN: 0-87691-222-6

Library of Congress Cataloging in Publication Data
Main entry under title:

All about small-game hunting in America.

Includes index.
1. Hunting—North America. I. Tinsley, Russell.
SK40.A38 799.2'97 75-38768
ISBN 0-87691-222-6

Published by Winchester Press, 205 East 42nd Street, New York 10017

Printed in the United States of America

Contents

All About Small-Game Hunting in America

Introduction

by Russell Tinsley

HAPPINESS IS THE YELP of an excited Beagle violating the quiet of a dewy, cool autumn morning as he races pellmell through briers and undergrowth on a hot bunny track. Happiness is stealing silently through somber woods at daybreak, scrutinizing the treetops for anything unnatural which might announce the presence of a squirrel. Happiness is steadying the crosshairs of a scope sight on a distant woodchuck.

Happiness, my friend, is small-game hunting, serve it up any way you desire. And the options are many and varied. Hunt alone or with companions; use virtually any weapon you choose, from bow and arrow or primitive muzzleloader to the most sophisticated far-shooting varmint rifle; enlist the aid of a trained dog or improvise as you go along; prospect close to home or travel a long distance to pursue your favorite pastime; make the hunting as complex or as simple as you might desire.

The other day Dr. C. H. Richey, a veterinarian friend, and I were hunting cottontail rabbits. We walked, one on either side, along an overgrown fence row and flushed the bunnies into the open. When one of the diminutive critters squirted from the underbrush it offered only a brief and elusive target as it zigged and zagged through the tall grass and weeds. Often we caught just a quick glimpse of a white tail.

Once, when we paused for a breather, Dr. Richey succinctly summed up the outing by observing: "You know, a person needs a little bit of the kid left in him to enjoy this hunting."

True. Someone usually inaugurates his hunting career on small game such as rabbits or squirrels. He eventually might graduate to bigger things—deer hunting perhaps—but those earlier days afield leave a permanent imprint in his memory. And one day probably he will come back, for the joys of small-game hunting never are erased.

Or maybe he never covets "bigger things." He is content with small-game hunting, a deep-rooted satisfaction that is difficult to fault, for it is hard to improve on perfection.

Yet this isn't something we have belatedly learned. Small-game hunting is rich in history. Plentiful small-game species provided the primary subsistence for our earliest settlers. Black powder and lead balls were scarce and this made men into better marksmen, for each shot had to count. Such shooting skill proved invaluable. Pennsylvania squirrel shooters were the crack shots who embarrassed the Redcoats; Kentucky squirrel "barkers" made the Indians think twice about attacking precipitately; Western Indian fighters occasionally practiced on prairie dogs. Even many soldiers of the two major world wars attributed their shooting accuracy to lessons learned afield while small-game hunting.

Big-game species—deer, elk, moose, etc.—hog most of the fanfare and publicity, however. Elaborate records are kept of the biggest taken of each species. Much ballyhoo is made of bagging "one large enough to hang on the wall."

No such lofty quest confronts the small-game hunter. His hunting really isn't that big a deal. His quarry often can be stuffed in a coat pocket. No trophies to brag about, his sport merely is a personal fuel source for relaxation and contentment.

Yet that is the charm.

"I hunt because it is fun and I like to eat wild game," said my colleague Bruce Brady, field editor for *Outdoor Life* magazine. "And I apologize for neither."

So it should be. Even in this day of a spreading civilization which threatens habitat, small-game species are fecund and adaptable and can take considerable hunting pressure. In fact, hunting is a viable management tool and recognized as such. The various species are widespread and fairly abundant. No matter where you live you probably can find something to hunt close to home. It is sport for the budget-minded.

Availability, then, is the primary key. But it goes beyond that. This hunting is leisure sport, the challenge of search and pursuit, the skillful application of stealth and know-how, a pastime to get totally submerged in, a brief reprieve from everyday stress and worries.

A person can grope for some mystic description to bring the issue into sharper focus, yet after much mind searching it is difficult to come forth with anything more apt than just "fun."

Plain, unvarnished fun sport. Yes, happiness is small-game hunting, and to make your hunts more successful and thus happier, I am both proud and pleased to present what I feel is the finest collection of small-game hunting know-how ever put between covers of a book, contributors who are the most knowledgeable in their field, people who not only are accomplished hunters but who can write about their specialties in a most informative and entertaining manner.

Yet most important perhaps is that they are fine gentlemen and ladies who are conservationists first, hunters second. They believe in protecting this rare heritage for your grandchildren and mine to enjoy. Please, let's all do our fair share.

I

The Small-Game Outlook—Forecast for the Future

by Byron W. Dalrymple

Abundance or dearth of small-game animals is a quite different problem from that which confronts the big-game hunter. The large animal populations do not fluctuate year to year as drastically as small species may. They are much longer lived, and stability through careful scientific management allows rather accurate prediction of what hunting will be like for a number of years.

Conversely, some small-game species are cyclic. Nonetheless, small-game management, though less precise and more difficult than that for big game, can keep the general trend of population levels at least reasonably predictable. The hunter who bases his activity plans upon surveys and projected animal population expectations will always be the most successful.

As a rule, but not always, small game is hunted closer to home than big game. However, nowadays many enthusiasts of the smaller species do leave their home states to pursue small game elsewhere, or they combine hunts for small animals with those for deer or elk. In a few instances, also, summer vacationers can find pest-shooting opportunities during fishing and camping trips, if they know what to look for and have some idea of what the species population level may be.

Father and son hunt fox squirrels. These squirrels may experience a slow decline as habitat in farm country is lost.

Further, because certain animals have drastic high and low cycles, prospects can be quite accurately forecast as to when a high may be expected after a low. Thus, the hunter might put off squirrel hunting in a given region for this year because the prediction is that squirrels will be scarce. Yet he would know that most likely three seasons from the low end of the cycle there probably would be a bonanza.

What are the population trends among small-game animals? Which are expanding their ranges? What is the overall situation among small game continent-wide? What is the hunting picture for the foreseeable future? The outlook for the small-game hunter is exceedingly optimistic.

Rabbits

The cottontail hunter could not possibly wish for a brighter future for his sport. The most important fact is that cottontails can and do live almost everywhere, and do not require a vast amount of territory to serve as home to a good many of them. Although highways, urban sprawl, industry and the general crowding of civilization incessantly nibble away at wildlife habitat by hundreds of thousands of acres annually, the cottontail is able to hold its own.

The trend toward subdivision of large land tracts near cities does only minor harm to this ubiquitous animal. Even with the subdivision trend continuing, owners and friends will be able to hunt with bow or shotgun on tracts of this size for the foreseeable future. Bag limits and seasons will continue about as in the past, the limit substantial and seasons long. In some states where cottontails receive no protection, it is conceivable that at last they may be placed on the game list, with a season. But if so, the closed season is not likely to be very restrictive.

This animal is to some degree susceptible to cycles. When it becomes supremely abundant, crowding generates disease, which causes a down trend. However, these cycles are invariably local, and the animals are so prolific that it does not take long to build back again. If in your area cottontails are now low in population, you can be certain that from two to four seasons hence there will be another high. Weather can give you an assist in planning, too. A moist, green spring, but not too wet, and a continuing good summer with no drought conditions, invariably puts a bumper fresh supply of cottontails into the thickets.

On the bad news side, certain land-use trends will continue to harm the cottontail population. Soil Bank lands, vast a few years ago, now

Cottontail rabbit hunting should continue to be excellent. (Russell Tinsley photo)

have been mostly put back into production. And wherever these lands are clean-farmed right to the fences cottontail habitat is destroyed. The same thing occurs in the clearing of bottomlands, and also in tree farming areas. Mixed woodland and understory and edges that have been replaced by pine plantings, for example, are not conducive to a good cottontail crop after the trees get several feet high. If any of these practices are occurring on a large scale in your area, it will be wise to look elsewhere for cottontail hunting grounds for the future.

For those who have long been enthusiasts of the larger swamp and marsh rabbits, the future, while not entirely gloomy, certainly will not compare with the past. These animals inhabit the lowlands, the stream bottoms and the cane patches of a number of Southern states. The Carolinas, Georgia, Florida, Kentucky, Missouri, Arkansas, Oklahoma, Alabama, Mississippi, Louisiana are their major strongholds. Again, changing land use is their worst enemy. Stream courses are cleared and channelized more and more. Dams form impoundments that wipe out much habitat. Cutting of hardwoods across the South and planting of more and more soybeans further destroy living room. These highly specialized rabbits continue to be plentiful in what is left to them. But huntable populations will be more and more confined, and the general population will continue to decline.

Bow hunting might become more popular in areas of population. (Russell Tinsley photo)

A very bright spot almost entirely overlooked by small-game hunters is the fine hunting available for the tiny pigmy and brush rabbits in the West, chiefly in Oregon, California, Idaho and Nevada. This reservoir of good sport is barely dipped into. The sagebrush and grass and brushy draws where the animals live are not likely to be much changed over the next few years, especially on the vast BLM lands. As with all rabbits, there may be localized up and down cycles, but most of the time hunting will be topnotch.

The big snowshoe hare so popular in northern forests will remain abundant over most of its broad range in coming seasons. Happily, the conifer "swamps" as they're sometimes called in the Great Lakes area, and the mixed forests and the stream and lake shores so important to these big rabbits will see no drastic changes. As long as habitat remains, so will the hares. And the state and national forests and other public lands where they dwell are secure at least for the next decade.

There will unquestionably be more hunting for these big rabbits in

Lands for snowshoe rabbit hunting appear secure.

places where up to now they have had little pressure. In New England and the Great Lakes States they have always been popular, but until recently many hunters did not realize that they are also available elsewhere. Pennsylvania has a substantial and fairly stable population, and the range runs on down the mountains in the East clear to northern Georgia. In the Rockies and the Coast Ranges this hare is also present, high up, although usually not in abundance. The varying hare, or snowshoe, is highly cyclic. But from the bottom-out period, hunting predictably improves gradually to a new high in a three- to five-year period.

Jack rabbits everywhere, again except for up and down cycles, will be plentiful. The large cattle ranches of the West, and the BLM and other public lands where they range should see few changes to affect abundance. However, an upswing in coyote population which has been in progress since control by poison was drastically cut down may in spots pressure the jacks hard, for they are a staple of diet wherever the two animals occur. Jacks have been introduced spottily in some states outside their natural range, for example in the East. However, don't look for much hunting. The introductions are undoubtedly ill-advised anyway, and besides the animals seem unable to adapt to Eastern habitats.

Introduced European hares also have not done well, furnish poor hunting, and are unlikely to add anything of note to the hunting picture in coming years. Wherever they have made progress, they have become pests.

The "hot" rabbit states in terms of annual harvests will remain the same: Maine, New Hampshire, Vermont, New York, Wisconsin, Michigan for snowshoes; the Eastern, Southern and Central states for cottontails. Again, however, there is a great deal of hunting for both species that is not utilized. For example, rabbit hunting on the West Coast is not pursued with the vigor it might be; the same is true in some of the Plains States, and in Texas. In several Eastern states also there seems to be little hunter interest, although animals are plentiful. These areas, if utilized by hunters, will be capable of adding to small-game recreational opportunities during coming seasons.

Squirrels

There is not likely to be any radical change in squirrel hunting on a national scale. Overall, the forecast is for excellent hunting. However, several influences may spottily degrade hunting for both gray and fox squirrels. In some states—South Carolina has been an example for some years now—the removal of hardwoods and planting of pines has already contracted the squirrel hunter's domain. This trend will without question continue, especially across the South. It harms both varieties, but may cut into gray squirrel habitat more than that of the fox squirrel, because the gray is more abundant over larger areas.

Several aspects of forest and timber company management are not favorable to squirrel populations. Clear cutting certainly is not, nor is controlled burning as a management tool, and both are now more than ever in vogue. There may be a bright spot, however, in the new emphasis on retaining or growing wooded areas suitable for recreation near the cities. It is of course too early to tell whether or not these sites will be large enough and abundant enough to have effect, or if hunting will be allowed.

The truly important reservoirs of squirrel production—the state and national forests over the better squirrel ranges—will probably remain over coming years about as they are now. The gray squirrel will con-

Squirrel hunting will remain in good shape, but there may be some localized declines due to changing land use. (Russell Tinsley photo)

tinue to be dominant, for the gray is a forest animal. Fox squirrel populations may decline gently. This squirrel, so common and abundant in farm woodlots, is having difficulties because of habitat removal.

The same areas that now see most squirrels harvested will continue to lead. Some of the best areas for gray squirrels are New York, Virginia, West Virginia, North Carolina, Georgia, Kentucky, Tennessee, Florida, Alabama. Maine and most of the southern portions of New England states will remain fair. Squirrels in Michigan, once a topnotch state, are having "people" troubles. For a mixture of grays and fox squirrels, the hot states are certain to be Pennsylvania, Wisconsin, Ohio, Indiana, Illinois, Iowa, Missouri, Arkansas, Oklahoma, Mississippi, Louisiana.

Much squirrel hunting now passed up may see some takers in coming seasons as the need for recreational opportunity expands. All hunters have to do is seek it. There is good squirrel hunting to be ferreted out on the West Coast, and in some of the Plains States such as the Dakotas, Nebraska, Kansas, especially along stream courses. Texas, which has few squirrel hunters and numerous counties with no closed season, should see more protection and management, and a keener hunter interest.

A squirrel little known to hunters, and hunted presently only in the yellow pine forests of parts of Arizona and New Mexico, may draw more hunters looking for a different variety. It is the Abert, or tassle-eared squirrel—a big, handsome creature. It will almost certainly remain abundant in its restricted habitat where only a few hunters molest it each season.

Squirrel hunters, especially those after gray squirrels, should check with local game authorities prior to each season concerning the cycle situation. In certain areas, particularly across the South and in the Ozark forests, grays reach astonishing population highs, then suddenly all but disappear. Recently, in the Mark Twain National Forest in Missouri, a prime gray squirreling ground, they literally overran the forest. Then immense migrations, probably to locate new feeding grounds, began. These movements have been recognized since Colonial days.

The Predators

The next decade will almost certainly see unique changes in attitudes toward coyotes, bobcats, foxes, and it will definitely see additional regulations concerning hunting them. Predator populations will almost certainly continue to increase over the next several years. But there may also be a return to severe population control attempts, particularly upon coyotes, in some states or localities.

The coyote has lost no range to crowding civilization. It is extremely abundant over much of its western range, and it has expanded into areas where once it was not known. Notably in New England the coyote will continue to create a stir, and some problems, and will undoubtedly furnish at least some hunting in the East. These animals, those well established all through the Great Lakes region, and those on across the Rockies will continue to expand population as well as range, and will also be taken in sizes much larger than their Southwestern counterpart.

Hunting coyotes with greyhounds will probably disappear from the scene, chiefly because fences and trespass laws make the practice more and more difficult. Calling, a sport that has zoomed in popularity, will continue to grow. But there may be more and more restrictions. Using a light and call at night is already being nipped in the bud in some areas, because it has too often been used as an excuse by persons actually poaching deer. It is also conceivable that the so-called "protectionists" may attempt to outlaw mechanical calls, or even all predator calls. Hunters will be well advised to remain alert to these attempts, and to fight them.

With poisoning now mostly stopped, coyote numbers are high and might get even higher.

The coyote has avoided extermination by all man's ruse, so there are certain to be ample numbers for hunting. However, sheep and goat raisers especially will be pushing hard to go back to use of poisons, and science will keep trying to develop a surefire method of reducing coyote populations with chemicals that interfere with the breeding process. These influences are likely to affect hunting only locally, where coyotes have become too plentiful. Hunters who intend to take up the calling sport will have to try harder over the coming years, and become more adept and expert. The high incidence of calling is swiftly developing a coyote population harder and harder to fool.

Fox hunting for both grays and red foxes will unquestionably remain very good in coming years. For one thing, attention will continue to be centered on the coyote because it can be destructive. This takes attention from the smaller foxes, and game biologists have by now pretty

Both the gray fox, shown here, and . . .

The red fox may increase in number. (Red fox photo by Bob Gilsvik)

well won their battle over foxes versus game birds. It is doubtful that bounties will return. Almost certainly more protection will be given to foxes. Already several eastern states have them on the game list. Others in the Midwest have placed them on the list of fur bearers. Both listings give seasonal protection, and in some instances limits. This trend may well continue. All told, hunters interested in foxes, by whatever hunting method, have little to worry about. The fox population is more likely to increase than to decrease.

The bobcat outlook is also excellent. There is a definite trend toward protection for the bobcat, with a season, just as there has been recently for the mountain lion. Several states already have the bobcat on the seasonally protected list, and more are predicted to follow. Governmental policies toward predators also enhance the chances for enlarging or at least stabilizing bobcat numbers. Of course they are never plentiful in

Bobcat, here with jack rabbit kill, will get more protection and in some places become a game animal.

the sense that coyotes are. But their extreme secretiveness argues well for their future.

Opossum and Raccoon

The opossum has pulled off a remarkable feat over the years of this century, having expanded its range from its original domain in the Southern States clear north to parts of southern Ontario. It has also pushed east as far as eastern Colorado and bits of the Southwest. Introduced on the West Coast, it has steadily plodded up to the Canadian border.

This does not mean that New England or Washington 'possum hunters are going to find animals abundant in coming years. The northern areas are precarious range for the creature and it may never be able to sustain itself in more than token numbers. However, from Texas across the South and the Midsouth it can be predicted with certainty that the opossum will remain as plentiful as ever.

Raccoons will likely be even more plentiful. This animal has also spread its original range and now is found over practically all of the U.S. and southern Canada, except for the high Rockies. In numerous places, populations have skyrocketed even to nuisance proportions. The raccoon has learned to live easily on the very fringes of cities and towns, and to survive in small woodlots as well as larger expanses.

The present trend away from furs by protectionist groups, and the low price of raccoon pelts has given the population a big push. In a few states of the East and South it can be predicted that bounties may be urged for this animal because of its overabundance. Game managers are not likely to go for that, however. The opportunity will certainly be available over almost all of raccoon range, and particularly across the South, the East, New England, the Great Lakes States and the Midwest for all the raccoon hunting anyone could wish. More management may well be given to the raccoon, with attendant regulations. In some of the states with greatest abundance this may mean urging harder hunting.

Chucks, Prairie Dogs, Ground Squirrels

For woodchuck addicts, there will be a stable number of targets over the coming decade. The states in which woodchucks are most abundant are ones not likely to change land use drastically for some time. However, woodchuck hunters may find some restrictions appearing here and there. It is conceivable that as human population grows and subdivision of lands with it, rifle shooting may be outlawed in more areas than it now is. This, however, would still leave woodchucks to the bow hunters.

Marmot will continue to thrive on public lands of Western states. (Erwin Bauer photo)

But the chief trend regarding the woodchuck is more protection. In the East there has been talk in several states of elevating the animal to game status, of establishing a closed season to protect females during gestation and after the young are born. There is even some inclination toward bag limits. Pennsylvania already has a closed season from late fall through mid-June, and the precedent may well influence other Eastern states.

The rockchuck of the West will remain stable in numbers. Its rather specialized habitat is not likely to be invaded by any overwhelming number of hunters, and enthusiasts of rockchuck hunting are so few that hunting pressure has little effect on the overall population. It is doubtful that any very restrictive regulations will enter the picture.

Prairie dogs are on increase due to protection and ban on poisons. (Russell Tinsley photo)

The prairie dog future is somewhat cloudy. Poisoning so severely depleted this animal that even in Texas where early dog towns stretched for several hundred unbroken miles, a few ranchers recently began setting up small oases or refuges where the animals were left alone. The change in control policy due to government influence has already brought the dogs back in numbers in spotty areas of the West. Certainly land owners where large towns evolve will need some method of control, and it is reasonably predictable that the hunter may be urged to assist.

The numerous varieties of ground squirrels, with the great bulk of their numbers spread over the West, have never caught the attention of pest shooters to any high degree. Nor has control by poisoning or other methods done much to reduce their amazing numbers on their best ranges. For those who wish to shoot ground squirrels, there's no question whatever that especially in such states as Wyoming, Montana, Oregon and Washington and many others they will be there by millions over the long future.

Javelina

The forecast for the javelina couldn't be better. In Arizona its range, much of it on public lands, is assured of remaining unchanged for the foreseeable future, and the state gives very careful protection, with hunting on a quota and drawing system. The past reflects the future in that numbers have long remained remarkably stable. In New Mexico, although the population is modest, introduction of animals from Texas a few years ago has reestablished the animal permanently in a few southwestern counties. The game department meticulously monitors the herd and issues permits for limited numbers. It is likely that in New Mexico javelina hunting will expand over the next few years.

Texas, with the largest number of javelina, has been slowly giving this animal more attention. In most counties it is now accorded a season as a full-fledged game animal. There is a growing landowner respect for it, a tight clamp on hide hunting, which was supposed to have been outlawed—but wasn't entirely—years ago. The prediction is that Texas will within a short time require license tags for javelina just as for deer. Fee hunting for javelina, unheard of in Texas some few years ago, is now growing, and that means more and more protection for a valuable resource, and without question better hunting over coming years.

2

From Cottontails to Canecutters

by Erwin A. Bauer

FOR SEVERAL MINUTES we watched the pack of eager Beagles scour through the thick green brier patch and that proved to be more pressure than the cottontail crouched inside could stand. From the corner of one eye I saw it bounce out of the thicket—a gray-brown blur with a white tail—and then vanish over a low bluegrass knoll in the distance. No one had time even for a snap shot: the action came so suddenly. Before I could flip the safety, the four mini-hounds—Timmy and Towhead, Mamie and Myra—were baying in wild pursuit.

There are plenty of good reasons to go afield on bright autumn days, beside the fact that hunting seasons are open. Companionship of old friends is one reason, and the cool, invigorating days are another. But among the greatest rewards of all is listening to a pack of Beagle hounds hot on the trail of a cottontail rabbit. No matter how you view it, here is one of the most exciting sounds in all the outdoors.

At first Towhead was leading the chase, but when the bunny swapped ends and headed for an oak woods over toward the east, Mamie was first to solve the mystery of lost rabbit tracks and all at once *she* was leading the chase. Her high hysterical bawl is unmistakable even from very far away. And so is the almost bird-like voice of Myra.

Beagle sounding off to start a wild chase.

"Let's find some stands," Nat Franklin said, "in case that bunny comes bounding this way."

Maybe the target was just long-winded. Or maybe that rabbit was feeling the pressure of four fast dogs—or probably both. Anyway it led them on a long run completely through the woods, cleared a small brook (where the Beagles briefly lost the trail again) and then began to circle around to the starting point of the chase. Once the dogs had been almost out of hearing. Now all at once the cottontail was aimed our way in high gear; we could tell because the hounds were baying closer and closer.

For a few minutes the suspense of waiting was as thick as molasses. Then I caught a flick of motion and a split second later saw the rabbit race from one small thicket to another—and then directly toward my partner. The dogs were not far behind. Another moment and I heard Nat shoot and then he was holding up a fine fat cottontail. His Beagles were barking and jumping up all around him in pure canine glee.

"How can you beat that for starting a November morning?" Nat asked.

"There'll be a rabbit banquet tonight," I answered.

What followed the rest of that golden day in eastern Tennessee should happen to absolutely everyone who enjoys small-game hunting and loves the great outdoors. We found enough game to keep the dogs running from early morning until dusk. Altogether it was a happy hunt—a glorious time I wouldn't forget during the bleak winter days which were certain to follow.

Still it was a typical hunt rather than something special for a great game species.

I like to think of cottontails as the greatest target since the bullseye and a whole lot faster. Without serious competition, the cottontail rabbit is the most popular game animal nationwide in North America and that isn't any wonder. Cottontail range includes every state in the U.S. except Hawaii and Alaska. It also extends into parts of southern Canada and throughout a large portion of Mexico.

Millions of cottontails are bagged every year in America. It is *the* game animal of every sportsman's salad days, the first challenge for a beginner, and a favorite of older hunters (who have a tougher time negotiating the uplands?) as well. Pursuing cottontails may lack the reward and sudden explosiveness of grouse hunting—or the wonder of sitting in a duck blind at dawn—but it has immense charm all its own. And no game species on this continent is more available. Still—hunting rabbit is not as easy nowadays as during a generation ago, before pesticides and modern farming methods, when every patch of cover concealed a bunny or two. A modern hunter works a little harder now for his rabbit dinner.

Actually the cottontail is eight different rabbits and this has nothing to do with its almost legendary reproductive capabilities. It's simply that there are eight different species of the genus *Sylvilagus*, ranging from the pygmy (which is the smallest, averaging less than one pound) to the swamp rabbit or canecutter (which is the largest and may reach six pounds). Most abundant of all, however, is the Eastern cottontail, *Sylvilagus floridanus*, which inhabits the eastern two-thirds of the United States and weighs about 2½ pounds when full grown. The moun-

Widespread cottontail is No. 1 quarry of small-game hunters. (Russell Tinsley photo)

tain and desert cottontails inhabit the western United States and their ranges overlap with one another, as well as with the eastern species. But in any event, at least one kind of cottontail lives everywhere. Only an expert biologist can tell them apart. American sportsmen do not find any other game species so widely distributed and so available.

Perhaps one other rabbit which isn't a rabbit at all should be mentioned here. It is the varying hare, or more commonly the snowshoe hare—Jerome Knap tells you all about its habits and how to hunt it in Chapter 4.

To hunt any wildlife successfully, it is always important to know something about the quarry. All of the cottontails thrive best in scrub or brushy environment—or in what is often termed "edge." This may be the edge of agricultural lands, of a woodland, a swamp or even the edge of a small town where it lurks around gardens. The list of plant items on which rabbits browse is almost endless, but in summertime they concentrate on green herbaceous plants while in fall and winter the menu turns to bark and twigs. A hunter can often easily tell if there are many

Western cottontail is well hidden in thorny bed.

rabbits in any vicinity by the telltale gnawing and stripping of bark at the bases of small trees and shrubs.

Cottontails are far more nocturnal than generally suspected and a good way to locate them is to drive about after dark and watch in the beams of the headlamps. (But carrying a firearm in the car at the same time is illegal in most states.) During daytime cottontails remain motionless, crouched (often very well hidden) in "forms" or "squats" of grass or other dense vegetation. You can practically step on some without spotting them. When the weather becomes very severe or the snow very deep, they retreat underground into holes or dens built by other mammals, especially those excavated by groundhogs or marmots, or perhaps by badgers. Sometimes rabbits remain underground for extended periods and tracks in the snow at the den entrance may reveal that they emerge only briefly or not very far.

Of course the best time of all to spot or to census (for future hunting) cottontails in northern parts of their range is as soon as possible after a fresh snowfall. The telltale footpads explain much about where the animals are concentrated and how many are living in any one patch of cover.

Beagle whiffs fresh cottontail track in snow and soon will be off and running in full cry.

But rabbits will often use brushpiles and similar dense thickets for shelter instead of going underground. It is not unusual for quite a number of rabbits to be inside a honeysuckle bush or a single brushpile. The larger the brushpile, the more likely it will house more than one bunny.

Some extremely productive places to find cottontails are abandoned farmlands and orchards, on the fringes of cropfields or all vegetable gardens, or along the borders of second growth woodlands from which most of the timber has been recently harvested. Given the suitable heavy, mixed cover which soon grows lush in such places, rabbits will eventually multiply and maintain populations high enough for good hunting year in and year out. The same is true of the swamp rabbits which are native to moist places of the Southeast and therefore prefer a slightly more swampy habitat.

Unaccountably, cottontail rabbits almost everywhere are subject to fluctuations in population. These ups and downs occur for no apparent reason: in other words abundance for several years in any region may be followed with scarcity, even though pressure from hunters and their dogs does not vary in the least. Nor has the presence of predators proven to be an important factor. The fluctuations just happen and nobody really knows why.

There are as many ways to hunt rabbits as there are different types of autumn cover in North America. The simplest, most widespread method is to get out and walk through blackberry thickets and along brushy fencerows, through tangled second-growth woodlands, abandoned orchards, stubble fields—anywhere there is enough vegetation to conceal the animals. This way you flush the bunnies as you do game birds and hope for a quick shot as the white-tailed target bounds away in or through the cover. Occasionally sportsmen with keen eyes spot the quarry concealed in their forms before they flush without warning. However a hunter's first sight of a rabbit is usually when it is well underway and often almost out of shooting range.

Make no mistake that this jump-shooting alone requires a fast and accurate hand with a scattergun. I have known great wingshots and high scorers on the trap or skeet fields who fared very badly during their first encounters with cottontails. Probably it was only overconfidence.

Two men can cooperate to make jump-shooting somewhat more productive, as well as companionable. The rabbit which one man flushes may give the other a passing shot—and vice versa, if they walk out on parallel courses. Especially late in the season, when all farm crops are harvested and the cottontails may be concentrated in isolated islands of cover, driving them may be practical. In this, one or more shooters wait on stand while others attempt to flush and drive rabbits toward them by

Rabbit leaps wildly past Beagle after being surprised from mid-day siesta.

Cottontail takes off with Beagle hot on its trail.

beating the cover on foot. At times it works well; other times it doesn't.

But everything considered, there is just one *best* way to bag bunnies anywhere and that is with a four-footed ally or two, specifically a Beagle or brace of them. There are a good many sportsmen in this country who believe it isn't really rabbit hunting without hounds and maybe I'm one of them.

For the really serious cottontail gunner in cottontail country a couple of good Beagles make all the difference in the world. But hunting with Beagles is slightly different than going afield without them. Normally, both hunters and hounds wander out into rabbit cover until a bunny is flushed by one or the other. Some Beagles are much better, or enthusiastic, about trying to find and flush rabbits than others. They only run a hot trail. In some cases it may be necessary for the hunters to find and flush all of the bunnies. Once a cottontail is on the move, the dog or dogs smell the hot tracks and follow, giving tongue all the way, to some sort of conclusion.

If the Beagles (or they could be Bassets, or even coon or foxhounds) are good tenacious trackers, and most Beagles naturally are, they will keep on the track no matter how the rabbit dodges and changes direction, until it eventually returns to the territory from which it was originally flushed. Meanwhile the hunters take up stands, perhaps on top of

Cottontail stops during chase to listen to baying of hounds which gets closer and closer.

stumps or brushpiles for better vision all around, and wait for the dogs to "push" the rabbit back.

Beaglers use colorful phrases to describe their dogs' voices. Consider "chop mouth" for one example, which is a rapid, frantic kind of barking on a steaming track. Then there are "bawl mouth" Beagles and "yodelers," both of which hang onto high (or low) notes for a longer time than a nervous "chop mouth." Nobody ever refers to a Beagle (especially one belonging to his close buddy) as a "babbler"; that means the pooch is lying—is baying for the hell of it and not because it's on a genuinely hot trail. Fast friendships have been strained—even dissolved forever—by careless use of the word "babbler."

It is always tense and exciting to wait on stand. Sometimes the target will run far in a difficult challenging race; sometimes it will double back quickly and give one hunter a shot before the chase has hardly begun. There is never any definite pattern. You just listen to the dogs and from their voices try to determine how far they are running behind the rabbits. You also try to figure which way it will approach and how soon.

Although the target is small, waiting on stand is rarely dull or unexciting. An older cottontail with previous Beagle experience is not likely to give a gunner any easy opportunities, even when coming close. It will take every advantage of existing cover and when that seems to fail, may dart into the nearest groundhog hole.

A hunter can increase the odds in his own favor by getting up on an elevation for better vision and field of fire. Brushpiles, boulders and atop old farm machinery are all good places to stand above ground. Listen carefully to the hounds' voices because it is possible, by the urgency, to tell if they are trailing far behind or are really pushing the rabbit. That way you know better where to watch for the target to pass. I have had rabbits circle as many as six times past my stand and within easy gun range without getting a shot because of heavy cover. But the skill and persistence of the dogs is important here to keep right after the cottontail. The longer a chase lasts, the colder the trail is likely to become and the dogs may drag farther behind until they lose out altogether.

Most Beagles will naturally chase rabbits and begin doing so at a very early age. Here is one breed which does not require extensive and elaborate training. As in all breeds there are both good and bad individuals, but surely the percentage of Beagles which can trail good enough to put rabbits in front of the gun is comparatively high. The surest way to obtain a good hunting Beagle is to buy one of known, proven ability. Of course, such dogs can run high because few owners are willing to part with top quality dogs for a small consideration. There simply is too much demand for such Beagles today.

Hunter draws down on bunny that Beagles send scurrying past.

Because of its great abundance, probably, the cottontail is not always considered great game. It's a lingering, but unfortunate, attitude. In some places rabbit hunting isn't "status," as say waterfowling. Some writers have claimed that the cottontail is not an elusive target and is certainly not in the same class with our highly rated game birds—the grouse, pheasants and bobwhites. Well, that is pure, unadulterated bunk. Beginners simply do not go out and start busting rabbits just as novices have little luck with grouse until after considerable experience in ruffed grouse cover.

There really is no suitable substitute for actual shooting in the field to become a good marksman on the bounding will-o-the-wisp targets. But shooting skeet in advance of opening day is a very good practice for the different types of crossing and going-away shots a rabbit hunter is likely to get. Another good drill is to go afield with a companion carrying a hand trap and a bag of clay pigeons. While walking out through typical rabbit cover, without warning the friend tosses out the clay birds, as low as possible and just skimming the vegetation to try to imitate a flushing

Classic cottontail hunting scene: Beagle flushes bunny in Midwestern snow, then starts chase as hunter watches.

cottontail. This sharpens a hunter's reflexes and will greatly increase his bag once the season is underway.

Obviously there will be disagreement about which scattergun is best for cottontail hunting. That isn't any wonder because there exists a very wide choice. Most outdoorsmen eventually become acquainted with one type or another—say a double or an autoloader—and so eventually become more familiar and finally more proficient with that particular piece. Hunters also come in different sizes and shapes, with varying reflexes, and this can make a difference. But by far the best advice to any rabbit hunter is to use (or buy) a high-quality reliable smoothbore which best suits his own physique and preference. A consensus of the most experienced rabbit hunters I know would suggest a double gun, side-by-side or superposed with fairly short barrels (say 26″), either 12-or 20-gauge, one improved cylinder and the other modified choke. Let's let it stand right there.

No matter where, when, or how it's hunted, the cottontail is a prolific game species which has everything. It's our most abundant target by far, whose only close rival is the squirrel. Cottontails survive in wilderness as well as close to man, so the future of the species appears bright.

Beagle flushes rabbit from depression just below hunter.

Rabbit hunting is one of the greatest events of fall. It combines bright cool weather with companionship, action, and music of Beagles.

Hunted with or without hounds, they are tough targets, but delicious (rather than tough) on any outdoorsman's table.

Summed up, rabbit hunting is a fascinating game anyone or any number can play almost anywhere in America.

3

Dealer's Choice, Jacks Wild

by Russell Tinsley

A TRAINED SPRINTER couldn't have gotten a more explosive start, and what the 100-yard dash record for a rabbit might be, I don't know, but if a stop watch was clocking this lean and muscular jack, I am confident it navigated the distance in less than five seconds.

I'd sighted the jack rabbit perhaps 200 yards away and I steadied my 6mm Remington over a rotting log and centered the crosshairs of the 4X scope on the critter's shoulder. But I'd misjudged the distance or jerked when I should have squeezed the trigger or something else, because the slug struck ground just beyond the rabbit and showered it with dust. The startled hare made one frantic leap, accelerated in mid-air, and hit running at full throttle. And when a jack rabbit has its mind on moving, it can really get with it!

What the top speed of a jack might be is anyone's guess. I suppose it depends on the individual rabbit and the circumstances. I've been traveling backcountry roads and had jack rabbits galloping in from my automobile and the odometer registered better than 35 miles per hour. Nature blessed this long-legged animal, primarily an inhabitant of open plains and desert, with superior speed and uncanny hearing and sight for eluding its natural enemies such as the coyote and eagle. Unlike the cottontail, the jack would much rather run than hide.

Not enough hunters purposely pursue jacks, which is a shame. They don't realize what they are missing. And opportunity certainly is there, jack rabbits being widespread and plentiful. I have shot jacks in such diverse places as the sand hills country of Nebraska, near alfalfa fields in California, and in the semi-arid brush country of southern Texas and

Jack is a rangy animal that depends on its speed to elude danger.

northern Mexico. When I was a kid in central Texas, friends and I used to eradicate jacks that were raiding watermelon patches and we took their livers to use as catfish bait. I can recall the many delightful hours I spent hunting jacks in the desert country around Alamogordo in southeastern New Mexico. But no matter where I have sought it and what subspecies it might happen to be, the jack rabbit still is the same familiar long-eared speedster with the jet afterburner.

I've also hunted jacks in many different ways. Just the other day I got into an argument with a friend debating the sport of shooting jack rabbits with long-range varmint rifles versus stalking them with a .22 rimfire Magnum handgun, which is like saying a red-haired woman is more passionate than a blonde, or vice versa. To each his own.

Certainly there is no "best" method for hunting jacks. How you go about it depends on personal preferences or perhaps circumstances. I've jumped them from their hiding spots and rolled them with a charge of No. 4 shot from a 12-gauge shotgun and I have tested my long-range shooting skill with various varmint rifles and I've even stalked and bagged them with a handgun and bow and arrow. It is the challenge I enjoy.

Some pseudo-conservationists have questioned my motives for advocating the hunting of jack rabbits anyway. The jack is a harmless creature that does no harm, they argue. But try telling that to a farmer or maybe a rancher. Jack rabbits can be very destructive to crops like wheat, alfalfa, watermelons and young fruit trees. Dr. William B. Davis in his book *The Mammals of Texas* (published by the Texas Parks and Wildlife Department) observed that 128 jack rabbits can consume as much range vegetation as one cow or seven sheep. I have seen haystacks which toppled because hungry jacks gnawed away the foundation. A plague of jack rabbits hits the landowner where it hurts most, in the pocketbook.

But other than being a pest, the jack also is a very fine game animal. The species is a master of multiplication and sport hunting certainly isn't going to make any inroads into the population. Nature itself is much more cruel. I've observed jacks in areas of no hunting and there will be fluctuating years of few and plenty, as with any wildlife. But fast-multiplying jacks (a female might have two to four litters a year) have a much better recovery potential than most mammals. There are times when jacks are conspicuous by their absence; they seem to be about extinct in an area. Then lo and behold, the very next year they are abundant. If dedicated men using poisons or organized drives can't eliminate the jack rabbit, then a hunter armed with nothing more than a rifle can't be of significant consequence, no matter how efficient he might be.

There are three subspecies of jack rabbits, the blacktailed variety being the most widespread and plentiful, found from western Arkansas and Missouri to California and Oregon and south into Mexico. Jacks generally are creatures of lower-elevation grasslands and deserts. The blacktailed jack rabbit is about 18 to 24 inches in length, weighs four to 7½ pounds, and has ears six, maybe seven inches long. Its pelage is brownish-gray with white along the belly and underside of the tail. Ears are tipped with black.

The whitetailed jack rabbit ranges from south-central Canada into

New Mexico and from Wisconsin to the Sierras. In places its bailiwick overlaps that of its blacktailed cousin. During the summer the coloration is a light brownish-gray along the back, not so dark on the belly. In the winter, however, northern inhabitants often turn completely white and the jack is confused with the Arctic hare. Yet not all go through this alchemy; at lower elevations some simply turn to a softer buff-white. The whitetail is the largest of the jack rabbits: 22 to 26 inches in length, six to ten pounds in weight, ears five to six inches long.

The antelope jack is a smaller rabbit, lean and muscular through the flanks, weighing only four to six pounds. It is an inhabitant of the southwest desert country and is easily confused with the blacktailed jack, although it will have longer ears, maybe eight inches or more, and they lack the black tips.

Yet while their range might be slightly different and ditto their coloration, the everyday habits and characteristics are the same, and a jack rabbit is a jack rabbit no matter where you might find it.

If you live or travel into areas where jack rabbits are known to roam,

Jack rabbit squats and draws long ears down, making it difficult to see.

you shouldn't have much trouble finding a place to hunt. Most ranchers and farmers welcome those who demonstrate they are safe and will help in eradicating these pests, although a few slob hunters have made it tough on all of us when it comes to getting places for hunting. There is no closed season in most of the prime jack rabbit states and you can go after them when you please.

Late summer and early fall are likely times to hunt them. The population is at a peak. Young of the spring are large enough to fare for themselves. And an immature whitetailed jack isn't bad to eat, although with a blacktailed jack, if you boiled an old boot and a tough adult rabbit together, I'd prefer if you'd throw away the jack and serve the boot. In other words, this rabbit on the dinner table hasn't got much to offer.

A jack rabbit is primarily nocturnal, prowling at night. In places where it is legal I've hunted them at night with spotlights and either shotguns or rifles. But even during the summertime jacks will be up and about early and late in the day, and of the two periods, I prefer the first hour of daylight best, especially on a cool, dewy morning.

Stump makes a steady rest for the long-range shooter.

No special weapon is needed for jack rabbit hunting. A gun simply is a tool for delivering the bullet, a means to an end. Practically any weapon and any cartridge, from the .22 rimfire Long Rifle up, can be utilized if you realize the capabilities and limitations of the rifle or shotgun or whatever you might use. Yet a jack is a tough hombre and you don't want to be undergunned, which is just inviting crippled game, the cardinal sin.

Jack rabbit hunting is not a sport restricted to the purist. It is a simple, uncomplicated pastime or as complex as you want to make it. The means and methods are as varied as your imagination.

Maybe you want to use your deer rifle on jacks, this for a twofold purpose: it is sporty to use and such hunting allows you to become familiar and proficient with the weapon you'll be utilizing later during the big-game seasons.

C. L. Kennedy with pair of jacks he bagged at long distances.

Or perhaps you prefer a long-range, flat-shooting varmint rifle. In my case the two above are the same. I hunt deer with either a .243 Winchester or a 6mm Remington. Both are also fine varmint guns.

Any of these hot centerfire cartridges, from the .222 Remington on up, are okay for jacks, and the rifle-cartridge combinations that Carlos Vinson recommends for woodchucks in Chapter 15 are equally as potent on jack rabbits. In body size and structure the two critters are much alike, although of course the jack rabbit is more lanky and muscular.

If you do much off-season shooting you might want to consider handloading your own ammunition. With a cartridge the most expensive component is the brass case, which can be reused over and over. So reloading ammo just makes good sense. It saves money, in addition to being a fascinating hobby. You might want to start with one of the simple Lee loaders, to see if you like reloading, before graduating into the more complicated bench presses. The Lee loader is a hand operation and rather slow, but it serves the needs of most casual shooters and helps them utilize the brass they otherwise would discard. The loader is compact, fitting in a small box that can go into a bureau drawer. Many

Author bagged this jack with a .22 rimfire handgun loaded with Long Rifles.

books have been written about reloading and you probably can find a copy at your local library.

Other than saving money, reloading also permits you some experimentation, as long as you remain within the bounds of common sense. Most reloaders stick with standard factory loads until they get more confidence in their abilities, which is a smart route to take.

One possibility is to "tone down" a load to reduce impact damage. Suppose you are hunting rabbits to eat. Hit one solidly with a fast-moving, quick-expanding .243 slug and there won't be much left. The alternative, then, is to use a load/bullet combination which kills adequately yet does negligible damage to meat.

With most calibers the only solution is to reduce the powder charge, as recommended by a reference guide. But if you own a .22-caliber centerfire such as the .22 Hornet, .22-250 or .222, you might be interested in the full-jacketed, 55-grain bullet developed by Speer, Inc., of Lewiston, Idaho. The point is formed by the solid jacket with no hollow or soft point. If this bullet isn't driven at ultra-high velocities, it won't cause much damage, yet will get the job done. Speer recommends a velocity of 2000 fps or less. I have a friend who hunts jack rabbits with a .22-250 and he brewed some handloads using the 55-grain Speer bullet and 11 grains of IMR 4759 powder. Muzzle velocity is only about 1700 fps but my friend says accuracy is adequate up to 200 yards and the bullet kills quickly and humanely with very little meat damage.

But as I previously said, jack rabbit hunting need not be this complicated. Just get your pet deer rifle and maybe a pair of binoculars and you're in business.

It is early morning, just enough light to make shape from shadow, and I am standing on a low-slung ridge, using my fieldglasses to sweep the brush-studded prairie below. Nearby is a field where the young, tender sprouts of milo maize are attracting destructive jack rabbits. A farmer friend had asked me out to help eliminate some of the problem.

Then a hint of movement stops me. I look intently through the 7X35 glasses. Yes, there's a jack rabbit! If it hadn't hopped across a small clearing I might never have seen it.

I reach for my 6mm loaded with factory 100-grain cartridges. Sitting down, I rest the weapon across an upturned knee and try to find the jack in the 4X scope. The temptation is to find a nice steady rest to make my aim more accurate, but that would be defeating the basic purpose. I try to simulate field conditions for hunting most game and steadying the rifle over a knee is more in character than resting against a tree or on a tripod, although if you prefer that kind of shooting, help yourself.

One way to hunt jacks is to find a high vantage and glass the countryside.

Close-range stalking paid off with this pair of jacks for handgun hunter.

The rifle I know is sighted in to hit the bull's-eye at 250 yards. How far is the rabbit? Maybe 200, 225 yards. Another advantage of this hunting is that it teaches a person to judge range accurately. Despite its size, the jack rabbit nonetheless is a small target when it is way out there.

I center the crosshairs, suck in breath and hold it, and gingerly s-q-u-e-e-z-e the trigger. The blast of the rifle is immediately followed by that telltale plop of bullet meeting flesh. The jack never knew what hit it.

I was feeling pretty smug after that auspicious beginning, but the next jack deflated my ego. This one I estimated to be about 300 yards away; so I held just over its back and fired. The bullet hit right where I aimed, high. Obviously the range wasn't as far as I guessed it to be.

By the time the temperature had warmed enough to dampen my brow with sweat, I had three jacks on the ground and had missed two others. Nothing was stirring now. The rabbits were taking a siesta, seeking the shade of small bushes to squat comfortably and idle away the mid-day hours. A change in habits called for a change in strategy.

I began walking, pausing occasionally to look, the same technique I use when stalking deer. The idea was to try and spot a rabbit before it sighted me, to gain enough time for a quick shot, or if one spooked and ran, to try and hit the moving target. When a jack shifts into high gear and I'm shooting at it, I usually don't make anyone happy except maybe the rabbit and ammo manufacturers. The old eyes and reflexes are not what they used to be.

Sometimes an alarmed jack won't impulsively run. Instead it squats and folds those long ears back and seems to "disappear" into the landscape. Nature has blessed the jack with wonderful camouflage and unless one moves you likely will never see it.

This stalk hunting can be classed in degrees of difficulty. With a shotgun loaded with No. 4 or No. 2 shot, any rabbit which flushes within range you likely will down. A big hare isn't that hard to hit with a scattergun. But switch from a shotgun to a rifle and the challenge becomes much more formidable. With a handgun it is even tougher. And the bow and arrow . . . well, I wouldn't recommend it unless you're long on patience and short on ego. It can be a frustrating sport, yet richly rewarding.

The possibilities are limited only by your imagination. It is a sport of dealer's choice, choose your own technique and weapon—a delightful, fascinating game of jacks wild.

4

Hunting the White Hares

by Jerome Knap

"TAKE A STAND somewhere on that knoll," Ned Simmons said as we snowshoed along an old logging road. "I'll take the hounds into the bush and get a chase going. It won't take more than a few minutes. The rabbits are pretty thick here this year."

There was no doubt that the snowshoe hare population was high. Tracks crisscrossed the road in every direction.

Ned unsnapped the leashes from our two dogs and all three disappeared into the thick cedar and black spruce swamp. The snow on the evergreens hung in huge puffs. The woods in the brilliant January sun looked like a postcard scene.

I was starting to daydream just a little when a hound suddenly howled in the swamp below. My shotgun was still empty, but I lost no time in cramming the two chambers full. The other hound gave out a loud bay, and then both dogs opened up in full chorus. The chase was on.

Holding my gun for instant action, I looked up and down the logging road. A white form suddenly streaked out and cleared the road with two or three jumps. It all happened so fast that I didn't even get my gun up.

Snowshoes over deep snow paid off with these snowshoe or varying hares.

That was my first introduction to hunting snowshoe hares. The hare that had streaked across the road was not even the one the hounds were after. It was just a bystander fleeing for quieter and safer places. I later learned that this happens frequently with snowshoe hares.

It didn't take me long to discover that, in many ways, snowshoe hares are ideal rabbits to hunt with hounds. They run faster and in bigger circles than cottontails. They never seem to tire and they never hole up. They give the hounds a real run for their money. And if anyone considers a bouncing cottontail hard to follow with a shotgun barrel, he should try a snowshoe. There's no doubt in my mind that snowshoes offer more challenging hunting than their cousins the cottontails if they're hunted with hounds.

The snowshoe hare is one of our most neglected game species. Wildlife biologists throughout the animal's range proclaim them to be underharvested. The only other hare that gets less hunting pressure is the Arctic hare of the far north. The reason why both hares are underharvested is largely their geographic range.

The snowshoe hare is found from Newfoundland (where it was introduced by sportsmen,) across all of Quebec and northern Ontario, down through New England, upper New York State, and Pennsylvania, southward through the Appalachians into Tennessee. From northern Michigan, the hare's range extends westward into North Dakota and northward across all of forested Canada. The range also dips southward in the western mountains through Washington, Oregon, northern California, parts of Idaho, Montana, Wyoming, Colorado, and Utah, and as far south as New Mexico. Northward its range extends into the Northwest Territories, the Yukon, and the forested areas of Alaska. By and large, the snowshoe hare's range is primarily wilderness area, or perhaps what might be termed semi-wilderness. It bypasses the major areas of human population. This, in part, is the reason why the snowshoe hare is not as popular a game animal as the cottontail.

The Arctic hare lives in even more remote areas than the snowshoe. Its range extends from northern Newfoundland across Labrador, the Ungava of Quebec, the tundra of the Northwest Territories, and right up into the Arctic Islands, including Greenland. This hare is also found across the coastal tundra of Alaska.

Very few sportsmen even see an Arctic hare, let alone shoot one. But it is an important species to the Eskimos. For one thing, it is the principal prey species of the Arctic fox, which is a valuable furbearer to the Eskimos. The hare is, at times, also an important source of food and bedding material for the Eskimos themselves. These native people seldom waste ammunition by shooting hares. They snare them. The hare has a unique habit of never jumping over a wire or rawhide string. It always crawls under, where it's easily snared by nooses hanging down.

Both the Arctic and snowshoe hares are true hares. The leverets are born fully furred and with their eyes open. Both species are susceptible to cyclic fluctuations in which their populations rise over a number of years and then crash. The cycle for the snowshoe hare is about 10 years, while that of the Arctic hare seems to be shorter, about four or five years. Both species of hares turn white in winter. This is where the snowshoe gets its alternate name of varying hare. It varies in color from season to season.

However, here the similarity between the two species ends. The snowshoe hare is an animal of thick forests in their early stages of growth. The thicker the forest is, the better snowshoes like it. The Arctic hare, on the other hand, is an animal of the open, treeless tundra. In winter, the Arctic hare seeks higher elevations, exposed hillsides where the snow has been blown off by the wind.

The snowshoe hare is a solitary animal, but it will tolerate other hares near it. It is nocturnal in habit. The Arctic hare is gregarious. It is commonly seen in family groups, or even in lots of two or three families together. Bands of over 100 hares have been seen on Baffin Island.

The hares are quite different in size as well. The snowshoe hare is not

Different color phases of snowshoe rabbit, as one on left is turning white.

Snowshoe hares are inhabitants of wilderness and semi-wilderness.

much bigger than a cottontail. It is somewhat rangier and, of course, leggier. But it's not significantly heavier. The Arctic hare, though, rivals the big western jacks in size. The average Arctic hare runs a shade over 10 pounds, and 12-pound animals are not uncommon.

It is the rangy frame and long legs that, of course, make the snowshoe hare such a tremendous game animal, particularly for houndsmen. A hare will take a brace of hounds on a merry chase for many hours. I've never had a hare hole up in front of my hounds, but I've heard of wounded hares going to ground. When the snow is deep, the advantages are with the hare. The hounds may wallow and flounder, and become quickly fatigued, but the hare with its big snowshoe feet will wisk over the snow without difficulty.

There is much dispute about the best hounds for snowshoe hares. Beaglers claim that their breed is best, but I have reservations about this, largely because I hunt snowshoes most often with Beagles. Beagles are fine during the early season before the snow becomes too deep. After that, they flounder too much. Even the big, 15-inch class Beagles get played out too quickly.

The bigger hounds—Blueticks, Redbones, Walkers, and the "grade" hounds of mixed ancestry—are far better in deep snow. I have always suspected that the English Harrier, an old hound bred to chase the big European hares, would make an excellent snowshoe dog. The Harrier is a powerful, muscular dog, halfway between a Beagle and a foxhound in size. Harriers are rare on this continent. I've never heard of anyone using them for snowshoes.

Weather plays a big role in hunting snowshoe hares, as it does in all rabbit hunting. During very cold weather, snowshoes tend to sink lower in their forms and are reluctant to run. The hounds can hardly root them out.

Weather also dictates how well the hounds work. In dry, cold weather, they have difficulty in keeping on the scent. Moderate temperatures with a bit of dampness in the air are ideal for trailing. After very cold nights, the hounds work better later in the morning when the temperature has risen and the first inch or two of snow loses its crust and becomes soft and damp.

Snowshoe hare hunting differs from cottontail hunting largely because of the thicker and wilder cover. The best snowshoe hare hunting is invariably in thick sapling growth and thick cedar and balsam swamps cut by alder and willow thickets. Choosing a place to hunt has to be done with care. If the swamp is too vast, the hare will run a circle all day but will rarely offer a shot. Swamps and forest stands that are bisected by forest roads, hiking trails, fire lanes, and even small creeks are best. Sooner or later, the hare will cross and offer a shot.

Hares are creatures of habit. They have favorite crossing places which are easy to discover by tracks in the snow. These are ideal places to stand. The snowshoes will cross there first. The trick in picking a stand is to choose one just inside the cover that the dogs are working. You are more likely to see the rabbit just before it streaks across the opening. When a hare runs, he can cover eight or 10 feet in one bound. A hunter needs all the help he can get.

You must also stand still. The hares are frequently 300 or 400 yards ahead of the dogs. They sit up and watch what's ahead. If a hare spots

In winter snowshoe rabbit hunting, everything from terrain to quarry is white.

any movement in front of him, he'll rebound back into the bush. So don't move around, even when the chase is going the other way. The hounds frequently stir up other hares which try to quietly hop out to a less disturbed spot. I've bagged a great many hares that were not being chased by the hounds.

It is likewise important that a hunter on a stand keep a sharp vigil. The white hares on white snow are not easy to see. The beady, black eyes and the black tips on the ears are a bit of a giveaway. But many a snowshoe has passed by without a hunter ever seeing it. When that happens and the hounds come howling through on a hot track, scarlet faces oftentimes match scarlet hunting jackets.

Gunfire doesn't bother the hares. I've actually seen them stop out of curiosity when the first shot missed them. It's also not unusual for a hound to have two, maybe three hares in front of him when the population is high. I have, at times, shot three hares from one stand in less than five minutes. And once on Michigan's Beaver Island, my hunting

For this hunting a .22 rimfire rifle is plenty potent.

partner and I bagged two hares apiece, both almost doubles, from two stands 30 feet apart.

A shotgun, of course, is the best weapon for this type of hunting. The shooting is fairly difficult. The gauge is not important. A 12-, 16-, or 20-gauge gun is fine.

Of greater consideration is the choke. I prefer an improved cylinder because a 35-yard shot is a long one. But some hunters prefer modified. Double guns choked improved cylinder and modified are ideal. A full choke is definitely not the best choice for snowshoe hare shooting.

The best shot size in my book is No. 6. Some hunters prefer heavier shot, but I don't think it's needed. I prefer dense patterns to coarse shot.

Snowshoe hunting with hounds is not a good rifleman's sport. But occasionally, when the Knap freezer is amply stocked with the makings of hassenpfeffer, I switch to a rifle. The hound chase then becomes more important than the shooting. A .22 rimfire is ideal, all a hunter needs. I use a .22 semi-auto. The action is not at all important as long as you can repeat your shots fast. However, the sights are important. I use a Weaver K 1.5 'scope for a wide field of view. The 'scope makes the white rabbits on the white background easier to see. Open sights are a handicap. It's hard to focus on the leaping white hares in the snow. A scope with a narrow field of view and critical eye relief are worse than useless for this type of hunting.

Snowshoe hare hunting is not all a houndsman's game. The hares can be hunted by a dogless hunter. However, hunting the hares in winter is difficult. With the coming of snow, snowshoes change their personality. They become wary and shy. They keep hopping in front of the hunter, through thick cover, seldom exposing themselves for a shot.

In the fall, however, they're animals of a different color—literally and figuratively. They are still brown then. When a hunter kicks one out, it is not likely to streak off. It may make a few fast bounds, and then sit up to see what has frightened it. Or it may jump away slowly, showing little concern. It is not unusual for big-game hunters to encounter snowshoe hares at dusk or dawn along a game trail. The rabbits usually sit where they are and act unconcerned.

On top of this, nature occasionally hands the snowshoe a bad turn. The hare turns white, but the snow is late in coming. This really makes the hares conspicuous and easy prey for all predators, including man.

Hunting snowshoe hares without a dog is much like hunting other rabbits without a dog. Move slowly and look a lot. You don't need to jump on brushpiles as you do with cottontails, but don't neglect thick cover. On rainy or drizzly days, stay in bed; the snowshoes will be in theirs.

Beagles are as adroit on snowshoes as they are cottontails.

It would be sporting sacrilege to shoot a snowshoe in the fall with a shotgun, unless he was ahead of a hound. The snowshoe at that time is game for riflemen, handgunners, and bowmen. These weapons are far more challenging. Again, a .22 is hard to beat. But any rifle will do if you confine your shots to the head. I've shot more than a few hares with big-game rifles. Certainly big-game hunters who want to bag the odd snowshoe for the pot should load up some small game loads.

In handguns, a .22 is again a good choice, but a .32-20 is a fine small game load with lead or jacketed bullets. Even a .38 can be used if loaded down. The action type is not important, except that revolvers are more practical for loaded-down small game loads.

Not being a bow hunter, I can't give much advice on bows and arrows. However, I'm sure that even a light bow has ample power to kill a rabbit. Arrows with blunts are recommended. Field points are not a good choice. They don't deliver much shock nor do they cause much hemorrhaging. Wounded hares are not unusual with field points.

When white landscape goes, so does the white pelage of snowshoe.

Many snowshoe hunters prefer long-legged dogs because of deep snow.

Aside from a gun, a hunter after snowshoe hares needs little other equipment. A small game knife is a must, of course. In winter, snowshoes become indispensable. My favorites are the Maine or Algonquin style, but in very thick cover I prefer the oval-shaped beaver-tail type. The clothing for winter should be warm, and of the type that can be opened or loosened when you're snowshoeing. It doesn't take long to work up a sweat on snowshoes. Footwear is also critical. It should be warm, because waiting for the hounds to bring the rabbit around can be cold business. Ideally the boots should be at least water resistant in case the snow is wet.

The snowshoe hare, regardless of how it is hunted and with what weapon, is a fine game animal. The fact that it is neglected by many sportsmen does not bother me at all. Actually, I think it's great. It means that the season can be long and the bag limits generous. Snowshoe hare seasons generally open in early or mid-fall and stay open all winter long. In some states, they never close. The limits are equally generous—seldom less than six hares a day, and frequently there are no bag limits at all.

There is no other small-game animal with so few restrictions on its harvest, at least none that tastes as good as the snowshoe hare on the dinner table. If you ever have a chance to try this recipe for snowshoe hare hassenpfeffer, I think you'll agree with me.

Get a bag of snowshoe rabbits like this and you've got some eating supreme.

In a large, earthenware crock, combine the following ingredients to make a marinade: 1 cup wine vinegar, 1 cup water, 1 teaspoon salt, ½ teaspoon pepper, 2 teaspoons sugar, 4 whole cloves, 4 bay leaves, 2 medium onions sliced, and 6 juniper berries. Cut 1 large or 2 small hares into serving pieces, and let stand in the marinade in the refrigerator overnight. It's preferable to turn the pieces several times to ensure even flavoring. After marinating, remove the cloves, juniper berries, and bay leaves from the marinade. Save the liquid for later.

Drain each piece of rabbit and dredge it in seasoned flour.

Brown the rabbit on all sides and place the browned pieces in a large casserole dish. Pour half of the marinade over the rabbit, cover, and cook over low heat for one hour or until tender. Additional warmed marinade can be added as the hare is cooking. Finally, just before serving, add ¾ cup of commercial sour cream and stir until thoroughly heated. The hare should be served at once, with brown rice or old-fashioned European bread dumplings. A side dish of wild cranberry sauce adds a delightful touch as well.

5

The Squirrels, a Strong Runner-up

by Bob Gooch

"SQUIRRELS ARE ALL RIGHT for young boys to hunt."

I bristled.

The speaker was a bird hunter, a state trooper by profession, a crack wingshot, and an even-tempered law enforcement officer. I had the utmost respect for him—both as a hunter and as an officer.

But he obviously didn't know much about squirrel hunting.

Sure, the usually available squirrel is fine game for the beginning hunter. No game animal will give him better training in hunting fundamentals—stalking, concealment, woodsmanship, and shooting and gun handling. And should he become so fortunate that he has a chance at them, those early lessons will serve him well on this continent's most prized big game animals.

The training values of the squirrel are beyond question, but to many veteran hunters periodic sessions in the hickory groves are equally important. Frequent jaunts to a convenient squirrel woods season the long and colorful careers of many of our most famous hunters. For in addition to providing nostalgic trips to yesteryear, the therapeutic values of a hickory grove resplendent in its autumn yellow, and tasty food, the little game animal is just plain fun to hunt.

The hunter pussyfooting through the squirrel woods is not seeking a trophy animal, is not concerned about the behavior of an expensive bird dog, nor is he attempting to impress a hunting partner with his wing-shooting. He is in the hardwoods for the pure joy of hunting. A strong case can be built for a game animal that provides this kind of hunting pleasure.

Wildlife managers and outdoor writers generally rank the squirrel

Hunter armed with .22 scope-sighted rifle takes aim at squirrel. (Russell Tinsley photo)

second in popularity among the many game animals on this continent, edging only the cottontail rabbit ahead of the frisky little tree squirrel.

I feel somewhat responsible for this ranking of our two most popular game animals, and occasionally my conscience nags me a bit. I suggested this in my story "America's No. 2 Game Animal," published in the November 1969 issue of *Field & Stream* magazine, and later I expounded this idea in my book *Squirrels and Squirrel Hunting.* Many writers have since picked up the thought.

It is true the cottontail is the No. 1 game animal in America. Even the most avid squirrel hunter will not deny this, but much of this popularity stems from the wider distribution of the cottontail rabbit. While the great majority of our 50 states offer hunting for at least one of the several species of cottontails, the range of the two major game squirrels, the fox and gray, is limited generally to the eastern half of the United States.

Within its domain the squirrel is often the No. 1 game animal—ahead of the cottontail. For example, in top squirrel states like Arkansas, Illinois, Kentucky, Louisiana, Maryland, Mississippi, Ohio, South Carolina, Tennessee, Virginia and West Virginia, the gray squirrel is the most popular game animal. The gray squirrel is the official state mammal in North Carolina, and in many good squirrel states such as Missouri the squirrel and the cottontail run neck in neck.

Such matters are of more value to the biologist responsible for the management of the game species in his state than they are to the hunter, but they are interesting.

Suffice it to say that where its abundance warrants the hunter's attention, the squirrel's status soars when rated against the factors that designate a wild animal as a species of game.

The gray squirrel, particularly, is a highly adaptable animal that has learned to live on the very heels of civilization. By preference an inhabitant of the dense hardwood forests such as early settlers found in eastern America, the gray squirrel is just as much at home in a city park. City suburbs, farm wood lots, large forests—all are acceptable to the frisky little tree squirrel.

The gray squirrel, the true bushytail, was abundant in the vast rich forests of early America, and the plucky little animal quickly won the respect of the hardy pioneers. Though hunted primarily in those distant days for its food value, good, clean fun soon became a by-product of squirrel hunting. The popularity of squirrel hunting is said to have created the demand for the Kentucky rifle, an extremely accurate weapon capable of putting a ball through a squirrel's head at 50 yards.

Probably never as abundant as the gray, the larger fox squirrel is not nearly as adaptable to changes in its environment.

The fox and gray squirrels are the major game squirrels in America. The handsome Abert squirrel of the Southwest is popular within its limited range and hunted mostly in Arizona. The big western gray is found mostly in the Far West—California, Oregon and Washington. It too is a handsome animal, but not avidly sought by westerners who do not have the same appreciation for squirrel hunting that easterners do.

The gray squirrel is the most popular and most widely distributed of the two major squirrels. The typical gray weighs approximately one to 1½ pounds, and measures 18 to 20 inches from the tip of its nose to the tip of its bushy tail. The typical animal is a salt-and-pepper gray with a white belly frequently tinged with yellow, tan or brown. A healthy gray may live to a ripe old age of 15 years, but the average age is much less.

Bushytail is alert and agile, adept at racing through the treetops and leaping expertly from one swaying branch to another—a difficult target for even the crack wingshot and his scattergun. Often it chooses to freeze and flatten against the gray bark of an oak or hickory instead of running. It is then extremely difficult to spot, though a light breeze rippling the long hairs in its bushy tail may give it away. The gray barks and chatters when disturbed, and its harsh *quak-quak-quak-a-a-a-a* and scolding *chir* are welcome sounds to the hunter moving quietly through the woods.

The gray's habits are fairly predictable though foul weather may disrupt them considerably. The squirrel is up at dawn and headed for an early breakfast in a favorite nut tree or the ripe cornfield of some unhappy farmer. It will feed until mid-morning, and then it is siesta time—back in the den tree or high on a sunny branch of a big oak. It feeds again in late afternoon and then heads for home with the approach of dusk.

The fox squirrel, the jumbo member of the tree squirrel family, is lazy, deliberate, and awkward when compared to the smaller gray, though the two squirrels often share the same range.

Its size makes the fox a hunting prize. Many healthy specimens exceed two feet from the tip of the nose to tip of the tail, and mature fox squirrels may weigh as much as 2½ pounds. Generally, the fox is about twice as heavy as the gray.

The fox's color is more varied than the other squirrels, ranging from a yellowish rust to a more characteristic gray. In parts of its range it is almost black. Its coat has a more hairy, unkempt appearance than that of the little gray.

Less wary by nature, the fox squirrel's status as a game animal suffers among hunters who enjoy the challenge of the stalk.

It prefers a more parklike habitat than the gray, living near the edges, in mature hedgerows and in the small wood lot with openings in the canopy and limited ground cover. While the fox and gray squirrel may share the same range, they do not often share the same habitat. In

Cleaning the kill in a creek after a successful squirrel hunt. (Russell Tinsley photo)

This trail hound has a gray squirrel treed in the Missouri Ozarks.

fact, heavy logging operations may make a dense forest less desirable for the gray and more desirable for the fox squirrel because of the breaking up of the canopy and added open areas.

The lazy fox squirrel is a late riser and feeds and retires earlier in the afternoon. It is not the provident, always busy harvester that the little gray is, and often suffers the consequences during long, harsh winters. It relies more upon a heavy layer of fat than a cache of nuts to carry it through the winter.

Still, the fox squirrel is also fun to hunt, and many hunters travel long miles for good hunting. The fox is generally not as readily available as the more abundant and more widely distributed gray squirrel.

Many hunting methods take squirrels, and therein lies the secret to much of the animal's popularity. Riflemen, shotgunners, bowhunters—all find the squirrel a true challenge.

I personally prefer the little .22 caliber rifle for the best in squirrel hunting, but I refuse to argue the point. There are times—such as the fast gray scampering through the swaying treetops—when the shotgun is a better choice and just as much of a challenge. And the bowhunter will find the frisky squirrel a true challenge for his primitive weapon.

The challenge of the stalk, a true test of woodsmanship, is one of the joys of hunting, and the stalk is one of the most interesting ways to take squirrels. The deer hunter calls it still-hunting, a term some confuse with stand hunting which will be discussed later. There is a difference between stalking and still-hunting. The stalker has located his game and is trying to get within shooting range, while the still-hunter is employing the same general tactics to move quietly through the woods hoping to surprise game before it detects his presence.

The stalker has ordinarily scouted the territory prior to the hunt and knows the usual location of his game. Having spotted a squirrel at a distance, he attempts to get within range, employing all of the woodsmanship at his command. This means selecting his route carefully, using trees, cliffs and ravines for concealment and moving as quietly as possible. When he moves he concentrates on the move, keeping his eyes on the ground and placing his feet carefully so as not to rustle leaves or snap dry sticks or twigs. He pauses frequently to study his game, and if it has not become alarmed he moves on, continuing to select his route carefully and moving as quietly as possible until he has reached the proper shooting range.

Irrespective of how quietly he moves, the squirrel hunter is going to have to keep some kind of concealment between himself and his sharp-

Successful North Carolina squirrel hunter studies a trail marker.

Still-hunter has to be alert to see bushytail before it sees him. (Russell Tinsley photo)

Still-hunting or stalk hunting is one of the most fascinating ways to hunt. (Russell Tinsley photo)

eyed quarry. If the squirrel shows signs of being alarmed he should freeze and wait for it to resume feeding before he moves again.

The still-hunter uses the same stealthy move, pause and look technique, the only difference being that when he stops he studies the woods thoroughly, hoping to sight game. When he does he too becomes a stalker—unless his quarry is in range, or spooks.

Still-hunting is advisable when the hunter is working woods he has not had a chance to scout.

Ideally, the forest floor should be wet underfoot for the best still-hunting or stalking. Dry, newly fallen leaves are loose and noisy to move through. Stalking and still-hunting conditions are best after an early snow has packed the new leaves, but a heavy rain will also help.

In areas where late summer and early fall, or spring hunting is legal, the leaves are usually well packed from the previous winter, and the hunter has the additional advantage of the full foliage for concealment. Concealment is more difficult in late winter after storms have stripped the hardwoods of their foliage. Then the hunter must resort to large trees, cliffs and hollows for a covered approach.

My personal preference for stalking or still-hunting is a late fall or early winter day when the leaves are reasonably well packed and a light drizzle rain falls from cloudy skies. Squirrels move well on such days and some of my most memorable hunts have come under such conditions

While I tend to stick with a rifle for still-hunting, it is here that the shotgun is at its best. The moving hunter often spooks squirrels, sending them scampering through the woods. They are tough targets for the deliberately aiming rifleman, but the shotgunner will find them a challenge.

The best stand hunting is done in territory that has been well scouted. Active den and feeding trees assure the hunter squirrels will be there at certain times of the day. The entrances of active dens will be well worn and close scrutiny will reveal loose hairs. Binoculars are helpful in this kind of scouting. The ground beneath nut trees will be littered with "cuttings"—nut fragments dropped there by the feeding squirrels.

Once he has located such an area, the hunter need only figure out the squirrels' most active feeding time and then get on a well concealed stand in advance of that period. The stand should be within good range of the tree. If he wants to catch the morning feeding period he should be on his stand before dawn. Mid-afternoon is early enough for the evening feeding period. Also it is well to keep in mind that the fox squirrel feeds later in the morning, but earlier in the afternoon.

Nut trees are productive only during the late summer and early autumn when acorns, hickory nuts, pecans and other nuts are ripe and clinging to the trees.

Handgunner watches squirrel come tumbling from tree. (Russell Tinsley photo)

The late fall and winter hunter will fare better if he takes up his vigil near a den tree. This means getting there a little before dawn and staying later in the afternoon. Fortunately, winter days are short and even the dawn hunter does not lose much sleep.

The action at a den tree is fast. The squirrel emerges from his den at dawn and tarries little as he dashes off to find breakfast. The nut tree hunter has substantially more time as his game scurries about the tree plucking ripe nuts from first one branch and then another. The late hunting is also often limited as squirrels may feed until dusk, and then rush to their dens as darkness envelopes the forest.

The knowledgeable stand hunter rarely retrieves his game as he drops it. He watches closely as it hits the ground, makes sure it is dead, and notes its location. He leaves it there for the time being rather than disturb his setup by leaving his stand to retrieve it. If he remains quietly on his stand the other squirrels will resume feeding within a few minutes, particularly if the hunter is shooting a .22 caliber rifle.

I have actually missed squirrels on my first shot, watched them stop feeding momentarily, but then continue almost immediately, giving me time for a second shot. The noise of a rifle does not disturb squirrels nearly so much as the sight of a hunter moving through the woods.

The stand is the ideal setup for the rifleman, and about the only effective way to hunt squirrels with the bow and arrow.

Still-hunting and the stand are the basic methods employed by squirrel hunters with the stand being the most deadly. Still-hunting is challenging and has more appeal for the hunter who cannot discipline himself to sit quietly awaiting action.

But these are not the only ways to hunt this versatile and interesting

Author Bob Gooch leaves Missouri woods with fox squirrels taken with scope-sighted .22 rifle.

little game animal. New methods have evolved, and others are probably just inside the fringes of some rich hardwood forest.

Both fox and gray squirrels frequent streams for water, and in lake country the timbered shores have just as much appeal for them. Many hunters have learned this while fishing, and I have yet to see an all-around outdoorsman who would not pause in his fishing to watch the antics of a frisky squirrel.

Drifting down a small stream in a light boat or canoe is a heady experience, and highly effective for squirrels, ducks and other game. It has particular appeal for the squirrel hunter, however. It is a game for the shotgun fan, as settling the crosshairs of a telescopic scope on a tiny target while moving along in a rocky boat or canoe is just about impossible. The shotgun is also the gun for ducks and other small game.

The light craft should be camouflaged or painted a dull color. Metal boats are noisy, but light, tough and otherwise ideal for this kind of hunting. The hunter should avoid shuffling his feet, and he should be alert for rocks and stumps and the fatal crashing noise they make when hit with a metal boat.

Boat hunters should hug the shoreline and use bends in the stream to surprise squirrels watering at the banks or playing or feeding in a streamside tree.

Generally, float hunting is a partnership deal with one hunter handling the craft while the other rides the bow, ready to shoot. They alternate frequently so as to share the shooting.

It has been my experience that squirrels go from their dens at dawn directly to a feeding area, watering after they have fed. This means that lake or stream hunting is best an hour or so after first light.

And don't worry about losing squirrels that drop into the water. Dead squirrels float well for a long time.

If the stream is too small to float the hunter can don hip boots and wade slowly down the stream—again hugging a bank and using trees, the shore and other concealment as much as possible.

Lake shores are a bit more difficult to hunt. In many states the use of outboard motors in hunting is illegal, so one hunter must paddle while the other shoots. A canoe is best for this kind of hunting. The lake shore rarely provides the high quality hunting that a stream does, however.

Game call manufacturers have come forth with all kinds of wildlife imitations in recent years—in addition to the more traditional crow, turkey and waterfowl calls. Today, imaginative call designers and hunters call fox, coyotes, wolves, moose, elk, 'coons, and many other animals. The squirrel has not been neglected.

Squirrels often can be fooled with call which imitates their bark. (Russell Tinsley photo)

There are two basic kinds of squirrel calls on the market, one being the mouth operated call and the other a manually operated bellows call. The slate-box turkey call can be used to imitate the bark of a squirrel, and some hunters successfully imitate the squirrel with half-dollar coins struck edge to edge.

The caller attempts to imitate the familiar bark of the squirrel. While a call may occasionally draw a squirrel within shooting range, that is not the purpose of the call. Instead, the object is to make old bushytail sound off, revealing his location.

Expert squirrel callers say the fox squirrel is more vulnerable to the call than the gray.

The squirrel call is an interesting and helpful item in the hunter's outfit, but it is not likely that squirrel calling will ever develop to the degree that varmint and gamebird calling has. The squirrel is not that difficult to locate and get within shooting range.

Dogs also play a role in squirrel hunting, though not as much so as in other kinds of small-game hunting.

Beagles and other trail hounds can be trained to trail and tree squirrels. I once hunted with a venerable Ozarks hillsman that owned just about every kind of hound imaginable, including squirrel hounds. He

This call you tap with a finger to imitate squirrel bark. (Russell Tinsley photo)

Fox squirrel bounces around tree trunk to answer the call.

put a pair of his squirrel dogs down in the woods behind his farm house, and we enjoyed several good chases and bagged one or two grays.

House dogs, pets, or mongrels often make good squirrel dogs, but they usually hunt and follow the squirrel by sight, keeping a sharp eye on it in its flight through the treetops. They will tree squirrels, however. Some mongrels make top squirrel dogs.

For some reason squirrels tend to freeze when treed by a dog. The presence of the barking dog seems to have this effect on the squirrel. Possibly it feels safe well beyond the reach of its tormentor.

The hunter's job is locating the well concealed squirrel flattened against the matching gray bark of a hardwood. It is not often easy. I was able to locate one of the Missouri squirrels my Ozarks friend's dogs treed when a light breeze ruffled the long hairs in its tail.

The adaptability of the squirrel to the dog owner's kind of hunting pads its case as one of America's top game animals.

The squirrel hunter's clothing and equipment are not demanding upon a family budget. Besides being appropriate for the weather, clothing should be of a dull hue, or better still, of a camouflage design. A head net is handy for stand hunting. The boots or shoes should have rubber soles or soles of some other soft material that facilitates quiet movement and good traction in hilly country.

I prefer hollow-point bullets for my scope sighted .22 caliber rifle, though I know many hunters feel the hollow points are too destructive of the fine meat. If these hunters can limit themselves to head shots, then more power to them, but I have seen too many squirrels, drilled through the body with solid-point bullets, make it to a den for a slow and lingering death.

You can get a good argument going as to whether size No. 4 or 6 shot is the best shotgun load for squirrels, but either load should carry plenty

This Illinois shotgunner has just scored on a squirrel.

of powder. Squirrels are tough to bring out of a tall oak with light field loads.

I don't often use a shotgun for squirrels, but if I did I would go with a modified or even tighter choke.

Many bowhunters recommend blunt-tip small-game arrows for squirrels, but others insist upon broadheads. The blunt tips are effective at close ranges, but the squirrel is a tougher critter than the cottontail—

Author Gooch skins squirrel taken with bow and arrow.

even if he does have to accept second place in the national polls. Flu-flu fletchings to retard the flight of the arrow after the initial burst of speed are a necessity unless you want to lose a lot of arrows. And if you use broadheads plan on losing a few that lodge high in the trees.

American squirrel seasons are long, often controversial, and not always biologically sound.

While there is some mating every month of the year, the bulk of the annual offspring of squirrels comes twice a year—first in late winter or early spring, and again in late summer or early fall. This will vary slightly between the fox and gray squirrels, and in different parts of the squirrel's range. The trick in good squirrel management is to wedge the

Gray squirrel scampering through treetops makes difficult target even for shotgunner.

hunting between these periods, giving the animals time to rear their young to the point where they can make it on their own. Unfortunately, too many game departments ignore this in setting their seasons.

Squirrel seasons vary tremendously. The Texas seasons are split, opening on May 1 and again in October and finally ending December 31. The Missouri season opens in late May and continues through December 31. Georgia has a one month early season opening in mid-August and another season running from mid-October into February. The southern Illinois season opens August 1, and neighboring Indiana opens its squirrel woods August 15. Both are top squirrel hunting states. The Kentucky and Tennessee seasons also open in August. In Virginia where the squirrel is the No. 1 game animal, early two-week seasons open as early as September 1 in some counties; and somewhere in the state there is hunting from then until the end of January.

Most game managers favor October for the opening of the squirrel season, and many agree a spring season, sandwiched between the early and late breeding periods is also feasible. But generations ago squirrel hunters learned that the most productive time to hunt was late summer when the hungry little animals were feeding on ripening acorns, hick-

Fox squirrel is the largest of all tree squirrels. (Russell Tinsley photo)

ory nuts and corn. Seasons are often set to take advantage of this peak period, and the custom is hard to break down.

The mobile hunter, if he desires, can find squirrel hunting somewhere in America from early May through February—a long ten months of hunting.

The range of the gray squirrel blankets the eastern half of the United States. Starting near the rocky coast of Maine, it extends to the tip of Florida and then along the Gulf of Mexico to eastern Texas. It then runs due north to the northwestern corner of Minnesota, dips into Canada and follows the United States–Canada border to Maine. Few acres of suitable habitat within this vast country are without at least a few squirrels.

The range of the fox squirrel lies a bit more south, but further west than that of the gray. It begins generally in southern New Jersey, runs south to Florida and along the Gulf Coast to western Texas and the Rio Grande River. From there it shoots north through the Texas Panhandle, claiming most of Oklahoma, Kansas, Nebraska and South Dakota. From South Dakota it runs eastward through Minnesota, the Lower Peninsula of Michigan, Ohio and the southern edge of Pennsylvania.

In very little of its range is the fox squirrel as abundant as the little gray, however.

There are spotty populations of both fox and gray squirrels beyond these natural boundaries, but the prime squirrel hunting country will still be found within the natural range of the animal.

Widely distributed, often abundant, suitable for many styles of hunting, and tasty on the table, the squirrel is not popular among some hunters only because they have not given America's No. 2 game animal a chance.

6

Calling All Predators

by Russell Tinsley

Once I attended a state game and fish department hearing where a motion was being discussed to prohibit the use of a predator call in a certain county because, as the eloquent opponent of calling said, "It just makes me sick to think that someone can dupe an unsuspecting and innocent animal to its execution."

If it hadn't been for the seriousness of the discussion, I might have doubled over with laughter. Take unfair advantage of a predator by using a call? Never!

Consider the cunning coyote, for example. Despite man's long-time and most dedicated efforts to eradicate the critter, using everything from guns and steel traps to the most virulent poisons, the coyote not only has flourished, but also has greatly expanded its range. Now where such insidious means have failed, a hunter with a predator call is capable of "duping a coyote to its execution." What is most unkind and unjust about such comments is that it doesn't show proper respect for the coyote, nor to any other survival-wise predator, for that matter.

Put in proper perspective, calling is just another hunting technique, not too unlike stand hunting or stalking or even hunting with hounds.

Camouflage clothing is a definite aid in concealing the predator caller.

Yet it is a fascinating way to hunt. There is nothing, absolutely nothing, quite like the drama and thrill of seeing a hungry predator coming toward you, almost hypnotized, its guard down briefly, as it heads for what it thinks is a quick and easy meal. But the crafty critter doesn't throw all caution to the wind. Make no mistake about that! One blunder by the hunter and the animal will vanish even quicker than it appeared on the scene.

Although refinements have been added to both the technique and equipment through the years, the basic motivation remains the same: imitate something that will bring a predator toward you, either preying on its need for food or perhaps have it respond more from curiosity than anything else. The old reliable is the distress cries of a rabbit in trouble. All predators feed on the widespread rabbit.

Some hunters can mimic this dying-rabbit cry merely by sucking against a hand, although the majority of us must depend on mechanical help, either a mouth-blown call or a battery-powered electronic unit, in places where such a calling device is legal.

A blown call is the most rudimentary. For someone who knows what he is doing, this economical contraption is as effective as any electronic player. I normally carry one in my hunting jacket, never knowing when opportunity for its use might present itself.

Murry Burnham brings young coyote within handshaking distance. (Burnham Bros. photo)

Various sounds will attract predators. There is a high-pitched squeal, to imitate a cottontail, and a deep-voiced call that sounds like a jack rabbit in trouble. Experienced callers usually employ the sounds which mimic the food sources of the predators they are after, such as cottontail cries for foxes, maybe the jack rabbit call in open western lands where the quarry is a coyote or perhaps a bobcat. Simply adjusting the call's reed can vary the tone and pitch. A predator call can be purchased at most any sporting goods store.

All types of electronic equipment also are available and the hunter can make calling as simple or as complex as he wishes. A calling cassette, for instance, can be used in any of the small recorders/players which are commonplace in businesses and homes nowadays. While the volume on most of these units is at best just passable, there are auxiliary plug-in speakers which can increase the player's volume tenfold, to broadcast the distress cries over a much wider area.

A portable phonograph probably still is the most widely used gadget, but it has drawbacks, bulk and weight being one, and phono records are more susceptive to scratches. The trend seems to be toward eight-track and cassette callers.

I have accompanied Murry and Winston Burnham, the brothers of game-calling prominence, on several trips to collect authentic calling sounds. One advantage of the electronic unit is that it instantly makes

Henry Howell with pair of bobcats duped by dying-rabbit call.

anyone an expert caller, as far as the right sound goes. It is the real thing, those piteous squeals of a frightened rabbit hollering off the tape.

One time the brothers heard of some jack rabbits trapped on an island in the middle of a large central Texas impoundment. Obviously when the fluctuating lake was down the rabbits made it to the island, which at the time was connected to the mainland. When the water level abruptly came up, they only could swim to escape, and several elected to remain on the isle. A jack was run into the water and caught with a long-handled dip net. Captured in the net, the rabbit squalled

Winston Burnham brings in a bobcat at night. (Burnham Bros. photo)

and the brothers recorded the frantic cries. Later the creature was released unharmed. Another time a roosting meadowlark was similarly pinned with a net and its cries of distress recorded before it was freed.

Another advantage with the caller is that sounds can be changed simply by substituting one cassette cartridge for another. Thus a dying-rabbit tape can be used for foxes; a bird-in-distress tape is good for raccoons, which are attracted more by the bird than a rabbit. Eight-track cartridges often have different sounds on four channels and the caller can change back and forth just by pushing the channel-selector button.

An electronic caller also can be placed away from the hunter, which helps avoid detection, and it leaves both hands free for shooting, an important consideration if the weapon is bow and arrow.

Electronic callers are prohibited in some states and areas, however, and it is wise to get a copy of your state's game laws and find what is permitted and what is not. But even if such a device isn't allowed, ob-

Gray fox that answered a predator call on winter night.

tain a cassette or eight-track cartridge and listen to these authentic sounds and learn how to imitate them with a mouth-blown call. This is much superior to attempting the right sound from written instructions.

Night calling is very effective in areas where it is legal, and among the latest development for this sport is a red-lens light. Predators are primarily nocturnal, prowling at night, and thus they are more susceptive to a call after dark, with foxes, bobcats and coyotes responding best when there is no moon. The red-light idea was developed by the Burnham Brothers after reading how the utilization of various colored lights in the Bronx Zoo made some animals believe night is day and vice versa, to have them active in the daytime when people visit such places. The theory seems to be that animals can't see the light and are oblivious to its presence. All predators, with the exception of maybe the bobcat, are color blind and when red is photographed with black-and-white film, it comes out black, or an absence of color. Whatever the reason for its effectiveness, the red light definitely works and is much superior to the conventional white light, although the latter can be used effectively if it isn't too bright and harsh. When calling with a conventional headlight, tilt the beam upwards so the ground is faintly illuminated by the outer edge, and swing it in a circle about you as you call. This is sufficient light for detecting eyes, yet not so harsh as to spook the light-shy critter. A gray fox doesn't seem to mind a light all that much, but a red fox and coyote are plenty wary.

As for weapons, since usually targets will be quite close, many hunters arm themselves with full-choke 12-gauge shotguns loaded with No. 4 or No. 2 shotshells, aiming at the critter's head. The scattergun is especially popular with gray fox callers since this little jittery critter bounces around and is difficult to get in a rifle sight. As Murry Burnham once jokingly said, "There's a lot of air around a gray fox."

Actually for this short-range shooting, any weapon from bow and arrow to handgun or your favorite deer rifle can be utilized, depending upon your desires and the circumstances. But a predator is tough and the caller shouldn't be undergunned. I use a .222 or something in that class for foxes, a 6mm or .243 for bobcats and foxes. Smaller .22 centerfires such as the .22-250, .222 and .22 Hornet simply do not have enough wallop for the larger predators I have found. One might drop an animal in its tracks nine out of 10 times, but that's not good enough.

Yet even using an electronic caller doesn't guarantee instant results. There is more to calling than merely having the proper equipment and being armed with the right weapon, although these are considerations not to be taken casually.

Coyote senses something is wrong and leaves scene in a hurry. (Burnham Bros. photo)

Duping a predator like the fox, coyote or bobcat is comparable to hunting the white-tailed deer—only possibly tougher.

If that statement raises some eyebrows, it should. I am convinced this is the single most common costly mistake made by the inexperienced predator caller: he does not show his quarry the proper respect.

Typical is the fellow I hunted with recently. I parked the pickup in an area which appeared promising and the loudmouth climbed outside, slammed the vehicle door, and proclaimed in a booming voice: "Sure hope we call something here."

I cautioned him to silence. He stifled the impulse to talk for maybe five minutes, but he stomped into the woods, making no effort to be cautious. After we got hidden and I commenced blowing on the dying-rabbit call, he squirmed about and even raised up a couple times to look about. Finally in a complaining voice that could have been heard in the next county he announced: "We ain't going to call anything here."

No, I thought bitterly, and you ain't going to get the chance again—not with me anyway.

It is odd, really, but this same man is a fairly proficient deer hunter. I have been in the woods with him and he slips about and keeps quiet and acts as if he does carry some substance between his ears. He respects the deer's cunning and this is reflected in his cautious actions. That is why I didn't hesitate to take him along when he asked to go predator calling.

If anything a predator is more crafty, wary and sly than the whitetail. It must be, persecuted as it is, being fair game year-round in most places, this being particularly true of the coyote. Bobcats and coyotes and even the ubiquitous fox to some extent are blamed for every foul deed from a decline in quail numbers to the loss of domestic stock.

Because it has been a victim of attempted eradication, a sort of "super breed" predator has evolved. Soon after the spring-born young are old enough to fare for themselves, the dumb ones are killed. Only those a cut above the average wariness survive to breed and propagate the species. This cycle is duplicated generation after generation. As a result only the super-wary have made it.

But the predator does have an exploitable weakness: it must eat. By imitating a small animal in distress—a rabbit, rodent or bird—the predator is lured into a false sense of security, rushing for the easy meal before another animal gets it. But if the caller somehow fouls up and the predator senses it has been had—that's it, brother. A predator once fooled by a call isn't apt to make the same mistake again anytime soon. In its precarious world there seldom is the luxury of a second mistake. The first one usually is fatal.

Most neophyte callers attach too much importance to the call itself and ignore other, more important fundamentals. I know a man in my hometown—and I have talked and corresponded with many others like him—who bought a brand-name call, spent considerable time practicing on it, and went into the woods—just one time, mind you—and blew on the contraption for a few minutes, then later told me "the damn thing won't work." Upon questioning he admitted he didn't know whether or not any predators were present to hear the call; he went where he "thought" there should be predators.

He should have done his homework and been reasonably assured there were predators where he was hunting, or failing to do this, he should have moved around a lot and tried many different places, relying on the law of averages to hapchance try a spot where a willing animal would be within hearing range of the call. Ideally, the caller improvises a strategy which incorporates both of these.

There are several ways of locating likely calling territory. Visual sightings are perhaps the best. If you should sight a fox running across a backcountry road, for example, then this area would be a good spot to call. Predators generally are creatures of fairly limited range and should you see one, you almost can assume that it lives somewhere close. Another method is to look for telltale signs such as tracks and droppings, along country roads and well-traveled trails and around waterholes. Learn what type of terrain each predator prefers and its food preferences. The more you know about your quarry the better are your odds of success.

But suppose someone invites you on a hunt into territory neither of you is familiar with. Time is limited and you want to—and should—utilize most of it actually calling. If you have sought predators before, probably you can get, by just looking, some inkling as to where to call; but if you lack the necessary experience, freelance about, stopping occasionally to call, then moving to try again. But in doing this many callers make two rudimentary mistakes: they spend too much time in one spot and, secondly, by moving in a circle or not journeying very far between attempts, they only are prospecting the same countryside again and again. When critters like the fox and coyote are going to answer, they respond in a hurry, in less than 15 minutes usually. Bobcats are more deliberate and require longer, 30 to 40 minutes, but the person who sets out to call cats exclusively has to know about where to concentrate his efforts because in any one trip he isn't going to make many stops because of the time involved, as John Wootters explains in Chapter 14.

Winston Burnham goes to work on a mouth-blown predator call.

Some of the different types of calls available to predator caller.

In calm weather the sound will carry for maybe a half mile and you should move at least this far between stops. A coarse, deep-pitched call, imitating a jack rabbit in distress, will reach farther than will the conventional high-pitched cottontail voice. If there is a wind don't travel quite as far between tries; any breeze muffles the call somewhat. A wind also sends the sound fartherest in the direction the hunter doesn't want it to go, downwind where any approaching predator will be spooked by a whiff of human scent. For this reason the optimum calling condition is calm or with a very light breeze. A mistake many callers are guilty of is to hunt during a strong wind. Actually this might be termed a "double mistake." The odds definitely are against any success in a high wind, and the caller is "wising up" predators in an area that otherwise might provide quality hunting under conducive conditions.

Vast Bureau of Land Management (BLM) lands, where sheep are raised in the western states, offer the best opportunity for calling, because of access and a large population of coyotes. But over most of North America, access to productive hunting territory is becoming increasingly more difficult and consequently the wise caller tries to beguile wily predators when he figures he has conditions in his favor. Another way he can gain some advantage is to call along the perimeter of the place he has access to, particularly if the farm or ranch is small, less than 1000 acres; this way the hunter is calling not only this acreage, but also attracts predators from neighboring lands.

With calling, like any hunting, there are various ways and means for the human to outwit his quarry. Hunting at the right time, for instance, is almost as important as being at the right place. I have seen predators called in mid-mornings of hot summer days, but such unexpected success is the exception rather than the rule. Since predators are habitually nocturnal creatures, it stands to reason that the best times for calling are

Bowhunter with 'coon he called and bagged just at dusk.

early and late in the day, or even at night if your state laws permit. These are the periods when predators are up and about, searching for food, and they are most susceptive to a call.

A mistake made by many callers is to start too late and quit too early. Of all the daylight hours, I prefer the very first one, from dawn to sun-up, when the weather is cold or cool and usually there is an absence of wind. But the late period, from after sundown to total dark, is almost equally as good. The best night hunting, as I stated earlier, is during the dark of the moon. If there is any moonlight try to arrange your calling schedule to take advantage of the darkness. Maybe the moon will set near midnight; so in this circumstance, sleep early in the night, hunt later. Except for 'coon calling, even a tiny sliver of moon will affect hunting. But a full moon is naturally the worst.

In night calling there are a couple of more common mistakes to avoid. Wear dark clothing, to make your telltale outline less conspicuous. Be very quiet when departing your vehicle and walking into potential calling territory. Animals moving about are more alert and are more apt to be frightened by unnatural noises. Have your light source near your eyes, which makes it easier to spot eyes, rather than holding it at waist level, like with a flashlight.

After nightfall is, actually, the most advantageous time to dupe predators. The critters are most active then and in darkness there is less likelihood of human error. The primary bugaboo is wind, and the caller's primary strategy must be adapted to the prevailing breeze. If the wind is from the north, as an example, the caller would travel to the south side of his calling territory before stopping. Otherwise, from the north, his scent would be scattered through the area from where he hoped to attract predators.

At night predators are found in different places than they are in the daytime. Under the security of darkness they head to open flats and prairies where rodents and rabbits are found; during daylight they'll be in their dens in rough country.

This calling demands the human know his country. On a dark night the hunter gets confused on his sense of direction and his view is limited, where he can't ascertain whether he is in likely calling terrain or not. If possible the caller should scout the countryside beforehand and mark potential calling spots by hanging easily seen white flags on branches of trees or bushes. Otherwise he might make this mistake: he moves about in a big circle and although he might stop two or three times, he only will be calling the same general area over and over.

On this hot, humid summer night, Murry and Winston Burnham and I returned to a spot we had marked earlier, near a rocky tree-lined creek. That afternoon we had hiked along the trickle of a steam and Winston showed me plenty of evidence that 'coons were present. Tracks were everywhere along the moist shoreline.

There were a couple of factors which made this different than the run-of-the-mill hunt. For one, it was late summer, an odd time for hunting, but there was a pragmatic reason for it.

"By late summer the 'coon population is at a peak," Winston explained. "The young of spring have grown up and they are naïve, easily fooled with a call. And they are gathered around water where there is a lot for them to eat in the summer. That makes them easy to find."

Also unique about this hunt was the fact that we were to hunt at night yet without any artificial light. A few days earlier the Burnhams and I were discussing 'coon calling. Murry said the optimum time for calling these ubiquitous critters is at night, when 'coons are prowling and are easily called.

Some of the electronic equipment that's available to predator caller.

Murry Burnham sets up an eight-track cartridge player for some nocturnal calling.

"Oh you might get one up early or late in the day," he went on, "but it's a hit-or-miss proposition; you have to be fortunate enough to be calling near one's den. At night calling a 'coon is almost a surefire cinch, however."

I told him that was unfortunate since many small-game hunters were missing out on a lot of fun since many states prohibit hunting at night with a light.

"Who said anything about a light?" Winston interrupted. "Shucks, just the illumination from a full moon is good enough."

The brothers offered to show me and that is the primary reason we were here.

We soon came to a likely spot not far from where we had parked the pickup beside a branch marked with a white rag.

"This looks good," Winston said. "Get ready with your bow and arrow and I'll call us a 'coon."

Winston put a call in his mouth and ruptured the quiet night air with one of the darndest sounds you'll ever hear, a shrilling shriek punctuated by harsh, high notes. If you have ever heard the desperate shriek of a bird caught by some animal, it sounds something like that, a piteous and painful cry, yet it is deeper, with a more coarse tone, to give it volume and range. Almost immediately a 'coon came running, a dark blob on the sun-bleached, moonlighted grass.

Maybe an hour and several stops later the third one appeared on the scene and I finally connected with an arrow and we called it quits and headed home. I learned something different about the 'coon, although calling the black-masked critters is nothing new to me. I have seen many duped by the crippled-bird cries. But it was either in the daytime or at night calling with a light. In fact, I always believed the odds were against calling *anything* if there was any moon.

"The 'coon is an exception," Murry said. "One will answer a call as readily in the moonlight as it will when it is pitch black. But you're right about other predators like the fox and coyote. They don't like the moon."

A 'coon isn't particularly difficult to fool with a call, especially if there is a fair population of the roly-poly animals. The more 'coons, the better are your chances of success. So by finding the tracks and thus determining some 'coons were available, we had improved our odds considerably.

Yet even if you give an area the look-see and find predator tracks, that is no guarantee of calling success. Many things can go wrong and they usually do.

Perhaps the caller unknowingly is prospecting an area already called recently. A predator once fooled by a call isn't going to make the same error again right away. Ideally the locale should be rested several weeks between calls. But if you hunt the same territory twice within a short time span, try different calling sounds. If you used the dying-rabbit call the first time around, go to a bird-distress cry for the second hunt.

As the sport of predator calling continues to increase in popularity, fertile hunting areas are becoming increasingly more difficult to find. Should you locate a prime spot, protect it zealously, for once game is pinpointed in huntable numbers, you are well on your way to success.

Actually predator calling is rather basic and uncomplicated and can be quite inexpensive. A mouth-blown call, maybe camouflage clothing and a weapon are all the tools you need. As you progress in experience you will learn ways to improve your technique, taking full advantage of camouflage, even a mesh headnet to cover your face, and scents to mask human odor. But despite what equipment you might obtain, results still depend primarily on hunting in the right place, at the right time, and being able to negate the critter's ultrasensitive defense system of smell,

Author takes aim at raccoon that was attracted by bird distress cries.

sight and hearing. Take care with every detail, no matter how insignificant one might be. There is a very thin line between success and failure.

Tape recorder with cottontail distress cries brought this bobcat in.

7

Hounds for Small-Game Hunting

by David Michael Duffey

HUNTED SINGLY, in braces or in packs, hounds produce game for the sportsman today in a manner little changed from the way hounds have been doing for centuries.

The pursuit of beasts chasable by keen-nosed, clear-tonguing hounds has long occupied men who needed meat for their families or simply thrilled to the contest enjoined when a sagacious hound was set on the track of a wild and wily critter. The excitement and reward that comes to men who follow hounds remains today what it always has been, a primal sport that grabs a man where he lives.

Down through the years hounds have been sorted out, through both natural and artificial selection, into breeds (or at least strains and types) that best satisfy hunters in widely scattered locations for use on various types of game. The criteria, as far as hound men are concerned, has always been the practical. If a hound does the job, the men who hunt with him care little about the color of his hide or the names and titles that spice up the pedigrees of other gun dogs.

There is more emphasis than there ever was on purebred and registered hounds. But sportsmen still cross one recognized breed with another separate breed if they think the crossing will produce what they believe they need for the game in their particular locality. The resulting off-spring are always, unmistakably, hounds.

Hounds, through experience and training, may become specialists, "straight" on one kind of game and not diverted by the scent of other animals. Others may be generalists or "combination" hounds whose masters use them on several game species.

It is difficult to categorize and classify hounds. Two hounds of the same breed, even out of the same litter, may each be used for hunting a different type of game. According "to the book," Redbone and Bluetick hounds, for example, are two of the officially recognized coonhound breeds. Perhaps the majority of Redbones and Blueticks are hunted on raccoon. But thousands are also put on the track of everything from rabbit and squirrel to deer, bear and mountain lion, which runs the gauntlet from small to big game.

Beagles rank as our smallest hunting hound and are generally thought of as cottontail rabbit specialists. So it might seem that they rank special attention in a chapter on hounds for the small-game hunter . . . and they do. But it should never be forgotten that in states where it is legal, many a buck deer has been brought to the gun of a stander by a Beagle pack. So Beagles can also be big-game hounds. This kind of overlap is evident throughout the world of hounds.

Also consider the fact that a dog referred to and used as a foxhound in northern climes is a different type of dog, does his fox hunting in a different manner and for a different purpose than does the foxhound of the south.

To avoid, as much as possible, confusion that may exist as a result of varied usage to suit local conditions and the multiple roles of individual hounds, it will be a lot clearer to the hunter who plans to use a hound on small game if we "name the game" and then indicate what hound breeds are generally most satisfactory for that type of hunting.

Hounds of various breeds are used on bear, boar, deer and mountain lion in North America. These species, being big game, are not part of our discussion, although hound breeds used for what we are going to arbitrarily call "small game" are also used to pursue big game.

For our purposes small game will include not only the furred and feathered upland game like rabbit, squirrel, pheasant, etc., but also such animals as fox, raccoon, coyote, etc., which more properly have their own designation as predators or varmints and which some sportsmen might consider closer to a big-game than small-game category. But there is great sport to be had by running such critters with hounds and they will be included as small game.

It makes good sense, in most instances, to call hounds not so much by their breed names as by the name of the game animal they are used to pursue. Thus we have rabbit hounds, raccoon hounds, fox hounds, bobcat hounds, etc. However, regardless of the kind of game they hunt, small-game hounds will be of stock stemming from Beagles, Bassets, coonhounds and foxhounds or mixtures thereof. There is only one breed of Beagle and one breed of Basset. But numerous breeds or, at least strains, of coonhounds and foxhounds with the proper prefix, such as Black and Tan coonhound or Walker foxhound, become specific instead of generic.

If, to you, small-game hunting involves rabbit, squirrel and possibly an occasional crack at upland birds, only Beagles and Bassets need be given serious consideration, particularly if you specialize in rabbits and hares. Just for the record there is extant a hound breed known as a Harrier, which might be described as a long-legged Beagle or an undersized foxhound. But it is practically unknown and next to impossible to acquire.

If raccoon, opossum, bobcat or any other animal that trees (including squirrel) is your quarry, your selection should come from among the six or more recognized coonhound breeds. If it's fox, coyote or any other long-running animal you are after, one of the foxhound strains will give you the most sport if you hunt southern style and might well be your choice even in the North. But for northern predator hunting, usually done on snow during the daytime rather than at night on bare ground, as is done in the South, hounds out of the coonhound classification or crosses between coonhounds and foxhounds usually prove most satisfactory.

With those general explanations and recommendations giving us a cold trail, let's try to warm up the line by getting a bit more specific. But always bear in mind that *some* Beagles *might* do quite satisfactorily on fox, for example, just as *some* foxhounds *may* do what *you* want done on rabbit and hare. In the hound game there is little agreement, only a consensus, so nothing is cut and dried.

Rabbits and Hares

If there is a universally recognized rabbit hound it is the Beagle. And for the man who likes something a bit different in terms of appearance, pace and tongue, Bassets are available. Both are honored as bunny spe-

Some hunters prefer the slow-moving Bassett hound to move rabbits. (Russell Tinsley photo)

cialists, but they can aid in putting game birds like pheasant in the bag, with training can become practical squirrel dogs and in some instances useful on such game as fox and raccoon.

Beagles have many things going for them. They start hunting young, they are hardy and easy to keep and their small size is advantageous when space and cost involved in keeping a hunting dog have to be con-

But a vast majority still vote for the little Beagles. (Erwin Bauer photo)

sidered. That also encourages many sportsmen to keep more than one Beagle. The little hounds can be worked in pairs or in small or large packs as well as alone.

Bassets, although they are only nine to 15 inches at the shoulder, are actually rather large hounds, for they may weigh up to 70 pounds. Their short, crooked legs keep them low to the ground. Bred from field stock, Bassets are capable and sure workers, although they are best known to the public as the result of media exploitation of their lugubrious appearance. Bassets are far less popular than Beagles, which rank as the most popular gun dog in North America, with probably half-a-dozen purebred but unregistered Beagles pushing out rabbits for hunters for every one of the about 80,000 annually registered with the AKC. The Basset is generally conceded to be more of a one-man hound than the Beagle (who will perform merrily for anyone with a gun), slower in moving a line and taking longer to develop into a good hunter.

As with most of our hounds, the Beagle's ancestors came from the

Beagle seems surprised as a cottontail leaps from its bed. (Erwin Bauer photo)

British Isles. France is credited with developing the Basset. General Richard Rowett, Carlinville, Illinois, who brought some Beagles over about 1870 is the man generally credited with introducing the breed to this country. Basset pioneers were New York stockbrokers Erastus T. Teft and Gerald M. Livingstone who established packs after World War I and Carl E. Smith, Xenia, Ohio, who is still breeding and publicizing Bassets at the time of this writing.

Raccoon

If you want to get mixed up in a knock-down drag 'em out argument, just stand up at a gathering of raccoon hunters and state flatly that you *know* one breed of coonhound, let's say the Black and Tan, is a hound that can't be beat and no other coonhound breed is fit to carry a Black and Tan's feedpan. Your assertions will be drowned out in the uproar and you may have to fight your way out. But when everything settles down, the survivors, for all their vociferous support of their favorite coonhound breeds will concede one thing: there are top coonhounds among every one of the six recognized and several less-known breeds of treeing hounds, regardless of breed and color. The requirements for a good coonhound are pretty much the same, and cross-breeding among the recognized breeds produces good and useful hounds. Differences in opinion boil down largely to some minor characteristics or refinements that particularly please an individual hunter, and others who think like he does and need what he needs.

The major criterion for determining what coonhound breed each hound belongs to is color. The physical and mental requirements are pretty much the same and the end result identical.

To put that 'coon up a tree requires a sagacious hound with a good nose, stamina and an inherited instinct to bark treed. The rest is up to the owner. There are few formal or mechanical methods of training coonhounds. Like all hounds, coonhounds properly bred have inherited the proper instincts. That means the oftener they are taken to the woods and given a chance on game, particularly in the company of other proven straight cooners, the better they will be at their trade.

The six recognized breeds of coonhounds are Black and Tan, Bluetick, English, Plott, Redbone and Treeing Walker. Other coonhounds you will hear mentioned include American Saddleback, Tennessee Treeing Brindle, Mountain Cur and Leopard Cur.

Good coonhounds don't leave any room for doubt when they stand on a tree and tell the world where Mr. Raccoon has taken refuge. (Larry Mueller photo)

If your choice in style of work by a coonhound involves what is often termed a "pleasure hunt" you probably will lean toward the Black and Tan or Bluetick. If you hunt more in the manner competitive night hunts for coonhounds are conducted you will prefer the Treeing Walker or English. Compromises between these two extremes would be Redbones and Plotts.

Fox

Fox hunters have much in common. But three distinct styles of hunting the red and gray rascals are in vogue and they call for a different style of hound. In the scope of this book, the formal hunts, with properly attired horsemen and women following a well disciplined pack, rate little attention.

Northern-style hunting hounds, started on tracks early in the morning, brought around this bobcat, left, and coyote.

But two distinct types of fox hunting, involving single or paired hounds, or packs made up of hounds belonging to different hunters, which can be termed northern- and southern-style foxhunting, need a bit of explanation.

In the North, foxes are hunted during the day, often over snow-covered ground, with the object being to bring the fox around to a stander who will shoot it. A single hound, cold-nosed, and sure about his work will be started on a cold trail. He may complete the hunt without the assistance of other hounds; or, once the fox is jumped, faster hounds may be slipped in on the hot track.

In the South, foxes are hunted during the night and packs of fast, hot-running hounds are cast. If the fox is killed, the hounds do the job. Shooting foxes before the hounds is no more acceptable by hunters who go this route than among the horse-oriented fox chasers. It is a chase, not a hunt.

Hounds more of a "true" foxhound type are used for southern-style hunts. There have been more than two dozen foxhound "breeds" or strains recognized in various localities from time to time. Today only

A mixed breed takes off through woods on the trail of a fox. (Russell Tinsley photo)

Fox hunting in north is done on snow and this pair of foxes was brought around by a Redbone, left, and a Walker.

three are widely recognized, the Walker, the Trigg and the July Foxhound. As with coonhounds, there are probably more "grade" than "registered" foxhounds. Grade hounds are dogs whose purity of breeding may be questionable or improbable. Registered hounds are certified as being carefully bred by the registry that lists them.

Northern foxhounds are more likely to stem from ancestors or belong to breeds now classified as coonhounds, or from crosses between the colder nosed, more deliberate trailing coonhound types and the faster hounds favored in the South who provide a hot, hard-driving chase. The type of hound chosen depends upon the preferences of the hunter as to the way he wants his fox moved and the situations imposed by climate, geography and local custom.

And verily, all of the hounds used on every kind of game in this country, with notable exceptions such as the Beagle, Basset and Plott, are descended from foxhounds. Southerners bred for hard-driving hot-scent running hounds that would strive to catch a fox, and northerners showed partiality for hounds that would carefully work a cold trail to

Hunters managed to intercept this coyote which was pushed by a Bluetick and a Black and Tan hound.

jump a fox and deliberately bring him to the gun. Hounds of the latter type, who possessed an instinct to stay at a tree and bark when their quarry went aloft, as gray foxes will do, were converted into hunters of raccoon, bobcat and other treeing game.

Coyotes and Bobcats

What has been said regarding foxhounds and, to a lesser extent, coonhounds in regard to northern and southern styles of hunting is generally applicable to "wolf" and "cat" hounds.

To sum up, it might be fairly said that a good coyote hound is a good foxhound only more so, while a not-so-hot coonhound in many circumstances might cut it as a hunter of bobcats. But other circumstances may require that a hound set on cats have a bit more of everything than the average coonhound.

Some Texas "wolfhounds" tear at one coyote that didn't get away just at dawn. Most are of Walker breeding.

It takes more of a hound to run bobcats in the terrain of the West and Southwest than in the northeastern and northcentral states, where a quick burst and abbreviated chase usually culminates in a treed cat. It takes a better-nosed, more determined dog to trail a bobcat over windswept rock and force him to tree.

Coyotes, whether run in open or timbered country, pose a real challenge, for miles mean nothing to them and they'll take hounds right out of the country. Seldom, if ever, is a single hound a match for a "brush wolf" or a "prairie yodeler." In addition, when wounded, run down or cornered, both the coyote and the bobcat are tougher customers for hounds to handle than a fox or raccoon.

Javelina

The collared peccary of the Southwest is a marginal animal as far as providing hunting sport with hounds is concerned and is more frequently hunted with locally developed dogs of the "ketch-dog" type than with generally recognized breeds or strains of hounds.

It more approaches herding or driving runaway livestock than a deliberate working out tracks and turning a trailing job into a hot chase.

This suggests that some locally famous breeds like the Catahoula hog dog of east Texas and Louisiana, the Lacey cur and the Leopard cur get first consideration.

Hounds used on wild boar or feral pigs, which rate as big game animals, should also be considered for javelina. This involves individual hounds rather than breeds or strains. But because of its heritage, among the recognized hound breeds the Plott hound, which was converted to 'coonhunting after starting as a bear and boar specialist, has to rate the nod.

Upland Birds

Hounds are not bird dogs. Nonetheless, there are hounds that can aid a hunter greatly in bagging feathered as well as furred game, particularly in providing bonus shots at birds a hunter would never know were about if they sneak off or sit tight.

Cur dogs, trained for the part, trailed and bayed these three javelina in southern Texas brush country. (Russell Tinsley photo)

The idea of hunting upland game birds with the larger foxhounds and coonhounds should largely be discarded. Anyone using these hounds, out after a quarry that will provide him with the kind of chase he likes, won't be geared or garbed to cope with the flush of a bird.

But a sportsman out on a rabbit hunt is something else. He'll be in cover where game birds are found and the gun and load that deals disaster to a hopping bunny can also grass a flying bird.

So it goes without saying that if the hunter hopes to pop a bonus in his game bag, in the form of a pheasant, grouse or quail . . . or if he is partial to rabbit hunting but enjoys an occasional bird hunt, the hound for him is the big or little "B," a Basset or a Beagle.

Birds share coverts with rabbits and a busy Beagle, casting about for a line or jumping a bunny from a brushpile or form, may inadvertently flush a tight-sitting covey. Because pheasants like to use their legs to escape detection, they leave a line for a hound to follow. If the hunter will stir his stumps he can keep up with a Basset (or Beagle) and be within shotgun range when the hound forces the runner into aerial flight.

Some Beagles and Bassets can also be taught to retrieve. One who will, or who will catch and hold a wounded bird, does his bit for conservation and good sportsmanship by assuring the recovery of shot birds. When a hunter learns to read his hound, he will know from the change in tonguing or actions whether a bird or a rabbit is being trailed and conduct himself accordingly. Small hounds can provide some interesting and novel mixed-bag shooting.

Squirrel

Squirrels are furred upland animals and therefore fair game for hounds. But there are various techniques of hunting squirrel with dogs that do not require that the dog be a hound. Terriers, spaniels, farm shepherds, feists and curs and mixed breeds of every description, even some pointers and setters, have been trained to be good squirrel dogs. But you can pretty well bet that a mixed-breed squirrel dog will have received a shot of hound blood somewhere along the line.

It would seem reasonable and logical that smaller hounds, like the Beagle and Basset, would be best utilized for squirrel hunting. They can be, but they are not necessarily best bets because few Beagles or Bassets possess an instinct to tree. They can be taught, as can many smart dogs of different breeds.

But the coonhounds possess a treeing instinct to a high degree and can provide almost uninterrupted hunting for a man who just doesn't like to get out of the woods, day or night. Because squirrels are diurnal and raccoons nocturnal it won't harm a straight 'cooner to hunt squirrel during the day and turn him out after dark on the masked, bushy-tailed rascals.

It's a way to get more fun and use out of a hound and still not have to worry about him running off-game when he's after his primary quarry.

Because of the northern method of hunting fox in the daytime, it is possible for Yankees to have one hound that is virtually straight on *both* fox and 'coon, since a smart hound soon learns he is set on a fox track during the day but after dark when cast for raccoon he's to ignore Reynard's calling cards. But both southerners and northerners can have a "combination" hound if they hunt squirrel in the light and raccoon in the dark.

Beagles are affectionate, hardy little gun dogs and proficient deliverers of rabbits, as evidenced by this bag of Wisconsin snowshoe rabbits.

The purpose of this chapter is to introduce sportsmen to the possibilities and advantages of hunting small game with hounds. It is by no means a comprehensive and complete treatise. But it should give a line on what's best for what game and guide a man who is going to put down some money for a started or trained hound or gamble on a puppy.

If buying a started or trained dog who demonstrates he does what you want done the way you want it done, disregard any recommendations as to breed or type. If the dog does it right pay the man and take the hound home. But when starting with a puppy, it pays to heed advice that will increase the percentage of chance that the pup will grow up into a hound of merit.

If this chapter has stimulated your interest so you want to delve deeper into houndology, learning about the history, selection and training of hounds, you may want to read more on the subject. Most books written about hounds were limited editions and are now out of print.

Beagles, boys and bunnies are a mix that is hard to beat.

There is one comprehensive book available, however. It is *Hunting Hounds* by yours truly, published by Winchester Press.

With the possible exception of another type of hound, the sight-hound (as epitomised by the Greyhound, which courses rather than trails the quarry), trail hounds have been used for hunting by man longer than any other type of dog we have. In fact, it would be difficult to name a gun dog of any breed that was not traceable to a hound.

Today, there is more hunting available to men with hounds than is possible with any other type of dog and the possibilities are greater. Hounds are used to hunt game that landowners consider threats or pests, so permission to hunt is easier to obtain. A wealthy man can enjoy hounds. But so can the less than well-to-do, whether working shifts in a city factory or living close to the land in a rural setting. During vacations or days off, hounds can be hunted. But the hunter whose daytime hours are limited can enjoy great sport with hounds after dark when he has the woods and fields to himself and there is no priority on his time.

It is a natural thing for hounds to hunt and they do it with no concern for reward or praise. The only crime they might be charged with is the fact that in doing what comes naturally they provide hours, days and nights of enjoyment for men who share their hounds' fascination with the chase.

8

Handguns for Small Game

by Hal Swiggett

ALL OF MY SMALL-GAME HUNTING would be with handguns, if I had my 'druthers. I know I'm expected to have likes and dislikes as to whether a hunter uses pistols or revolvers, and I do. I like to use them all and dislike anyone telling me one is definitely better than the other for hunting these smaller species of animals.

Any shooter will do a better job with a gun he has confidence in. So long as the caliber is fitting for the purpose, don't let gun design get in the way.

A revolver is as the name implies. Cartridges are inserted in a cylinder which is held in the frame by a pin. Cocking the gun rotates that cylinder, causing the next chamber to come in line with the barrel. The bullet jumps from this cylinder into the barrel.

A pistol chambers the cartridge directly in the barrel. There is no jump from a chamber. In theory a pistol should be more efficient, since there is no escaping gas. Semi-automatics are pistols; single-shot handguns are pistols. Any handgun where the cartridge fits into a chamber which is part of the barrel itself is a pistol.

Some may disagree with these descriptions, but under no circumstances do I consider all handguns pistols.

Hunter with .22 rimfire revolver aims at squirrel. (Russell Tinsley photo)

What about caliber?

Probably more .22 rimfire ammunition is used than all other calibers combined. Much of it in handguns. I'm guessing here but I believe the larger percentage of handgun .22 ammo is probably fired through semi-automatic pistols.

Semi-automatics, or autoloaders, are a bit more dangerous, especially for beginning shooters. Every time a shot is fired a fresh cartridge is cycled into the chamber ready to fire again. The handgun is cocked, loaded, and ready to go—instantly.

Revolvers are safer. To get a fresh cartridge under the hammer it either has to be cocked manually or, in the case of double-action guns, the trigger has to be pulled.

There is a difference in revolvers. Some are single action, meaning the hammer has to be cocked manually to rotate the cylinder to a fresh cartridge. Others are double action, meaning they can be cocked as the single action or the trigger can be pulled through the revolving cycle and the gun fired without the individual motion of cocking the gun.

Neither has any advantage over the other as a hunting gun. All hunting shots are fired from a cocked gun for increased control of the shot. Double-action trigger pull is so excessive that a carefully aimed shot is impractical.

A hunting handgun should have a barrel at least four inches long. I like six inches better, though I confess to killing a lot of small game with three-inch barreled guns. Barrel length makes little difference if the rest of the gun fits the shooter.

Even this potent Smith & Wesson Model 29 .44 Magnum can be used on small game if toned-down handloads are used.

Sights should be adjustable. If they aren't, most handguns demand the use of "Kentucky windage"—aiming off the point intended to be hit, as few will print to the sights for every shooter.

Since the kill area on small game is really quite small it is imperative that sights be adjustable so the point of impact can be precisely set. Take a squirrel's head, for instance. If shots can't be held within 1½ inches, the squirrel is a lost cause.

Where should shots be placed? I know chests are bigger, and easier to hit, but I also know heads make better targets for animals to be eaten. A .22 doesn't shoot any animal up much, but it can cause meat to be bloodshot. Since there isn't a lot of meat to start with, why waste any?

Head-shot squirrels and cottontails drop in their tracks. Chest-shot animals may or may not drop in those same tracks. Shoulder-shot animals will of course drop where they are hit but this does destroy some meat.

I'm not all that fired up about shooting hollow points in handguns. The velocity simply isn't there to cause them to expand on a sure enough basis. If your gun shoots a particular brand well, fine, shoot

Author Hal Swiggett with javelina bagged with S&W .45 ACP target gun.

them all the time. If a solid bullet shoots better, stick to it. The important thing is to place the bullet in a deadly spot and not to put all that emphasis on expansion and so called "killing power."

Many years ago I used .22 rifles for all my squirrel hunting. They were loaded with standard-velocity ammunition in every instance. The slower bullet is more accurate, on the average, and it is bullet placement that kills cottontails, squirrels, or whatever, and not "killing power" as talked about by some companies in advertising their high-velocity hollow points.

These faster, hollow-pointed bullets are great on larger targets such as jack rabbits and the like, particularly in rifles, but are not necessary for handguns and small game.

Pot hunting, getting meat for the table, is best suited to .22 rimfire handguns for several reasons. Number one is the size and weight of the guns and ammunition. A box of 50 rounds takes little space in a pocket yet is sufficient for a lengthy, or many, small game hunts. Likewise about noise. Granted, handguns are noisier than rifles for any given caliber, but .22's aren't nearly so noisy as bigger bores.

The little .22 cartridge isn't up to dropping larger animals on a surefire basis. Particularly when fired from a handgun. Sure, many head of big game are shot with a .22; same goes for livestock in slaughtering pens. I know a Cree Indian in northern Saskatchewan who kills meat for his little community with a single-shot .22 rifle. His game is caribou and moose, primarily, and he uses .22 Longs because he sincerely believes Long Rifles are excessively powerful. In fact I hunted black bear with him on one trip. I was shooting a 6.5 Remington Magnum. He was backing me up with his single-shot .22 and those .22 Longs.

I know another Indian in that same community, a fishing village on a huge lake, who was working on a fishing boat when a moose was spotted way out in the lake. He wanted it so the boatman went to the moose. The Indian stuck his .22 single-shot down by the head and fired. The moose kept right on swimming. My commercial fisherman friend told the Indian to shoot him again. "Can't, only had one bullet," was his reply.

In my opinion nothing larger than cottontails and squirrels are fair game for the little .22 rimfire cartridge. I've seen far too many jack rabbits run off with .22 bullets through them, in many cases more than one .22 bullet. Sure, they die later but that's not what any true sportsman wants. Of course, the same thing happens with bigger handguns. I've seen jack rabbits shot through the middle look around a moment and go back to eating grass after being hit with a 230-grain, full-metal jacket bullet from a .45 autoloader. The same thing often happens with round-nosed regulation .38 Specials. Game larger than cottontails needs a fairly potent cartridge to do a creditable job killing.

The .22 WMR cartridge is a souped-up job definitely more damaging to whatever it hits than the standard .22. It shouldn't be used for pot hunting except maybe with solids and head shots. It is very good for small varmints, good to 100–125 yards on jack rabbits and the like, but not coyote-sized animals. There is also a .22 WMR shotshell loaded by CCI which does a magnificent job at close range, such as on snakes. It should also be good for 10-step cottontails, but I haven't tried it. Never, under any circumstances, shoot standard .22 shotshells at living animals, other than rats at extremely close range.

Once out of the .22 rimfire class it is best to move on up to the .38 Special if a revolver fan, or 9mm/.38 Super if a pistol addict. Those dresser drawer/night stand calibers of .25, .32 and .380 are good for nothing other than confidence builders for their owners.

The .38 Special can be loaded with target ammo, blunt-nosed bullets at low velocity, and do an excellent job on cottontails and squirrels. For jack rabbits and the larger animals it can be loaded with the newer high-velocity, light, expanding bullets and steps hard on the heels of magnum performance.

Jack rabbits are excellent handgun targets wherever the hunter finds them.

Idaho jack rabbit downed by Ray Speer, he of bullet-making fame.

If the shooter feels head shots aren't for him on small game, I encourage the use of a good .38 Special over .22's. This larger diameter, heavier, bullet does a terrific job with chest shots yet is slow enough to minimize bloodshot meat, even with a shoulder hit.

The .38 Special is probably the nearest thing to a perfect small-game handgun there is.

Many will have heard about .357 Magnums and their usefulness in shooting .38 Specials as low-powered loads, and on up to full-power magnum loads when needed. On paper this sounds great, but few guns will honestly handle those .38 Special cartridges as well as the slightly longer .357 case.

In turn, the .357 Magnum is powerful for any small game except long-range jack rabbits, javelina, turkey, fox and, of course, coyotes. It also does a grand job on woodchucks for the Easterner and rock chucks for the western small-game and varmint hunter.

It is possible for the handloader to make up light loads using those same .38 wadcutter target bullets and equal the results of the .38 Special, both in accuracy and killing potential. Any good handloaders manual will show the way.

Autoloader shooters will find excellent guns in both 9mm Luger and

.38 Super. Factory ammo in the 9mm can be had both as full-metal jacket, and soft or hollow point, depending on the manufacturer. These hunting loads are of recent manufacture. If your dealer doesn't stock them, have him order some.

The tried-and-true .38 Super is one of the finest autoloader cartridges to come down the pike, but there is no hunting ammo available for it. Slightly more potent than the 9mm Luger, it borders on .357 Magnum capabilities. Handloaders can use it with a great degree of success. I've taken a good many head of game with such a gun using 125-grain soft-point bullets. With factory full-metal-jacket ammunition it isn't even a good jack rabbit killer.

There is little use for any of the larger bores when hunting small game. The time-honored .44 Special and .45 Colt will do the job, no doubt about it, but even they are handicapped with their factory bullet—the ancient round-nose profile keeps them from being a deadly killer. The success of these big bores is based on bullet diameter. It doesn't have to expand to make a large hole.

The .45 ACP fits here also. It isn't powerful enough for big game, though there is one commercially loaded round that comes mighty close. It does a great job on medium game—javelina, coyote, fox and, of course, jack rabbit.

One of Swiggett's favorite hunting handguns is this Charter Arms .22 Pathfinder with Hutson Handgunner 1X scope sight.

No full-metal-jacket bullet shooting at live targets, please. It simply does not kill cleanly. If such a bullet must be shot, drop down to the target loaded semi-wadcutters. These have a clean-cutting shoulder and are decidedly more deadly on rabbits and the like than the more powerfully loaded full-metal-jacket bullet.

At this writing, Remington loads the only commercially made hunting cartridge, and it is truly a fine one. The 185-grain hollow-point bullet zips along at about 1,000 feet per second. It does a good job on whitetail deer, at least the smaller-sized animals common to my home state of Texas.

Handloaders can do well with the .45 ACP. Use hollow-pointed lightweight bullets for increased velocity and performance as a varmint cartridge, then sharp-shouldered semi-wadcutters for small- and medium-sized game.

If shooting a commercial or military Colt, good adjustable sights can be installed. Should you be lucky enough to own a Colt Gold Cup target gun you have the best and only yourself to blame when shots are missed.

There is no place, period, for the .44 Magnum where small-game hunting is concerned.

I do like to shoot the big guns and have bagged a good many javelina and a good many more coyotes with them, but a fully loaded .357 Magnum will do just as well on either and is much easier to handle. Same goes for the .44 Special and .45 Colt. Handloaders can turn either into a truly great small- to medium-game killer simply by loading to those same factory velocities and using a flat-nosed bullet.

Thompson/Center manufactures the fabulous Contender single-shot pistols with interchangeable barrels. Whatever I say will be wrong if I mention calibers available, as they are continually adding to the line, but I believe there are upwards of 20 and maybe even 30.

Contender barrels go from .22 rimfires to the almost discontinued 5mm Remington rimfire, .22 Winchester Magnum Rimfire through centerfire .17 calibers, most of the .22 centerfires through .222 Remington, and on through most all handgun calibers on up to several true rifle chamberings, including .25-35 Winchester and .30-30 Winchester. This last is one of my all-time favorite big-game hunting handguns.

I've taken a lot of game with T/C Contenders—from prairie dogs to deer. The priceless ingredient is those many interchangeable barrels. A man can start off on a trip with one frame and three or four barrels and be outfitted for whatever is offered. It takes only a moment to change barrels, giving an entirely different caliber for instant use.

T/C offers a shot barrel in both .357 and .44 caliber, making them comparable to 2½-inch .410 shells. These are legal barrels. They are deadly on small game out to 20–25 yards for the man not really sure of himself with a single bullet. Regulation bullet cartridges can be used in the same barrels by simply removing the choke device screwed into the muzzle.

I can't overrecommend the T/C Contender for the serious handgun hunter. For the price of a barrel a whole new gun is at the shooter's disposal. And it covers the entire range of calibers far in excess of those available in conventional handguns.

Scope one of those flat-shooting rifle calibers and 150- to 200-yard shots aren't at all impossible. I have a 2X Leupold on my T/C .30-30 barrel. It will knock off 250-yard metallic chicken silhouettes three times out of five all day long.

My .22 Hornet barrel is topped with Bushnell's 2.5X Magnum scope and turns in two-inch five-shot 100-yard groups regularly.

Swiggett with gray fox that came to call and succumbed to Star 9mm pistol with Hutson scope.

I have a .25-35 Winchester barrel topped with a 2.5X Bushnell that consistently shoots into three inches at 100 yards with factory ammunition.

That's why I'm so completely sold on these fine guns as hunting handguns. They are a specialist's handgun, but hunting with handguns is a specialty.

My 5mm Remington barrel decked out with a little Hutson Handgunner 1X scope will kill jack rabbits every shot at 125 yards. I'm hard-pressed to shoot like this with revolvers or autoloaders, or even scope-sighted revolvers.

I will admit that in reality not all that much small game needs to be shot at those distances. Ten- to 30-yard shooting with iron sights is still where it's at so far as true small-game hunting is concerned.

If I sound noncommitted you are reading it right. I like to hunt. I like to hunt with handguns. I don't really care what the gun, or caliber, so long as it is big enough for whatever I'm shooting at. Also, I prefer being overgunned rather than undergunned, if the choice has to be made.

Autoloaders in .22's are great. Most target shooters use nothing else. Colt, High Standard, Browning and Ruger all turn out guns at a price within reach of most any pocketbook. Guns made for the outdoorsman lack a refinement or two considered necessary by target shooters but they are lower priced and more than adequate for the small-game hunter. A few imports serve well here too. Stick to known brand names and buy from a recognized dealer so there will be someone to back up your purchase. This applies to American-made as well as imported guns. A few autoloaders put together in this country are not suitable by any stretch of the imagination, so put your faith in a reliable dealer.

Good revolvers are plentiful. Decide what you want to pay and take your choice. Proven names are Colt, Smith & Wesson, High Standard, Charter Arms, Harrington & Richardson, Iver Johnson, Dan Wesson, to name at least the best known. All offer guns suitable for small-game hunting.

A few imported revolvers of good quality fit here. Again, put your trust in known names and reliable dealers and not on the looks of the gun. Surface appearance can be very misleading to the inexperienced purchaser.

There are several good autoloaders on the market chambered for the 9mm Luger and .38 Super cartridges. Colt chambers for both. Smith & Wesson and Browning only for the 9mm. Both Llama and Star imported guns are available in both calibers. I shoot a Star 9mm and a .38 Super Llama regularly along with a Colt MKIV .38 Super. Also a Model

39 S&W 9mm, a Browning Hi Power 9mm and that Cadillac of autoloading pistols, a SIG P210-5 9mm with the extra-length target barrel.

Above these calibers, revolvers are it all the way. There is one big autoloader, the Auto-Mag, but it is far too much gun for anything we are concerned with in this chapter.

How to get good enough with a handgun to go hunting?

All it takes is practice. To be fair to the animal, don't buy a gun and rush out hunting. It might take a week, a month, or several months, but get so you know where your bullets are going before the handgun is ever pointed at a living target.

God gave us two arms with a hand on the end of each. Use both of them when shooting. One-handed shooting is for the target competitor only. Positively. No exceptions.

Grip the gun firmly with the shooting hand, but not so tight muscles

Swinging clay targets from a string in a tree and trying to hit one is good handgun practice.

quiver. Set this gun hand in the cup of the other one so that the fingers of the off hand come up to the trigger guard of the gun. This means most of the hand is underneath the butt. That's as it should be because it is there for support.

To get the most from this position as the trigger is being squeezed, push ever so gently forward with the gun hand. This causes a reverse action in the support hand making it pull back against that forward pressure. This action sets up the most solid offhand grip I know about.

This has been called the "Weaver Stance" by one well-known handgun writer, naming it after a West Coast lawman. Could be, but my grandfather taught me to shoot that way back in the late 1920s and I have no reason to believe he invented it. Be that as it may, it works.

Any offhand position should be used only as a last resort. Handguns place the hunter at a disadvantage from the start; so make up for it every chance you get. Always shoot with a rest of some sort. If on a range use sandbags for sighting in but then switch over to offhand because it is here you should do your practicing. In the field find yourself a fence post, stump, tree, rock; there is bound to be something nearby to support the gun hand, making a better shot possible.

Do not, under any circumstances, let the gun touch anything. Only the back of the hand, the wrists, forearms, depending on the support. The handgun must be free to work. Normally it will shoot away from anything touched that is hard.

If no rest is available, turn to the body. Shoot from a sitting position with forearms resting across, or inside, both knees. This works best for me with the ankles crossed. An individual's build will determine whether this position is worthwhile or not. My personal choice, if I feel

Prickly pear cactus pad makes an excellent target for sighting in a handgun.

the need to try a long shot with no solid support, is to use the kneeling position, with the left elbow on the left knee and my left hand supporting the gun as mentioned in the two-handed hold.

I've had little success with prone positions, but for some lying on the ground seems to work.

How do we sight in handguns for hunting?

Very carefully, believe me.

First let's talk about sights. If a choice is offered, have your gun outfitted with a Patridge-style front sight. This matched with a square-cut notched rear sight inset with a fine white outline makes the most precise shooting combination there is. The only thing that can improve on it is when that front sight is inset with red plastic, as on Smith & Wesson's big-framed magnum revolvers.

If you can have the rear sight cut a bit wider than normal, it will be to your advantage as a hunter. Targets are shot at in good light, with plain backgrounds. Few animals allow shots under those conditions. That extra bit of daylight to be seen alongside the front sight as you line up on game can be the difference between a hit or miss in uncertain

Testing bullet efficiency on a bar of soap, to find if you are getting any expansion from .22 bullets.

light. It *does not* decrease potential accuracy. Equal daylight on each side is all that's necessary. This is exactly the same principle as used by receiver-sight shooters long before scopes came into being.

Some oldtimers still swear by good receiver sights. In the field, target apertures are screwed out and only the frame hole is used. The eye automatically centers any object in a round hole so the front sight gets in the center regardless of the size of the hole. This within reason, of course, but it definitely works. Same for a wide-notched rear handgun sight. Either allows game to be seen, and killed, when conventional cut sights would make the shot impossible.

To get the most out of a .22 handgun I like to have mine hitting the point of aim at 25 yards. This means only a slightly low hold midrange and only very little holdover at 35 yards. In my opinion that's as far as .22 handguns should be used on small game. Maybe another five yards for the great shot, but that's it.

Centerfire handguns can be sighted in with high-velocity ammo to print right on at 50 yards, maybe even 60 yards for better shots. This means very little holdover at 75 to 85 yards and not much under at 35 yards. Few of us can hit jack rabbits beyond 75 yards and most shooters, if they are completely honest with themselves, ought to stop at 50 yards, or even a little less.

Only the shooter can decide his yardage to try shots. If shots can't be held within the size of the animal you are hunting on a range under ideal conditions at 30 yards, then that's too far to shoot at the animal in the field.

If you can hit a jack rabbit silhouette consistently on a range at 100 yards then it is safe to try a few in the field.

Let's do our practicing on paper rather than fur.

Until a shooter can consistently hit a quart oil can at 25 yards under adverse field conditions he should stick to targets. As experience increases, range can be extended.

A good way to increase hitting ability is to add a scope to your handgun. New shooters, folks who had never held a handgun before, hit targets the first shot by shooting a scoped handgun.

It isn't the magnification that causes scopes to be a success. It is the simplifying of the sight picture. Even experienced handgunners go through periods of bad shooting through trying to hold that perfect sight picture as the trigger is squeezed. Scopes do away with this. Simply put the crosshair on the target and expend all effort on a smooth trigger squeeze.

It sounds simple; it is simple.

It takes a good deal of thought, and concentration to place the front sight in the center of the rear sight, with equal daylight on both sides, then level it off on top so there is one straight line across the two—and to hold all this while trying to squeeze the trigger gently.

It's no wonder many folks try a handgun a time or two, miss their targets by many feet, and declare it too complicated for them.

Scopes make it possible for any shooter to score hits immediately. Since success in anything is required to some extent before any real interest can be created it stands to reason more folks can become addicted to handgun shooting with scopes than without.

This carries over to hunting, because a crosshair is much easier to see in bad light than a tiny bit of daylight alongside a front sight. A little practice and game can be found equally as fast with the scope as with iron sights.

Everyone has read about long shots with handguns. Not many believe such feats. Primarily, I guess, because handguns are thought of as short-range weapons. It ain't necessarily so. Since I've pulled off a few myself, I must believe what others tell me.

My longest shot with a .22 revolver came many years ago with two witnesses. Before I go any further, every shot mentioned here was witnessed by at least one other person. I'm not like the Baptist minister who skipped out one Sunday morning and played a round of golf. He shot a beautiful hole in one, his first, and couldn't tell anybody because he was alone and not supposed to be there. Everything I say here took place where I was supposed to be at the time and in front of critical eyes other than my own.

This longest .22 revolver shot came about while hunting in deep south Texas. My son and I had stopped to talk to a game warden on a ranch road. My S&W K22 was lying on the front seat of the car. As we talked the warden said, "There's a jack rabbit down the road, let's see if you can hit him."

"Down the road" turned out to be way down the road when I looked in the direction he was pointing. I got out, rested my forearms across the top of the car, prayed silently, and squeezed the trigger. After a slight pause there was a "plop" and the big jack staggered a bit, obviously hit.

I couldn't believe it—my son was watching and still didn't believe it—the game warden only muttered some unintelligible sound. Unfortunately, as was to be expected, it didn't kill the jack so I took off to finish the job. After such a great beginning I completely flubbed the finale by excitedly trying to hit him in the head with the remaining five rounds as he jumped around trying to get away from me. Had to end up catching him and finishing the job with my boot.

Javelina is a fine game animal and a real challenge for handgunner.

But, nevertheless, it was a good solid hit at a carefully stepped-off 168 steps.

Hunting coyotes one morning with a .44 Magnum Ruger single action I had called in three, got shots at two, and missed them both, at ranges of 50 to 60 yards. I've missed several shots in my life so didn't let these two new ones upset me much. At the next calling site one lone old dog coyote came on the run to about 100 yards, then something didn't ring quite true so he cut away and went back into never never land, so far as handgunning was concerned, and stopped to look the situation over.

He appeared to be content with his distance so I decided to wish him well with a bullet in his general direction.

Resting my arms across my knees I did my best to line up the sights, leaving most of that big front sight sticking up over the rear sight with the coyote sitting right on top.

As the hammer fell I had the feeling the shot was going to be good. A moment later the old dog flopped over. There is no way I could have hit that coyote, in my opinion, but felt I had to try. The big 240-grain handloaded bullet hit him square in the head going in only a little over one eye. I wasn't shooting at his head, honest, I was shooting at coyote but I willingly claimed the shot.

Bernie Dresden was with me. He could only say, "I wish I hadn't seen that because nobody is going to believe it anyway." Bernie stepped it off at 317 steps.

You probably think I'm bragging but bear with me for two or three more tales then I make my point.

There was the time when four hunters were shooting at a distant rock. This was during a lunch break before loading into vehicles and moving to a different location for the afternoon mule deer hunt. The rock really wasn't all that far off. It was maybe football-sized and give or take a little on 250 yards. None of the guys had hit it even though all four had tried several times. Not missing far but, unfortunately, far enough to miss, or cripple, a deer at that same distance.

I hauled out a Ruger .357 Magnum 6½-inch-barrel sixgun stuffed with hot handloads. Resting my forearms over the same pickup hood

Handguns and cottontail rabbits make a fine combination.

they were shooting from I turned one of those bullets loose. I wish I could say it hit the rock but it didn't. It was so close to the bottom edge they all willingly conceded it as a hit and it broke up the shootfest.

None of them had come nearly that close with their scope-sighted rifles.

Then there was the really recent incident, happening just before this written effort took place.

I used to own a Ruger Hawkeye .256 Winchester Magnum pistol. It was scope-sighted with Hutson's great little Handgunner 1X glass. I had killed several coyotes and a good many jack rabbits with it over the years but hadn't shot it in several years, maybe even three or four. It had been retired because of its rarity. My oldest son always liked the gun and had wanted one like it since he had used it on some prairie dogs in New Mexico several years ago during an antelope hunt.

The occasion was his birthday. I decided to give the gun to him but

Two-handed hold gives the handgunner less shake and better accuracy.

hadn't told him yet. I had to go to the ranch on that day, so I took him with me as he and his family were in town on their vacation.

We were shooting at silhouettes on our Mexican Metallic Silhouette course with a couple of rifles and knocking over 250-yard chickens, 375-yard turkeys and even a few 500-yard 18-inch squares.

Then I hauled out the Ruger.

My son tried those 250-yard chickens several times. A good many times I might say. He came close but no hits. Finally I asked to try one myself. He started to tell me where he was holding but I cut that off. I prefer my own mistakes. One shot; scratch one chicken silhouette. Feeling pretty good I committed myself to a turkey. Now these are life-sized silhouettes and those turkey birds were 375 yards, by measure, out yonder. I told him to watch close as I didn't think those light bullets would knock one off if hit.

A Thompson/Center Contender proved to be the undoing of this jack rabbit.

I squeezed the trigger, the bullet definitely hit metal, and number one son said, "If I were you I'd never shoot that gun again." My answer was easy and quick: "I'm not because this gun now belongs to you as a birthday present."

Now I ask you, how's that for getting out gracefully and not messing up the effect with a miss later on.

My point?

Surely you've caught on.

I've been shooting handguns almost 50 years and can remember those successful long-range shots as if they happened yesterday. That's how scarce they are. Sure, there have been others but not so many that I can't remember them all.

Handgunning is not a long-range effort. Rocks, targets, stumps, anything inanimate . . . have a go at it but unless you've a lot of experience don't thoughtlessly cripple any animal. My only illspent effort mentioned here was the one on the jack rabbit with the .22 S&W. On those others the bullet was heavy enough to kill most anyplace it hit so there really wasn't much danger of crippling, except for maybe a broken leg.

Take handgunning seriously. Get the best gun you can afford. Shoot up all the ammunition you can afford. In due time proficiency will come to you so a few of those shots I've mentioned here will take place and become imbedded in your mind for all time to come.

That's how scarce they are.

Do most of your shooting at sensible ranges with adequate calibers for the job at hand.

Handgun hunting for small game is great sport, provides many fine meals, and, as you might have already suspected, leads to big-game hunting. Those bigger animals are a thrill unto themselves, no doubt about it, but not all of us are cut out to be big-game handgun hunters. The only way to find out is to start with small game and a good .22 or .38 Special.

From that moment on let your conscience be your guide.

9

The Bow Hunter

by Russell Tinsley

It is one thing to take a custom-built, super-accurate varmint rifle—a sophisticated instrument almost capable of driving a tack at 100 yards—and standing off a considerable distance and taking deliberate aim through a powerful telescopic sight and ke-plunking an unsuspecting critter like a woodchuck, and quite another to stalk within 20 yards of the same jittery animal, raise a bow into firing position without the chuck becoming aware that something is amiss, and arrowing it when the slightest margin of human error will send the projectile off target.

But bow-and-arrow hunting never was meant to be easy. The demanding challenge is the appeal, its charm.

This emphasis on pursuit rather than the kill is one reason why bow-hunting is enjoying a phenomenal boom in popularity. Another is that, thanks to its limited range and inherent safety factor, the bow is permitted in places where a rifle and indeed even a shotgun often are not, especially in areas of modest population near and around cities and towns, places where small game thrives but receives negligible hunting pressure because of the hazards involved with firearms, despite any regulations and controls which might be applied.

Bow hunter takes aim at cottontail rabbit in underbrush.

Many sportsmen have become what bowhunting expert Fred Bear calls "two-season hunters." They hunt with both gun and bow, this primarily to take advantage of special and different big-game seasons, but the same philosophy applies equally to the small-game enthusiast. It simply adds another dimension.

Consider woodchucks. This animal long has been virtually synonymous with long-range gunning. But this isn't the *only* hunting method. Stalking a chuck and attempting to arrow same might not make any significant inroads into the groundhog population, yet it is sport supreme. The bow hunter can justifiably brag about any chuck he bags.

In many ways, surprisingly, the two pastimes are similar, although it might be difficult to convince either the rifleman or the bow hunter. There are certain steps to be followed before the hunting method or the weapon is decided. Like where to hunt. The rudimentary first step and probably the most important. You can't bag game where there is none.

A reasonable conclusion yet one step that often is glossed over, the factor that usually separates them-that-score from them-that-don't.

So we scout for a colony of the burrowing critters, concentrating on the food source, near pastures perhaps or cultivated fields or vegetable gardens. Once this requirement is satisfied we devise a "game plan" of attack. For the bow hunter this demands approaching close, within 25 yards or less (the chuck is a small target), employing his wits to negate the critter's formidable defense. This means he must study his quarry and be intimate with its habits. Thus the bow hunter creates his own luck—preparation meeting opportunity.

And once he approaches close, he has the proper equipment to not only connect, but to kill quickly and humanely. This means a bow of adequate draw weight and arrow broadheads honed sharp. In some ways bowhunting is like golf: a certain physical skill, a coordination of eyes and muscles, is required, and there is specific equipment for specific jobs. It is knowing what to use when, as we will explain.

Perhaps employing binoculars as an aid, the hunter evaluates the situation. He studies wind currents, not for the wind-drift factor on an arrow, but to stalk into the breeze, where the quarry won't get a whiff of

Compound bow is catching on big among bow hunters.

Winston Burnham with javelina he collected with bow and arrow.

telltale human scent. He tries to figure the best route where he can take advantage of any and all available cover. It is practically impossible for a hunter to go belly-scuttling across an open field without being detected.

Maybe the bow hunter will try a ploy of diverting the chuck's attention. His hunting partner, if there is one, remains upwind of the animal, far enough to make the woodchuck suspicious but not spooking it into its burrow. While the critter's attention is engaged, it is much easier for the hunter to come up on its blind side and hopefully get off an arrow before the human's presence is known. Many things can go wrong and something usually does. But as we said, it is a fascinating challenge. A raw-nerves game of anticipation, patience, stealth and, yes, frustration.

Again it should be emphasized that the bow and arrow is only a tool for delivering the *coup de grace.* The combination is as good or bad as the shooter manipulating it. Therefore it is important to learn the proper fundamentals and to handle the weapon proficiently. But there is more to bowhunting than that. Much more. The most important requirement is woodsmanship, being able to approach close, very close, to your quarry. That's the key to success. The closer you get, the better are your chances.

For some inexplicable reason most bow hunters haven't gotten the small-game habit. A sizable majority participates during deer season and that's about it for the year. Archers don't realize what they are missing.

If you have a bow suitable for big-game hunting, plus the usual accessories—arrows, armguard, shooting glove or tab—you are in business. Actually a target-archery bow, about 30-pounds draw weight, will suffice for smaller game—ground squirrels, cottontail rabbits, tree squirrels—but for bigger animals, from woodchucks and jack rabbits up, a bow designed for big-game hunting, something pulling 45 pounds or more, definitely is recommended.

And if you are interested in bowhunting but know nothing about the sport, don't let the terminology confuse you. Like draw weight, for instance. It is the method used for grading bows, and draw weight merely

Bow hunter doesn't bag many squirrels but he has a lot of sport.

indicates the amount of pounds needed to pull a standard 28-inch arrow full length.

We won't go into the complexities of obtaining the proper bow-hunting equipment and learning to use it properly here. Entire books have been written on the subject. In fact, yours truly authored one entitled *Bow Hunter's Guide* (Stoeger Publishing Co.).

It is important, however, to get started correctly. Bad faults are difficult to shake. For that reason we strongly recommend buying equipment from an established pro shop—some so-called "archery tackle" must be matched to your physical build, such as arrow length, longer for long arms, shorter for short—and get a cram course on shooting fundamentals from a professional instructor or at least an experienced archer.

If there is an indoor archery facility in the city where or near where you live, that's one place to shop for equipment and also get instruction. Yet if pro advice or even help from a seasoned bow hunter is not available, don't hesitate to get a competent book and follow the step-by-step guide. Learning to shoot a bow isn't that complicated. Once the basic procedure is mastered—draw, anchor and release—it is just a matter of repetitive practice.

The new generation of bows, those called compounds, have made learning somewhat easier. The old dependable recurve bow still is plenty good and don't hesitate to buy and use one if that is your preference. But the odd-looking compound with its pulleys and cables does have things going for it that the recurve does not, although the compound is more expensive. Among other things, it is easier to hold the compound steady for aiming, and it propels an arrow at a greater velocity than does a comparable draw-weight recurve.

A compound is patterned somewhat after the block-and-tackle principle—that is, pulling more weight with less effort. The problem with a recurve, particularly one in the 45-pound class, is that most people's muscles are not conditioned to the stress of pulling it and then holding steady. Little-used shoulder and back muscles come into play when pulling a bow. Unless the shooter strengthens these muscles by "dry firing" or pulling the recurve bow repeatedly for a long period before attempting to shoot it, he will find it requires undue effort to not only pull the arrow full length, but to hold it steady at the anchor point for aiming. This leads to the bad habit of a jerky release which affects accuracy.

But a compound, with eccentric wheels at the limb ends, has a rapid weight build-up which peaks through the middle of the draw. There is considerable resistance at the beginning of the draw, but as the eccentric wheels roll over in their 180-degree turn at mid-draw, the weight drops almost 50 percent on some models, less on others. Pulling a compound is a sensation. Suddenly the resistance is gone and the string comes on back effortlessly and it is no big deal to hold even a 50-pound bow steady for several seconds with no strain.

A hunting-style compound plus a dozen quality arrows will cost about what you'd pay for a standard-model centerfire rifle. A recurve bow is considerably cheaper. There is no reason to bend the family budget to get a fancy model for hunting; you'll only worry about scratching it anyway. But don't pinch pennies when it comes to purchasing arrows. Wood arrows are cheapest, but they are susceptible to warping, and one likely will break if it hits the ground at a sharp angle, and when small-game hunting you'll be shooting into the earth. Aluminum and fiberglass are much superior. Both materials are unaffected by weather and they are rugged. One often will ricochet off a rock or tree without bending or cracking. Aluminum is the most popular because tubing can be manufactured to produce arrows of the identical wall thickness and weight. This is critical because the arrow *must* be matched to the bow for stability and accuracy. All dealers have a chart

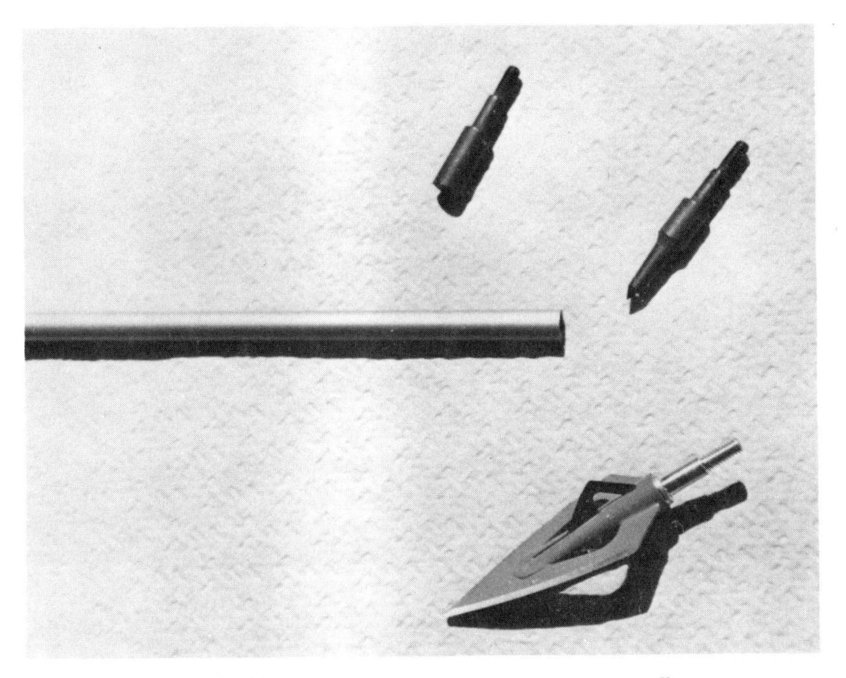

With the screw-in arrow the bowman can change points in a jiffy.

showing the weight of arrow (by code number) which matches any particular bow weight.

One arrow to consider is the screw-type with interchangeable heads. The bow hunter simply screws in a broadhead for bigger small game, a field point for practice, or a blunt for diminutive critters such as tree squirrels and cottontails. This way you can get by with a few arrows of quality rather than loading up with dozens of cheaper and inferior types.

Yet the arrow shaft is no more important than what's on the end. A field point should *never* be used for hunting. It passes through an animal, making a small hole, and there is a high risk of just crippling game. The broadhead for larger game should be constructed of quality steel that will take and hold a sharp edge. Ideally the broadhead edges should be honed to razor sharpness. Unlike a bullet, a broadhead kills by hemorrhage rather than shock. A dull edge does little cutting. It only forces flesh apart to permit entrance and negligible bleeding results. The idea is to hit a vital area and induce massive bleeding, depriving the animal of oxygen being carried to the brain and other organs. For smaller animals like squirrels and cottontails, a blunt is superior even to the broadhead. Dr. Saxton Pope, one of bow hunting's earliest pioneers, discovered this. When he shot a deer in the chest cavity with a sharp broadhead, death came quick; but a cottontail hit in the same area often ran off and only the arrow tangling in the underbrush prevented it from escaping. Dr. Pope, drawing from his surgeon background, concluded that a rabbit was less susceptible to a broadhead because of its minuscule vital areas and blood vessels. He reasoned that a blunt hunting point would kill much more quickly and humanely with its violent shock.

The blunt also has another advantage. Suppose you are hunting squirrels and you release an arrow at one in a treetop. The projectile misses and if the point is sharp it hits a branch and sticks and you've got to climb or write the arrow off. But a blunt simply bounces back. In the same reasoning, the use of a flu-flu arrow, one with oversized fletching, has more air resistance and won't travel far before falling harmlessly back to earth. With standard feathers the projectile is apt to carry a long way and drop where it can't be found.

But a blunt, even one driven by a powerful bow, isn't potent enough for anything including and bigger than a woodchuck or jack rabbit. For animals this size and those larger, use *sharp* broadheads.

Blunts come in different styles—from the typical solid-metal cylinder type to one with a wide, flat face from which a triangular blade juts forward to combine shock with a certain amount of blood letting—and are

Cottontail rabbit hunting with bow and arrow is a game of quiet stalking and patient looking.

Early and late, when bunnies are out feeding, is when the archer stands the best odds of success.

made of either metal, plastic or hard rubber. All will do the job and it is mostly a matter of personal preference. The most important consideration is to get standardized weights. If the field point you practice with weighs 125 grains, then a blunt or broadhead should weigh the same. This is necessary to get consistency and accuracy in your shooting. One advantage of buying a brand-name arrow with interchangeable heads is that all will be identical in weight.

Not much other equipment is needed, except maybe camouflage clothing.

Yet as we said earlier, becoming proficient with your equipment is just the start. After that you must call on all your ingenuity and know-how to approach close to your quarry, or in the case of predator calling, lure it to you. How you hunt will be dictated by circumstances and conditions. Maybe you'll hide alongside a nut tree where squirrels are feeding and wait for one of the arboreal critters to wander into the open . . . or stalk an unsuspecting cottontail rabbit as it nibbles on tender young grass in the edge of a clearing . . . or bring a gray fox close by duping it with a dying-rabbit predator call.

Whichever hunting method you select, it will be a formidable challenge, for with bow and arrow you earn, fair and square, every small-game animal you bag.

10

Muzzleloaders and Small Game

by George C. Nonte, Jr.

WELL, YOU'VE READ about how much fun and toothsome food can be had hunting small game with modern guns and ammunition of all sorts. But, in all the 600-year history of firearms, breechloaders and repeaters using metallic cartridges have been available for only a bit more than a single century. Really, for most of that 600 years, men in search of food and sport were forced to use front-loading guns, charged laboriously and slowly for each single shot with loose powder, ball, patching, grease, and percussion cap or flint.

And the homespun or buckskinned American settler, not to mention the silked and brocaded European gentry, didn't do too badly at the game, either.

The use of muzzleloaders on small game doesn't handicap one as much as might at first be thought. Remember all the emphasis that has been placed on making the first shot count? Remember, too, that lots of people favor single-shot rifles for small game.

Consider, then, that the muzzleloading rifle is simply a single-shot arm that just takes a bit longer to reload than a comparable cartridge gun. Think, too, about how many shots you might fire in a day's hunting

Some hunters decide to go all the way and combine complete period costume with their Kentucky squirrel rifles.

with a modern gun—the muzzleloader will do just as well in the same time. Think, too, back to the number of times when (if you *hunted* rather than just shot) you really *needed* a fast, second shot.

But mere adaptability to modern hunting isn't nearly all muzzleloaders have going for them. There is hardly one among us who doesn't occasionally wonder how he'd have performed in one field or another a century or three back in time. We like to think we're pretty damned good in the midst of today's advanced technology, and we are, but we wonder if we'd have kept our heads above water when mass transportation meant riding two to one horse and when central heating was a fire on the dirt floor beneath a smoke-hole in the roof.

Sure, we all wonder how well we'd have fed ourselves and our families on the frontier with a muzzleloader. Well, we can't learn how we'd have made out as armored knights or as sailing-vessel captains—but we *can* find out how we'd have fared in the woods with a muzzleloader, circa Lewis and Clark or thereabouts.

It's simple, in that instance, for there is still plenty of isolated woods peopled with small game; and, strange though it may seem, a plentitude

While the percussion gun is best for the neophyte, author George Nonte likes flinters as well, especially this Dixie Gun Works model.

of *new* muzzleloading guns looking and functioning just as did those of the dim and distant past during which our proud nation was forged from wilderness and strife. Somewhere within less than 100 miles from every one of you lie hills, creeks, and woods that once heard the bark of Kentucky squirrel rifle, Tennessee hawk rifle, or grizzly-busting Hawken. Somewhere near, there is an unmarked place where generations ago a man stood and slew food or enemy—a place where you, too, can stand and kill meat for the pot with essentially the same gun and ammunition. That you may find only rabbit or squirrel where he found deer, elk, or bear won't lessen your accomplishment in the least.

But enough nostalgia. Admitting that it's not only possible, but easy, and fun to boot, one must begin his hunting by obtaining a gun.

Not just any gun will do. In the old days a man bought or traded for what was popular and available in a given area or outfitting post. Today's choice is not so limited, and you can choose from a wider variety of guns than your ancestor ever dreamed of, and you won't have to wait six months for it to be made from bar iron and maple plank.

Traditionally, the small-caliber Kentucky or Pennsylvania rifle, gracefully slender and with up to a yard and a half of barrel, was the favored small-game gun. As the game got bigger, the caliber increased, the barrel shortened, weight went up, and the rifle lost some of its grace.

The choice today is the same: Kentucky style, with slender barrel and stock, and of small caliber. Unless you're a purist, though, the barrel need not be so long. We know now that an extra foot or two of barrel past about 30 inches increases neither accuracy nor velocity and power to any significant degree. So, the woods-handiness of a 30-odd-inch barrel outweighs the historical significance of a 44- or 50-inch tube. Really, those extra-long barrels are a disadvantage in thick brush and tangled timber; try carrying a five-foot-long rifle through a tangled blowdown or Tennessee laurel thicket and you'll be convinced.

Small caliber, as we said—but not too small. It isn't that a diminutive bullet won't kill game surely, but the smaller bores are harder to load and generally require very meticulous handling to produce top accuracy. I'd not recommend less than .36 caliber, and would advise larger, at least .40. As for myself, I use .44 and .45 almost exclusively because they shoot most accurately with least attention to load and loading.

There's another choice you must make that didn't concern Daniel Boone—between flintlock and percussion-cap ignition. If you're in the mood for advice, take mine, and make your first gun percussion. It's simpler to load, less likely to get out of order, far more certain of fire in damp weather, and a lot less trouble all-around.

There are plenty of guns available which meet all those requirements. Almost every maker and importer of "replica" guns offers one or more Kentucky rifles. Dixie Gun Works offers both Kentucky and Pennsylvania styles in both flint and percussion, .45 caliber, at prices from about $180 to about $300; DGW also has lower-priced guns of other styles that are quite adequate for small game. Other makers, principally Navy Arms and Connecticut Valley Arms offer Kentucky-style rifles from as little as $125 upward.

Some shops offer Kentucky-style rifles in carbine length with barrels as short as 22 inches. These make very handy small-game guns, but such short barrels hardly ever existed in the old days.

The gun alone isn't enough. With it you'll need round, lead balls of proper size; black powder in FFFg size; percussion caps to fit the

Typical modern replica of slender percussion Kentucky rifle is first choice of most small-game hunters, usually in .36 to .45 caliber.

Modern short-barrel Kentucky carbine is great for small game.

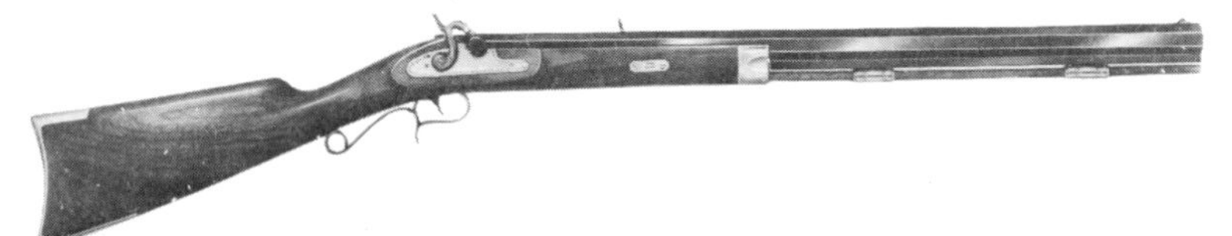

To be really old-fashioned, use a flintlock rifle, but be ready to accept its lesser reliability.

Modern copy of heavy, big-bore, Hawken-style rifles are available today. Lightly loaded, they also do very well on small game if caliber is under .50.

nipple, usually No. 11 or No. 12; cloth patching; and patch lubricant. Get all these items where you buy the gun and you'll be ahead.

You'll also need a few accessories to load and care for the gun properly. First is something to carry and measure powder. For convenience, stay away from the traditional powder horn and get a pistol-size copper measuring flask. Prepare the flask by trimming the brass spout to hold the amount of powder correct for your rifle. Pair this with a two-leg ball seater; a palm-size knob from which extend two bore-size dowels, one very short, the other three or four inches long. Add a nipple wrench, a piece of spring wire that will pass through the nipple, and a razor sharp knife for trimming patches, and you've a fair starting outfit. You'll find other items useful later, but not necessary now.

So, let's suppose you have a spanking new Dixie Kentucky Rifle, .45 caliber, and you want to get ready for the squirrel season—or maybe rabbits, javelina, coyotes, or what have you.

Consider first the game. If it's to be rabbits and squirrel for the table, you'll be taking them close in and won't want to tear them up too much. That calls for a modest load, say 40 grains of powder in .45 caliber. But if it's coyotes and similar varmints not intended for eating, they'll be farther away and you won't worry about meat damage. For that sort of work, you'll need a *heavy* load, one that extracts the most in range and velocity out of a round-ball rifle. Maximum powder charge would be 100 grains FFFg, producing well over 2000 fps, but a bit less will probably be more accurate.

So, for loads that have proven safe, practical, and accurate, let's settle on 40 grains (about 1400 fps in most guns) for edible game and 80 grains (about 2000 fps) for the others, both with a .445-inch diameter, pure

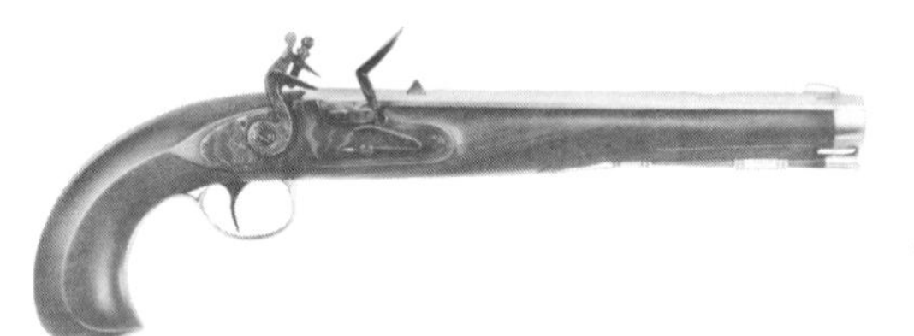

If you're a handgun fan, a Kentucky-style pistol also will bag plenty of small game.

lead ball and .015-inch patching lubricated with Crisco vegetable shortening.

The light load will have a mid-range trajectory height of only .77 inch when targeted at 50 yards, and will deliver 315 foot pounds of energy at that range; more than a .38 Special revolver. The heavy load will have a trajectory height of .37 inch for 50 yards, 2.12 inches for 100 yards. At those ranges, it will deliver 624 and 333 foot pounds of energy, respectively, and at 100 yards the ball will still be traveling 1066 feet per second. Even at 100 yards it's more potent than the .38 sixgun at the muzzle, and that's plenty to put a coyote or similar varmint out of action with any *good* hit.

Trim the spout of your flask to throw 40 grains of powder, then it's right for the light load, and if need be, you can throw *two* 40-grain charges to make up the heavy load.

Prepare the gun for its first firing by swabbing all the grease out of the bore with any good solvent. Pump plenty of solvent through the nipple to degrease it. Wipe dry and blow through the nipple to clear it.

Pull the hammer to half-cock (safety position) and press a percussion cap firmly, not roughly, on the nipple. Cock the hammer and pull the trigger, firing the cap, while pointing the muzzle at the ground. Enough gas should exit the muzzle to stir grass or dirt, showing the nipple to be clear. Repeat this to be sure the nipple is completely dry and leave the hammer down on the exploded cap.

Now comes the serious part, the loading. Rub Crisco into your strip of patch material—just enough to fill the weave—and keep it handy. Hold the rifle upright and pour the powder charge into the muzzle;

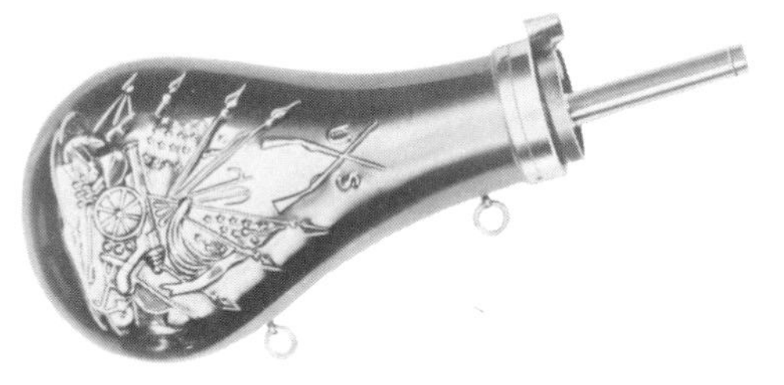

A pistol-type powder flask set up for the most commonly used load will be your biggest asset in the field.

don't spill any, get it all in the barrel. Lay one end of the Criscoed patch across the muzzle, then place a ball over it and thumb it into the muzzle as far as it will go. If the ball has a lump or flat spot (a sprue) where it was cast, center this upward as accurately as possible.

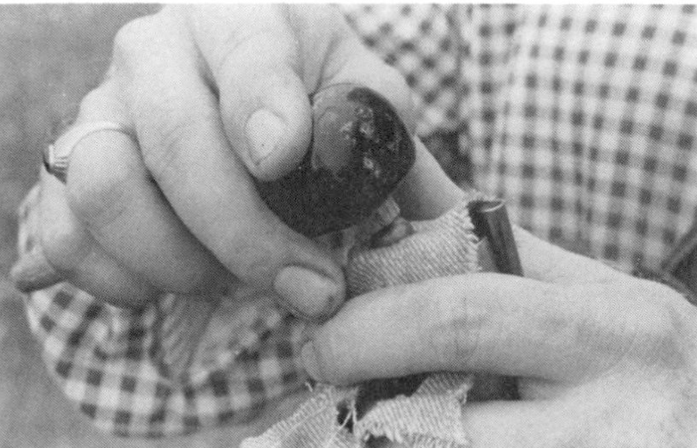

Key to easy, uniform loading is the use of a two-leg ball seater. Here short leg is used to seat ball just below muzzle prior to trimming patch.

Now, place the short leg of the ball seater over the ball; strike the seater a solid downward blow with the heel of your hand, forcing the ball and patch inside the muzzle. Gather up the excess patch material and slice it off flush with the muzzle with your *sharp* knife. Place the long leg of the seater in the muzzle and strike it again, driving the patched ball down the length of the leg.

Next, take the ramrod and place its brass-shrouded end in the muzzle, against the ball. Steadying the gun between your knees, use both hands on the rod and thrust smoothly downward, seating the ball firmly on the powder charge with a single stroke. Keep the thrust directly in line with the bore—the rod (if wood) may break and cut your hands if you're careless. Don't pound the ball with the rod or accuracy will be lousy; just push it down solidly against the powder.

Remove the ramrod from the barrel and replace it in its thimbles on the gun—yes, people *do* sometimes forget this and *shoot* the ramrod way out yonder. Imagine a rabbit already spitted on a ramrod when you pick him up, ready to hang over the campfire.

Now comes the last phase of loading. Ear the hammer back to half-cock and pluck the fired cap off the nipple. Seat a fresh one carefully. This operation corresponds to chambering a cartridge in a modern gun, so take care where you point the muzzle.

Always draw ramrod from barrel and place it back in its thimbles. Also note powder flask, hunting bag, and other shooting implements hung around neck.

Aim at a cottontail rabbit's head to avoid ruining any edible meat. (Russell Tinsley photo)

When you're ready, ear the hammer to full-cock, aim, and squeeze, just as with any other rifle. Keep in mind, though, that lock time and ignition time are slower than some modern guns—and this makes follow-through especially important.

If you've never shot a muzzleloader, the close-up 'crack' and smoke-puff (sometimes) of the cap might give you a start the first few times. Don't let it make you flinch. It may be different, but it shouldn't affect you any more than the cycling of any autoloader action, so just ignore it. It won't hurt you, so forget it. Actually, if you concentrate on sights and trigger pull as you should, you'll never notice it.

All other shots are just like the first one. Load carefully and uniformly, and a good Kentucky will shoot as accurately as lots of modern guns.

One thing to avoid when hunting is the legendary spit-patch. To be sure, guns shoot well when the patch is lubricated with saliva—but saliva is mostly water. Water rusts steel, and it also evaporates in time, leaving the patch without lubrication. When afield where shots might be hours apart, stick with grease or Crisco. Save spit-patches for plinking where you know they'll be shot out before they can cause trouble.

And of course your Kentucky rifle must be zeroed just as carefully and precisely as any modern gun. Target it for the range and load you expect to use most often, then shoot enough with the other load to *know* exactly how much Kentucky Windage or Tennessee Elevation is required to hit your target. Some rifles print two different loads surprisingly close together, others do not. I once had a .45 H&A rifle that

Squirrel is a small target, but modern-day replicas are accurate. (Russell Tinsley photo)

didn't seem to know the difference and put all reasonable loads in the same place at 50 yards.

With all the foregoing under your belt, you might ask "How do I hunt with a muzzleloader?" The answer is simple—*get as close as you can and shoot as accurately as you can.* In that essential regard, all hunting is the same, regardless of the gun and ammunition used. Generally speaking, sure hits may be obtained with a good muzzleloader to about the same ranges you'd expect with the .22 Long Rifle—so, just hunt as if you were using a .22 single-shot rifle, and you can't go wrong.

Just remember that you have only one shot, and don't fire it until the range and other conditions are such that you are sure of hitting your target in a vital spot.

In reality, using a muzzleloader causes (forces, actually) one to become a better hunter, more a *hunter* than a shooter. Considering that, sometimes I think everyone should try it for at least one season.

11

'Coon Hunts and Bonus 'Possums

by Bob Gooch

"A HORN, a flashlight and a pack of hounds—they'll make a fellow live a long life." Coming from the lips of an 87-year-old coonhunter, those words had a ring of credibility.

But now I was beginning to question that sage advice as we raced through the cold January night. Briers and vines tore at my clothes, low-swinging tree branches switched my face. I stumbled once as my foot slipped into a foot-deep hole left by a rotted tree stump. At this rate I would be lucky to survive the next few hours of that Virginia night hunt!

A couple of things about 'coon hunting set it apart.

For one thing, the coonhunter operates at night. His adrenalin starts pumping at sundown—as most hunters are racking their guns, tired and hungry from a long day in the field. He downs a quick dinner, fills a Thermos jug with hot coffee, loads his hounds into his pickup truck, kisses his wife good-bye and disappears into the night. Seemingly, he is bassackwards in his living routine.

Also unique to 'coon hunting is the minor role played by the firearm. An inexpensive .22 rimfire rifle with crude iron sights fills the coon-

Black-masked 'coon is a critter that is widespread and plentiful. (Russell Tinsley photo)

hunter's needs, and usually there is only one rifle to a hunting party—often four or five hunters.

My introduction to night hunting came back in the 1930's. A school buddy owned a fair trail hound with which we spent many nights under starry autumn skies—listening for the hound's throaty bawl to tell us he had the scent of game in his nostrils. The game in those days, however, was the lowly 'possum instead of the 'coon.

The coonskin fad of the roaring 20's had dug deeply into the raccoon populations, and there were precious few 'coons in the Virginia hill country where I cut my hunting teeth. So we hunted 'possums, often filling a gunny sack half full of the funny looking little animals with the scaly tails and long, white faces.

We usually took our quarry alive. Many were penned, fattened on corn, and butchered for the table. "Roast 'possum and 'taters" was a delicacy on many Depression tables. And 'possum skins brought a few pennies in the fur market.

But the 'coon outlived the coonskin coat fad and the romantic coonskin cap era of the pioneers, and bounced back from near extinction. Someone has estimated the 'coon population in the United States at five million, and today the busy little animals live in all of the continental states.

'Coons were introduced to the Ketchikan area of Alaska in 1945. They are scarce in the Rockies and absent from the deserts of the Southwest, but they are found along the Alberta–Saskatchewan border and are abundant in the timber country of southern Canada. 'Coons also inhabit Mexico and Central America.

Few are aware of it, but most Americans have 'coons practically in their back yards, roaming through the night in the nearest patch of timber. I have cussed 'coons that hauled away my camp utensils in Quebec and dug into my garbage in Vermont, and arisen in the night to chase them out of my food box at my camp in the Florida Everglades. But just last month I thrilled to the sight of a family of 'coons that ventured into the outer glow of my campfire on the Rappahannock River in Virginia.

The 'coon is highly adaptable, but he thrives best where there are mature hardwoods to provide him with den trees, and creeks and

The 'possum can be a bonus for the coonhunter.

swamps for his beloved water. Its diet is extremely varied, however, and its home range need not be very large. Food includes frogs, insects, rodents, wild fruit, corn, crawfish, eggs, vegetables, fish, worms and grass.

The 'coon has the most sensitive forepaws of any North American animal. With them it can hold food, lift the lid of a garbage can, and open a door latch. When overly abundant in residential areas 'coons can become a nuisance. The spectacle of a 'coon washing its food in a convenient stream is one that many outdoorsmen have thrilled to. If water is not easily available, however, the 'coon will forego this dining ritual.

The raccoon is identified by its black face mask and ringed tail. Its body is stout, and its grizzled appearing black, brown and gray hair is long, giving it a bushy-coated appearance. Its rounded ears are upright and its shiny black snout is pointed. When pressed, the rotund 'coon can bound along at 15 miles per hour.

The average 'coon weighs 12 to 16 pounds, with a shoulder height of approximately two feet and a body length of 30 inches to three feet. The Florida 'coon may weigh only three to six pounds, but some outsized 30-pounders have been taken in the Pacific Northwest and across the continent in Maine. One Wisconsin monster shot in 1950 weighed 62 pounds, six ounces and measured 55 inches in length. 'Coons can grow big.

The 'coon is an excellent swimmer and climber, very clever, and tames easily. It is also a fighter, but elusive, making it a quality game animal.

The raccoon is a scrappy fighter, particularly when cornered by a pack of hounds, though it is seldom a match for more than one. It travels mostly at night and is seldom seen except by hunters and campers.

Though it is more often silent than noisy, the 'coon does bark, growl and whine.

Early in my night hunting days I was thrashing through the woods following a group of older hunters who thought they had a 'coon treed. Breathless and almost exhausted, we arrived at the tree, a small but tall oak, and began sweeping long 'coon beams through the branches. Our yellow beams combed every twig of that oak, but to no avail. There was no 'coon in the tree, and we knew there was no den it could hole up in. The tree wasn't large enough.

"Tapped it," muttered one of the hunters.

Tapping a tree is one of the favorite tricks of the 'coon. It is intended to throw off the hounds. The pursued 'coon climbs the tree or taps the trunk with his paw, but then jumps on a long limb, runs to the end of it and takes off on the ground again. This breaks the trail of scent the dogs are following. The dogs tree, and by the time they and the hunters fig-

Virginia coonhunters wait for their hounds to hit a trail.

ure out what has happened the lumbering, but fast moving 'coon may be safely away, possibly holed up in a warm den.

Wise old 'coons also run along rail fences or logs, circle and double back, and cross streams, ponds, and arms of lakes. Another favorite trick is climbing aboard a drifting log. A 'coon in the water is a match for most dogs, sometimes drowning its adversary. To avoid this, some hunters release at least two or three dogs.

The hounds are the very heart of the 'coon hunt. Crack coonhounds command premium prices, and very good ones are much rarer than good fox or rabbit hounds.

'Coon hunting is demanding of the dog. Hounds are often called upon to work in water on freezing nights, hunt over rough terrain, and follow cold trails. And in addition to being infallible on a trail, they must also excel at treeing their game and staying with it until the hunters arrive.

There are six generally recognized breeds of coonhounds, the Black and Tan, Bluetick, English Coonhound, Plott, Redbone, and Treeing Walker. Of the six, the Black and Tan, Redbone and Walker are probably the most popular among American coonhunters.

The Bluetick is noted for its treeing ability, and the Plott probably gets more big-game duty—cats, bears, coyotes, and mountain lions. The Plott is a gutty and tough dog, but some coonhunters do not like its voice. Careless breeding practices among English Coonhound owners has brought this breed into disfavor among American hunters.

The kind of game found in Europe did not call for a treeing hound so early Americans had to develop one of their own. They quickly recognized the need for such a dog to produce food and clothing, and the modern coonhound is the result. The highly efficient coonhound is a product of early America.

The Black and Tan is the oldest of the coonhounds, and the grand old breed of the coonhound world. Generations of breeding refinements have developed a dog that is hard to fault. It is fast on the trail, has a wonderful voice, and is a top treeing dog. Some of the best coonhounds in America are Black and Tans.

Careful breeding has brought the Redbone to the front among coonhounds. The dog is noted for its loud, clear voice—sometimes a chop but often a bawl—its cold nose, tenaciousness, and strong treeing instinct. The Redbone is a beautifully built dog, agile and impressive looking.

The Treeing Walker is a descendant of the Walker Foxhound, and the range, speed, and aggressiveness inherited from that breed have

Herschell Hepler and Early Durham get ready to put their hounds down in 'coon country.

contributed to its success in competitive hunting. Walkers have become conspicuous among the winners in national competition. Unlike the Black and Tan and Redbone, both of which are tenacious trailers, inclined to stick with a trail and unwind it, the Walker is a drifter. When the trail gets cold the Walker likes to range out and pick it up where it is hotter. Some hunters dislike this trait, but it is an effective method of putting 'coons in a tree. The Walker, like the Black and Tan and Redbone, has a good treeing instinct, though many of them "tree coming," that is they bark treed even before they reach the tree.

In building his pack of coonhounds the hunter attempts to get dogs of like noses, voice, speed, and general ability. Such dogs will pack together better. Fast dogs discourage slow ones, and a cold trailer will have a like effect on a hot-nosed dog that will not hark to the strike of his cold-nosed partner.

The hunter who is short-winded himself should not own a wide ranging coonhound such as the Walker.

Hounds work best on warm, moist autumn nights when the 'coon populations are near their annual peak and very active, and the moist

Marshall Loving blows on 'coon squaller in an effort to fetch treed 'coon to the ground. It didn't work.

earth holds scent well. It is then that a full-voiced dog such as the Walker, Black and Tan, Redbone and Bluetick is at its best.

The coonhunter's gear is simple. Most hunters wear spelunker's headlamps, and it is debatable whether these modern headlights are built primarily for spelunking or for 'coon hunting. Most sporting goods stores that stock 'coon-hunting supplies carry these handy lights, more popularly known as 'coon beams among hunters. They are highly effective and leave both hands free for handling dogs, warding off tree branches and handling a rifle.

One open-sighted .22 rifle per hunting party is adequate. Even a .22 rimfire handgun will serve the purpose, and it is much handier to carry on a long hunt. In the old days it was a common practice to down trees with an axe or saw to get to the 'coon, but this practice has been long since discontinued, particularly with respect to valuable den trees. The rifle or pistol is needed to bring the game to the ground, but it is close-range shooting. Head shots are usually possible so solid point bullets are adequate.

Most hunters also own 'coon calls, the squaller being the most popular. With it the hunter attempts to imitate the squall of a 'coon and fetch the cornered animal out of the tree.

The hunter's clothing should be warm and tough enough to withstand the beating it will receive from briers, tree branches and barbed wire fences. Of particular importance is the hunter's footwear. Raccoons like water, so the best place to hunt them is near streams, swamps, lakes and ponds. This means often wading streams and mucking through marshes and swamps. Waterproof boots are a necessity. Modified hip boots, the tops of which reach just above the knee, are the mark of a knowledgeable coonhunter. Knee-length boots will get you through most of the tough going, however. Beyond these essentials the climate and weather will dictate the coonhunter's clothing.

While the successful 'coon hunt revolves around the hounds, this does not mean the hunter has no responsibilities. He has to exercise some control over his hounds, keep in touch with them, and hasten to the site once they have treed. He must also put his dogs down in likely 'coon territory though this can be just about anywhere in prime 'coon country.

"The first thing a 'coon does after it wakes is to go to water, so as soon as I put the dogs out, they start sniffin' toward the nearest water course," said one oldtimer who had just completed his 73rd year of 'coon hunting. Hunters like to put their dogs down in swampy or low areas and along woodland streams.

The veteran hunter has little trouble distinguishing between the long,

Early Durham pulls hound from downed 'coon while Herschell Hepler and Marshall Loving hold back their dogs.

Marshall Loving and Herschell Hepler let hounds have a taste of victory.

sometimes infrequent trail howl, bawl or chop, and the more frequent, highly excited bark that tells him his dog has treed.

Some hunters say 'coons move best after midnight, but many good chases also come in the early hours of darkness.

Raccoon seasons vary tremendously, but most are long. There are no closed seasons in many parts of the South, but where they exist 'coon seasons usually cover the late fall and winter months. October through February is a popular season. The 'coon does not hibernate, but it may become lethargic in the dead of winter, slumbering for days in its den.

The lowly opossum, a primitive creature equipped with a small brain and slow and stupid when compared to the highly intelligent 'coon, can be a bonus to 'coon hunting.

The 'possum is our only native marsupial or pouched animal. It too travels mostly at night, preferring much the same habitat that attracts the raccoon, though it does not have the same affinity for water.

The tasty meat of a fat 'possum makes it a hunting prize, though its coarse fur is less valuable than that of the raccoon.

The opossum is also widely distributed and found throughout the eastern half of the United States, though not along the Canadian border as is the 'coon. It is also found in the Far West, but not in the Rocky Mountain region.

Even a spreading civilization hasn't discouraged the opossum as many are found within city limits. (Texas Parks & Wildlife Dept. photo)

It is uncommon, but a 'possum will feed on a rabbit occasionally. (Texas Parks & Wildlife Dept. photo)

The 'coon population explosion has relegated the 'possum to a back seat in much of the country, though old-fashioned 'possum hunts are still popular in the South. And for those who long ago learned to appreciate the little animal, a good 'possum hunt can be just as exciting and productive of tasty meat—"roast 'possum and 'taters." The slow 'possum heads for the nearest tree when the hounds hit its trail so long chases are rare. The treeing can be just as exciting, however. Persimmon trees and their rich fruit are favorite hangouts.

The little animal's habit of feigning death—rolling on its side, mouth agape—when hopelessly cornered is amusing to hunters. But playing 'possum is a last resort. The 'possum can wage a fierce and convincing battle.

Autumn is the prime time for 'possum hunting also, and the hunting is usually best on a dark night.

Most coonhounds will tree 'possums—often to the disgust of their masters.

A competing coonhound may lose points if it stoops to 'possum chasing. Still, for the hunter who thrills to the chase and hunts for the pure joy it offers, an occasional 'possum is a welcome addition, giving him the bonus of a mixed bag.

The relative abundance of 'coons has considerable influence on

Call which imitates bird in distress brought this 'coon within bow-and-arrow range. (Russell Tinsley photo)

hounds going astray on 'possums. If the raccoon populations are high a crack coonhound will not waste its time on 'possums.

Calling wildlife has become increasingly popular in recent years, and the 'coon has not been neglected by those who favor this kind of hunting.

Animal calling enthusiasts like the famous Burnham Brothers of Texas say the widely distributed 'coon will respond best at night—the time it moves about the most, as any coonhunter knows.

The Burnhams like the heat of August and September for calling

It doesn't take a spooked 'coon long to climb a tree. (Russell Tinsley photo)

'coons, and since many states prohibit the use of lights for hunting at night, they recommend hunting on a moonlit night. But 'coons move better on dark nights, and where it is legal hunters employ red-lens hunting lights. The red light is not as likely to spook game.

"In late summer the 'coon population is at its peak," says Winston Burnham, "the young of spring have grown up, and they are naïve, easily fooled with a call. And they're gathered around water where there is a lot for them to eat in the summer. That makes them easy to find."

'Coons are less spooky than most animals, and a minimum of camouflage clothing is needed—even when the calling is done in the daytime. And unlike most animals, the 'coon does not seem to be wary of human odor.

The hunter can choose his weapon for this kind of hunting, for the animals can be called within easy range of even the bow and arrow.

The most effective 'coon calls imitate the distress call of a bird. The 'coon too is a predator and the caller appeals to the animal instinct to kill and eat some other creature.

Calling pits the hunter against the game. He has no dog to unravel a woodland trail, so he must understand the animal's habits, its affinity for water, its tendency to roam at night, and the fact that autumn is its favorite season.

Calling adds an exciting new dimension to 'coon hunting, and it is a sport the occasional night hunter can better afford. A mouth-operated call, a hunting light, and a bow or gun and he is in business.

With an estimated five million 'coons roaming the woodlands of America, the future of 'coon hunting appears secure. Fur trappers don't make a dent in the 'coon populations, night hunters and their hounds probably leave as many 'coons in the trees as they take home, and 'coon calling is still a budding form of hunting.

Night hunting draws men from all walks of life—doctors, lawyers, businessmen, public officials, construction workers, clerks and honest men of the soil. Social status is forgotten as they gather in the darkness, huddle beside logging roads, stamp their feet to keep warm, sip coffee, talk softly and listen for the full-voiced notes of a fine hound.

It all began in America where men who follow it gain a peg on "living a long life."

12

Foxes and Fox Hunting

by Bob Gilsvik

It's easy to get a "yes" to a request for permission to hunt when the fields and pastures are shrouded in snow and the quarry sought is the red fox. I'd just left the farmyard of one such cooperative farmer and was driving down the snow-packed road to where a fenceline bordered one edge of his property when, out of the corner of my eye, I sighted a red fox following the fenceline. He was about 200 yards out and approaching the road. I almost careened into the ditch in my haste to park the car out of sight below a high embankment.

Hurriedly I crammed 80-grain loads into my rifle, a new scope-sighted .243 in the Winchester Model 70. Easing the rifle barrel over the embankment I was greeted by the sight of the fox watching my every move.

The fox whirled and took off running. What a sight. His lush fur glistened in the winter sun and his tail stretched back like a great plume, the white tip showing stark against hues of black and rust-red. I got off three shots. The fox never faltered.

Later I found tiny drops of blood in the snow. One of the bullets had grazed him. I guessed it was not a serious wound, but I vowed to dispatch him as quickly as possible.

Hunter steadies himself as he takes aim at red fox in distance.

That was at 9:30 A.M. By 4:00 P.M. I was having second thoughts. I was a long way from my car. My legs seemed to plod along of their own accord. Foxes normally sleep during the day. Sooner or later this one would, I hoped, have to catch a few winks and then I could catch him napping.

Two other incentives prevailed: the fox was still intermittently bleeding, and he had been joined by a second fox. Then I saw them.

One fox was no more than a reddish lump in the snow, accented by two black-tipped ears. Curled in a furry ball with his tail over his nose, the fox was sleeping. The other fox was also bedded down but his head was up and he licked at his hind quarters. I guessed it was the fox I'd

Fox curls up to take a siesta in weak winter afternoon sun.

winged. The foxes were lying about one-third of the way down from the crest of a knoll that showed grass above the snow and which was situated along the edge of a plowed field.

It was the kind of heart-hammering scene I have experienced hundreds of times while stalking the red fox in winter, but which I can never quite get used to. I sank slowly into the prone position, and centered the more watchful fox in the cross-hairs of my 4X scope sight. The range was 150 yards. I squeezed off a round and he crumpled in the snow. The second fox leaped to his feet and, confused by the echo of the shot, ran straight toward me and raced by only 25 yards away. I scrambled into a sitting position and touched off a round. The fox spilled on his nose, sliding almost 10 feet in the snow.

Throughout most of the United States, seductive squeals on a varmint call, designed to imitate the cry of a rabbit in distress, will bring the fox

Find fresh tracks in the snow and you're in business.

running. Others like to chase it with hounds, still others like an organized drive and the congeniality of many hunting companions. Personally, I'll take winter and stalking the red fox as he naps on sheltered hillsides.

Admittedly the game has become more difficult in recent years. Snowmobiles on the winter scene have induced the adaptable red fox to lie where he has easier access to cover, but he still loves the open farmland and prairie, and the hunter who carefully glasses all possible bedding sites with binoculars and who is also endowed with a good deal of physical stamina can take him.

Basic equipment required is a scope-sighted varmint rifle, but if I were hunting in an area heavily populated with small farms I would be inclined to switch to a rifle in .22 magnum caliber. If the terrain is fairly rolling, it is not unusual to spot foxes within 100 yards. The .22 WRM is easily effective to this range.

But a varmint rifle is much more effective. A hot little number preferred by many is the .222. I like the idea of an all-round rifle and because I also use my .243 for deer hunting I use a 4X scope. For strictly fox hunting I would favor a 6- or 8-power scope sight on a varmint rifle.

Accessories include binoculars, usually 7X35, and snowshoes. I like the Alaskan model, 10X56 inches; they are easy to use yet large enough to support even a heavy adult. A half hour of walking and the most inexperienced soon has the hang of it. Tackling a barbed wire fence with these on takes a little longer.

Because you are usually on the move, lightweight clothing can be

Binoculars help in locating the reddish blob against the white snow.

worn. But I favor wool pants, despite their nagging weight, because of the final stages of a stalk that usually require crawling through the snow on elbows and knees. Wool pants have less of a tendency to become ice encrusted than blue jeans. I like a lightweight parka of goosedown. A hood is a must for conserving body heat when cutting winter winds send the wind-chill factor plummeting. Sunglasses or a visor cap will take the strain off your eyes from the often bright winter sun. Favorite footwear is the Soral boot. I like to tie my trouser legs around the tops of the boots with twine. This keeps snow out of my boot tops when I'm navigating deep drifts.

I usually hunt throughout the farming areas of Minnesota, Wisconsin and Iowa. This is sometimes flat terrain but often interspersed with country more to my liking: gently rolling hills with tree-lined fencerows and dotted with woodlots, potholes, and sloughs—country not unlike farming country in much of the United States and Canada. In rolling terrain it is easier to come upon your quarry without being spotted. As you near the crest of one hill your attention should be riveted on the next.

The wind is, curiously, the key to hunting these open country foxes. The red fox will lie where he is sheltered from the winter wind. They are very definite about it. There may be numerous niches where an animal the size of a red fox could lie and be sheltered from a crossing wind

When there is no rest handy, prone shooting is much preferred to off-hand.

Minnesota hunter pauses after a successful hunt.

but this character always chooses to lie directly on the leeward side of a hill. When possible, walk directly into the wind and, as each new vista comes into view, use your binoculars and carefully look over all upcoming hillsides, brushy fencelines, log piles and any place a red fox might lie without feeling too cramped. They do not, for example, like to bed down in a narrow sided ravine. They much prefer to nap where they have a good view of the surrounding terrain—and approaching danger—as well as shelter from the wind, no matter how slight that wind may be.

Recognizing a sleeping fox is not easy. The more snow there is on the ground the easier they are to see. I think that part of the difficulty, for a newcomer to this sport, is believing that it really is possible to spot a fox napping. The more confident you become in the knowledge that they can be hunted in this manner the more foxes you will see before they see you. Nocturnal, the red fox spends most of the daytime sleeping.

The fox sleeps curled in a ball. Look for a lump in the snow. A lump about one foot in diameter and with a soft outline. Rocks have hard, clearly defined outlines. The fox's fur gives him a softened look. In good light conditions the fox can appear as brightly red as he really is and be very easy to see. He can also look a dull gray or brown. A real giveaway are his black-tipped ears. If still in doubt, make yourself comfortable and just watch. Foxes are light sleepers. Rarely will ten minutes pass without the fox raising his head for a look at the surrounding terrain. Incidentally, the red fox will occasionally lie on his side on top of the snow if in a sunny spot. It is quite a sight.

Generally I'll spot a fox with my naked eye first. This usually occurs as I'm nearing the top of one hill and looking toward the next. If the fox

Although mostly nocturnal, red foxes do travel some during the winter daylight.

Although hunter can see fox, the wary critter also can spot human unless he is very furtive.

Alerted fox, tail puffed up, gets ready to run for freedom.

is close, I will recognize him for a fox instantly and drop to my knees out of his line of sight. If in doubt, I'll slowly rise up and take a quick look through rifle scope or binoculars. If it is a fox, my heart starts pounding and I begin moving forward at a crouch, finally crawling on elbows and knees in the snow until I can just barely see the fox while lying prone.

If the fox is alert he may also see you at this point but chances are he will see so little of you as not to be alarmed, only curious. Now is the time to catch your breath and let those heart beats return to something akin to normal. Then sink your elbows firmly in the snow for a steady hold. If the range is 200 yards and your rifle is sighted-in to hit point of aim at that range, hold the cross-hairs a little below where fox and snow meet. If you hold directly on that part of the fox showing above the snow your bullet may pierce only fur. The fox gives off body heat as he lies in the snow and he invariably sinks in a way. I believe I have missed most napping foxes by overshooting.

Even the best rifleman goofs once in a while, so let's say at the report of your rifle the red fox leaps to his feet and before you can even get off a running shot he is long gone over the next hill. Do not despair. You can track him down and get another shot. There was a time, back when my brothers and I first started hunting foxes, when trailing a fox was often just a matter of following his tracks over one or two hills and there he would be, fast asleep again on the next slope. But the winter

Stalk pays off as hunter puts a red fox down.

Talented caller Winston Burnham lures a gray fox within bow-and-arrow range. (Russell Tinsley photo)

scene is a lot more crowded nowadays, and foxes are used to being trailed or chased, so you may be in for an all-day tracking job, but it could be your most memorable hunt ever.

No matter which way the fox runs when first jumped, he will eventually turn and head directly into the wind. Follow his tracks and as before, carefully look over and glass each new hillside as it comes into view.

One of the nice things about winter fox hunting is the fact that you can see by their tracks in the snow if there is a good possibility that an area of say, one by three miles, holds a fox or two. I like to completely circle an area with my car before committing myself to hunting it. Watch for fox tracks crossing the roads. Watch for grassy knolls and hillsides within the area, as foxes feel more comfortable lying in such spots. One more thing, watch for foxes. Surprisingly, foxes can often be spotted from car windows; in fact, some hunters will spend whole days road hunting with powerful binoculars and spotting scopes. I keep my eyes open on the road but prefer to get out and hike for the kind of quality fox hunting I like best.

Hound Hunting and Calling

Although stalking red foxes in wintertime is my favorite, there are other fascinating methods for hunting the ubiquitous fox clan. "Riding to hounds" fox hunting dates back to our colonial forefathers, and while some of this still goes on, most hound hunting today is on a much more modest scale. There is something very special about standing on a ridge and listening to a hound pack unraveling a hot fox track in a wooded hollow below, trying to pick out the clear, bell-like voice of each hound as it sounds off. And although various breeds of hounds are used in pursuing foxes—Blueticks, Redbones, and Black and Tans—all have one thing in common—voice. In big field trials, when many hounds are turned loose together, each owner can pick his hound from the wild-barking chorus by its voice, for each voice is individually different.

Yet hound hunting really isn't that widespread and popular. Urban living has made it difficult to keep and maintain a large pack of hounds. Consequently, the enterprising hunter has learned to outfox the fox without canine help. Like calling, for instance.

Both the gray and red fox will readily respond to a predator call, although of the two the gray is much easier to dupe. Russell Tinsley in

Gray fox is less wary and easier called than its red fox cousin. (Russell Tinsley photo)

Chapter 6 (Calling All Predators) explains what equipment you will need and the proper technique.

Foxes are found throughout the United States, Mexico and most of Canada, with the red fox and gray fox being the predominate species. To a lesser extent we have the desert fox and the swift fox, sometimes called the kit fox because of its diminutive size. Both of these are subspecies of the red fox.

The red fox is more abundant in the northern states, since it can better tolerate cold, while the gray fox is found in greatest numbers in the South and Southwest. In places the range of the two overlap.

Foxes are omnivorous. Their diet runs the gamut from wild berries and fruit to small rodents, rabbits, birds, snakes, crayfish, insects, acorns, nuts and field corn.

Many people consider the fox a pest because of infrequent raids on a chicken house, but it really isn't the villain people often make it out to be. The fox plays a necessary and important ecological role, keeping pests like rodents and insects in check. It also provides a very sporting target for the hunter.

Size of the two major species is about the same, seven to 12 pounds, despite belief to the contrary. The typical red usually will be slightly larger, but probably no more than a pound or so. The gray is more a creature of the woodlands and heavily timbered forests, while reds are more prevalent in agricultural country, in open areas and along the fringes of woodlands. The red is more of a wanderer, five to six miles in its nocturnal travels, though it is more apt to be up and about in the daytime than is its gray cousin. A gray will readily climb trees while the red will not. The gray is a grizzled gray color along its sides, shading to white or gray along its belly with a touch of red around its throat; the red has a general coloration of reddish with a white-tipped tail. Of the two, the red is the more cunning.

The desert fox is buffy gray along the sides, with a plain buff underside. The most notable characteristic is its extra-large ears. It is a small fox, generally from five to six pounds in weight, and its range is primarily in arid areas of the West and Southwest.

The swift or kit fox is the smallest member of the fox family, averaging from three to six pounds in weight. It is found in many areas where the typical red fox roams, especially in the plains regions where

Red fox takes sun bath beside stacked logs which act as wind shield.

it lives on grassy prairies. Coloration is a pale buff touched with blackish, with a black-tipped light buffy tail.

All foxes, by nature, are cunning and sly, spooking at the slightest hint of danger; yet much of this innate caution is thrown to the wind when one hears the high-pitched shrieking of a predator call. And the drama of a wild-eyed, hungry fox racing toward you is a sight that you won't soon forget. The role is reversed; you are the *hunted* rather than the *hunter.*

13

The Ubiquitous Coyote

by John Wootters

NOBODY KNOWS how many coyotes exist today in the United States. Sheep ranchers will tell you there are several million too many. Most of them will state that *one* is one too many. Sportsmen who know the challenge the little prairie wolves can offer a hunter will say there aren't nearly enough coyotes, and, for once, the preservationists will agree with them. Biologists may say—cautiously—that coyote numbers are probably near optimum for the available habitat. There is no more controversial creature alive, and the controversy grows daily. Even the White House has been drawn into the fracas over predator (meaning coyote) control. So have various Federal courts, and (who knows?) someday the Supreme Court themselves may be called upon to rule on the coyote's place in the scheme of things.

Meanwhile, the coyote skips cheerfully through the countryside, uncaring of the storm which rages about his ears, knowing precisely his place in the scheme of things. It has always been thus, and I suspect it will remain so; judging from the historical record, the coyote will be yodeling at the moon long after mankind has gone the way of the dino-

Coyotes will respond to many kinds of calling, even the sound of gunfire when one learns about a dove hunter leaving breasted carcasses.

saurs, assuming man's demise leaves an earth for the coyote to inhabit and a moon for him to bark at.

Nobody really knows where all the coyotes are, either. We know he ranges from the shores of the Arctic Ocean to southern Mexico, covering the continent eastward to the Mississippi. In recent years, however, coyotes have steadily extended their range eastward and now infest all of the Great Lakes region, almost all of the Midwest, most of southern Canada, and even into New England, especially New York, New Hampshire, and Vermont. Distribution maps show him absent in the Deep South and the southeastern seaboard states, but I once made that statement in a magazine article and promptly received a flurry of snapshots and newspaper accounts of coyotes in the South. If the beast hasn't already colonized the entire North American continent, it's a pretty sure bet that he soon will!

His spread eastward in Texas has put even more pressure on the seriously endangered red wolf population there, through hybridization of the blood strains. In the Great Lakes country and eastward, he has apparently crossed with remnant wolf populations and/or domestic dogs, because he is a much larger animal in those regions than on his native western turf. The eradication of the wolf, in fact, may have opened the door to his little brother, the coyote, since wolves and coyotes will not occupy the same habitat, and the coyote seems to be taking over the historic range of the various species of wolves in the U.S.

Incidentally, coyotes also exclude gray foxes from the habitat, and may possibly have the same effect on red foxes. If so, the spread of the coyote bodes extremely ill for the nation's fox hunters.

Coyotes may exist for quite a while in a given area before even the woods-wise residents realize it; when his numbers are small, he tends to run silent, rather than advertising his presence by means of his famous singing. So the answer to the question "Where are the coyotes?" is likely to be everywhere, anywhere, perhaps behind your barn, or raiding your garbage can even in cities. He is the most adaptable, cunning, flexible, accommodating character in fur.

The hand of more than 50 generations of man (white man, that is; the Indians liked him and even revered the coyote) has been turned against him. He has been relentlessly shot, trapped, poisoned, and hounded since Americans first met him, and he's still around. He thrives in tropi-

Coyote is the craftiest, most adaptable, most cunning game animal in North America, and beyond question the most successful of all the larger predators.

cal heat and arctic cold, from Death Valley to 10,000 feet above sea level, in deserts, swamps, jungles, mountains, and residential subdivisions. I doubt that earthquakes, volcanic eruptions, or a reprise of the Biblical flood would be more than a temporary setback to El Coyote (he'd *own* the Ark by the second day!).

All this adds up to a most remarkable animal, whether you like him or not. The hunter who would take him in fair chase had better have his wits about him.

"Fair chase" emphatically does not include running him down on snowmobiles or in aircraft; that's legal in many areas, but about as sporting as strychnine. There are two major methods of getting a coyote on purpose, and several more which produce shots at the little wolves more or less accidentally. Probably at the head of the popularity list is the use of a predator call. If it isn't overdone, it can produce some wild and woolly action. I've called as many as eight coyotes to one stand, seven to another, and two or three to the same stand more times than I can count. In really good coyote country which hasn't been called within a year or so, I'm disappointed if I can't call up at least one coyote at every stop.

This kind of action involves knowing and respecting the animal you're looking for, and doing everything right. And having a little luck; a little luck is always a handy thing to have while hunting!

There are no weak spots in a coyote's sensory line of defense. His nose is superb, his ears are razor-sharp, and he is one of the few wild mammals which is capable of perceiving the motionless shape of a man as a *man*. Camouflage (including on face and hands) helps a great deal, but I haven't found it enough to fool a coyote if he could see all of me, no matter what my position. A combination of camouflage and concealment in shadowed brush—something to hide as much of my body as possible and to break up my outlines—is much better. Even then, there's usually not much time for leisurely gun-handling; better shoot at the first good opportunity.

Sometimes young coyotes will gallop straight in to the call, but most of them will circle to seek your wind. A little olfactory camouflage, such as an opened vial of pure, genuine skunk scent, set a few feet downwind, may confuse a coyote's nose long enough for a shot, but the best bet is to select a stand from which he can be seen and shot on the downwind side *before* he hits your scent-stream. Even better, pick dead-calm days (or nights) for your calling.

The way in which would-be coyote callers defeat themselves most frequently is disturbing the area and showing themselves as they approach the intended calling location. It pays heavy dividends to stalk

Tape-recorded calls produce on coyotes where law permits their use, but no better than mouth-blown calls in the hands of experts.

that stand as though you expected to find the coyote bedded down in the exact spot you plan to call. Make *no* noise, and never skyline yourself or even saunter across an opening. Hug the brush on the way in, ease into position like an owl settling on a branch, and keep still as you begin to call.

The second most common self-defeating tactic, assuming you've followed all that advice, is to use too much volume in the first few squeals from the call. I often begin with a short-range squeaker, blown as softly as if I believed there were a coyote on the other side of yonder bush . . . try it and you'll be surprised how many coyotes *are* just the other side of yonder bush! It's very common to have a yodel-dog in my lap within 30 seconds.

If not, then the volume can be increased gradually to full volume for a few bleats, but don't keep it up. On a still day, a coyote can hear a normal long-range predator call for a mile, although he may not come that far. Most of your calling should be distinctly on the soft side; too loud calling is an almost universal error with beginners, and even with many hunters who should know better.

Note that I haven't said much about what kind of instrument to use, or about the technique of blowing one. The reason is that I'm convinced

Utilization of full camouflage is crucial when trying to outwit a wily coyote.

that knowing *when* and *where* to call is much more important than what sort of sound is made with the call. I've tried 15 or 20 different brands and types, and most of them work about equally well. I also like the tape-recorded calls, where they're legal (which is in less than half the states), because they leave both hands free to handle a gun or camera. However, there's no magic in an electronic call (it's easy to play one of these too loudly, too) and I've proved to my own satisfaction many times that I can actually produce more coyotes with a mouth-blown call than with a tape player. I can "work" the game with the mouth call, adjusting my tempo, volume, and sequences to the actions of an incoming coyote, whereas with the recorded call I can only reduce the volume as the animal approaches. One great advantage to the electronic equipment, however, is the ability to set a camouflaged speaker as much as 40 feet away from me, to misdirect the coyote's attention. I need all the edge I can get on a coyote, and that's a good one.

Calling is essentially a self-regulating way of controlling coyotes. For every animal seen and shot, you can bet there's one or more which heard the call and investigated, usually downwind, which you never saw. That one has been educated; indeed, he just took the Ph.D.! He'll not only remember, but I'm convinced that a call-wise old bitch is capable of training her pups to stay away from that ersatz wounded-rabbit noise. However that may be, if you call the same area more intensively than about twice a year, you'll find you've run into the law of diminishing returns, even though sign, moonlight yodeling, and visual sightings prove the presence of a healthy coyote population. Once a year is better, for top sport. September and October, when the young dogs are as foolish as a coyote ever gets, and the "hungry time" in late winter are the prime calling seasons. Many devoted callers I know refuse to call during late spring and summer, when the females have dependent young in the dens. Even if the states won't give coyotes the protection of game-animal status, these sportsmen declare a voluntary closed season while the mother dogs are nursing.

The other popular method of hunting coyotes is coursing them with dogs. A few packs of greyhounds or one of the other wolfhound breeds exist, but the great majority of coyote packs are made up of trailhound breeds, most commonly Walkers with a few Black and Tans, Blueticks, Redbones, and others mixed in. Coyotes are not only smart and long-winded, but they have an unexpected turn of speed, being one of the few predators in the U.S. capable of catching jack rabbits regularly. They'll put a pack of hounds to the test.

On the flat Texas coastal prairies, hound-dog men have developed an interesting way of prospecting for coyotes. They've mounted police-type sirens on their pickup trucks, and they'll cruise the country roads, stopping now and then to crank the siren. Coyotes (and red wolves, too) seem unable to resist this siren call, and howl back at it, at which time the pack is put down and the chase begins. This siren technique is so reliable, as a matter of fact, that wildlife biologists are using it in southeastern Texas as a means of censusing both red wolf and coyote populations.

Running coyotes with hounds is a nighttime sport, and most hunters make no effort to follow the pack. They build a fire, put on the coffee pot, now and then pull a cork, and sit and listen to the music of the chase until dawn. Their joy is in interpreting the voices of their dogs, those psychedelic singers in the night, as the drama unfolds. Sometimes the coyote is run down and dies fighting; more often, he gives the pack the slip and lives to run another night. Hound hunters of coyotes hate predator callers.

Now and then, deer hunters encounter coyotes, occasionally still-hunting, but much more often while stand-sitting. I've hunted in prime coyote country for 35 years, and I've managed to still-hunt close enough to only three coyotes to get a shot. I've seen hundreds of them while sitting quietly, watching a deer trail or watering hole, however.

Only a couple of years ago, my wife was sitting quietly in the edge of the brush near a ranch pond in south Texas, when a pack of coyotes came to water only a few yards from her. She made no movement, and watched the pack, which appeared to be a family group, post a sentinel at the top of the earthen dam while the other dogs lapped their fill. When they were satisfied, one of them took the sentinel's post while the guard trotted down for his evening drink. The guard was a large male, accompanying his mate and three young-of-the-year.

Coyotes can be unbelievably bold when they sense a human is unarmed, and they have that same sixth sense which crows display that tells them not only whether a man is armed but what the maximum effective range of his weapon is. I've seen coyotes pay scant attention to a cowboy on his routine rounds, and have had them sit in plain view nearby while I dressed a whitetail buck, sensing that I meant them no harm. They watched the gutting with the same expression with which my poodle watches me prepare his dinner.

I've also had coyotes hang around me when I was shooting doves near

Author John Wootters called this huge old coyote bitch within seven yards and downed her with a .357 single-action revolver.

a water hole, rushing to get the breasted carcasses plus possible unrecovered kills before I'd walked more than 50 yards from my location at the end of the shoot. They knew I was dove-ing and not coyote-ing and they were right, but I'd love to know *how* they knew.

Coyotes do some damage to livestock interests and to game, no doubt about it. An occasional "rogue" can be a disaster to a sheep-raiser at lambing time, killing far more than it needs for food. An old three-toed bitch coyote once slew more than $4,000 worth of lambs belonging to a rancher friend of mine in 30 days, before he managed to trap her. I've called up and shot three different coyotes which were attacking livestock, and had the attacks end abruptly. Two of these rogues were killing goats and the other was harassing cattle, a very rare thing for an animal no larger than a coyote. There's no doubt that coyotes catch some whitetail fawns, at least in Texas, but their depredations are actually beneficial to our over-populated, unbalanced, three-million-plus deer herd. Stomach-contents analyses of Texas coyotes have consistently shown the proportion of game and livestock taken to be small, and much mutton and venison found in those stomachs was probably carrion. Killer coyotes do exist, but they can be dealt with without wiping out the entire population; such pogroms are like exterminating an entire human family because of the criminal actions of one member.

Although the average coyote is not as big as popular imagination would have him, he is a surprisingly tough beast to kill with a gun. The typical coyote of the Southwest and West weighs about 30 pounds, and the biggest I've ever weighed tipped the scales at only 46 pounds. Even so, I cannot recommend such centerfire rifle cartridges as the .22 Hornet or .222 Remington for efficient execution. I once shot a fairly large number of coyotes with a .17 caliber rifle, all at short range, to find out if this tiny hotshot was all I'd heard it was on medium-sized game. On coyotes, it isn't. The big-cased .224s—.224 Weatherby, .225 WCF, .22-250, and the great Swift—are adequate for most called-coyote shooting, with good bullet placement, but the .24 and .25 caliber rounds are far more reliable. My own favorite, among factory rounds, at least, is the 6mm Remington with handloaded bullets from 87 to 90 grains. No yodel-dogs escape this rifle when I do my part reasonably well.

Many predator callers (me among 'em) enjoy the challenge of the handgun, and why not? Shots are often short, at standing (momentarily) animals, and a pistol can be brought to bear with less alarming movement than a rifle. For such shooting, I'd call the magnums—.357, .41, .44, and the various Auto-Mag calibers, plus some of the hotshots available in the single-shot Thompson Contender—about right, although I've killed coyotes with carefully spotted shots from a .38 Super, .45 ACP,

About the only place where dogs have a chance with the swift coyote is in open plains country, not in cactus like this. (Johnny Stewart photo)

and even a .38 Special. For that matter, a called coyote is a prime target for an archer, although his reflexes are so quick that he'll occasionally jump the string (sound moves faster than the arrow) enough to sidestep the shaft.

Sport hunters are being accused these days of exterminating just about everything from the blue whale to the *Tyrannosaurus rex*, not to mention the dodo bird, the passenger pigeon, the Eskimo curlew, the bison, and dozens of other species which were *never* sought by sportsmen in significant numbers. However, the ubiquitous coyote seems to be one animal whose final demise not even the most ardent preservationist will ever be able to blame on sport hunters. The reason is that the coyote is going to outlive both hunter and preservationist, a thought from which I take a certain comfort.

In case you hadn't noticed, I love El Coyote. It's nice to know he's holding his own.

14

The Short-tailed Cat

by John Wootters

No other predatory wild animal has become so universally embedded in American folklore as what we call the bobcat. The saying that a man could "lick his weight in wildcats" was the supreme compliment to his fighting qualities even before American settlement reached the Mississippi River, and we still apply the term "wildcat" to impulsive, daring ventures, especially when they have an aura of individuality and of bucking long odds about them; a "wildcatter" can be one who designs non-standard cartridges, or who gambles his life savings on an independently drilled oil well. Americans have known the bobcat since Pilgrim days, and they have respected him. His toughness and independence still appeal to us, exemplifying some of the better qualities of the American national character.

Hunters, of course, have known the bobcat longer and better than anyone else, and they, too, have learned to respect this spotted, sinewy bundle of dynamite for the challenging game animal he is.

Today, bobcats are found in almost every one of the contiguous 48 states (although in limited numbers and in specialized habitats in a few of the midwestern and east-central states), all across the southern half of

Author John Wootters called this large male bobcat to within about six feet to take his picture.

Canada, and throughout most of Mexico. Because he is nocturnal and stealthy, he is remarkably inconspicuous in his habitat, however, and millions of people who live in good bobcat country have never seen one. Some don't even realize the cats are present, and most of them would be surprised to know how abundant they really are in most of the regions they inhabit.

I once asked the manager of a large south Texas ranch for permission to try a little predator-calling for bobcats. He told me to help myself, but added that his property didn't have many cats. "I shoot every one I see," he said, smugly, "and they ain't many left!" A companion and I spent five hours calling that night, and called up no fewer than six full-grown cats. The next night, we added four more to the total score, and subsequent expeditions on that ranch plainly indicated that we hadn't even made a dent in the population! The manager, who was a hunter and lived year-'round on that land, was hardly able to believe our results.

The wraithlike bobcat simply doesn't advertise his presence, except to the knowing reader of sign. Look for his round, four-toed prints along dusty trails, the edges of dirt roads, and the margins of streams, wherever the walking is easy. Males also make "scrapes" which are miniatures of those left by male cougars, small, raked-up piles of leaves and debris on which the cat leaves a urine signpost to mark his territory.

Old Bob is a very adaptable fellow, too, living in all sorts of terrain, sometimes quite close to human habitations. I've seen bobcats and bobcat sign inside the city limits of my home city of Houston, one of the nation's largest. I've encountered him in the thornbrush thickets along the Rio Grande, in aspen groves more than 8,000 feet above sea level in the Colorado Rockies, in the bare, stony desert of Arizona, in the tropical jungles of southern Mexico, in palmetto swamps in the Southeast, and on snowy ridges in the Appalachian Mountains. I've also met his larger cousin, the Canadian lynx, among the woodlots of rural New Hampshire. Everywhere, the cats are essentially the same, although biologists recognize several species and races. The coat is short to medium, depending upon the climate, reddish to gray, spotted, and the ears are tufted. Males, particularly, display a striped ruff around the face. The cat is long-legged, with the hind legs apparently longer than the forelegs. A very big male stands close to two feet high at the shoulder and may weigh 35 pounds or even more, although the average weight for

Cats' noses may be poor but their eyes are sharp. Author Wootters shows camouflage techniques as he calls bobcat for the camera.

the species is more like 20 to 25 pounds for large adults. Oddly enough, although the lynx is regarded as the larger of the two short-tailed cats, the heaviest recorded lynx weighed only 40 pounds, while the heaviest bobcat which has been reliably recorded tipped the scales at 69 pounds!

Also, wherever the bobcat is found, he exhibits the same inscrutable, secretive, yet occasionally arrogant personality. He is a silent and deadly hunter, mostly of rodents, rabbits, a few birds, and now and then poultry, and he is perfectly capable of killing young domestic livestock, especially lambs, kids, and pigs, and an occasional deer fawn. I've actually shot one big bobcat who was holding a dying gray fox in his jaws when the bullet arrived, so he's something of an opportunist where cuisine is concerned. There can be no doubt that most adult bobcats do some damage to livestock and game where they have the opportunity, and Texas studies have shown that the average bobcat is more likely to kill lambs and kids than is the average coyote, although ranchers paint the coyote as a villain and seldom pay much attention to the cats. Perhaps that's because bobcats don't run in packs, appear in broad daylight often, or bark at the moon.

Cats are much easier to trap than coyotes, but much harder to control through the use of poison, preferring to do most of their own killing. I believe they're easier to lure close with a predator call, too, although fewer callers know the special techniques necessary for consistent success on bobcats.

Cats come readily to the imitated sound of a terrified or agonized

Wootters says that every encounter with a bobcat is somehow surprising, even when you're looking for one, and sometimes a bit frightening.

rabbit or bird, but they come very deliberately most of the time. The caller who wants a bobcat-skin rug must plan to stay at each calling stand not less than 30 to 45 minutes, instead of the 10 or 15 minutes which suffice for most coyotes, foxes, and raccoons. It's very common to see a cat on his way to a predator call just sit down and stare in the direction of the sound, sometimes refusing to move for a full 15 minutes. Then he may begin moving toward the call once more . . . or he may amble away, apparently having decided that the whole thing is a hoax. One trick that will sometimes get one of these "sitters" off his rear end and on his way to the hunter quickly is an abrupt change in the calling sound, such as switching from a coarse-toned, long range call to a high-pitched squeaker.

Having opened the stomachs of scores of bobcats which responded to a predator call and having found quite a few of them packed full of cot-

Bobcat is a proud trophy, especially when it's lad's first "big" small-game animal bagged.

tontail or pack rat, I have some doubts that a bobcat comes to a call only because he's hungry. He also has a strong dash of curiosity in his make-up, and sometimes will come as well to a sound completely unrelated to any sort of animal. I frequently use a tape-recorded call during daylight so that I can have both hands free to handle a camera. My camera equipment is motor driven and makes a couple of soft clicks with each exposure, and I've had several cats become so intrigued with these mechanical noises that they walked right past the speaker from which my electronic call was issuing and ambled straight up to me as I sat motionless in full camouflage. On other occasions I've been able to draw a bobcat close by ticking two pebbles or a pair of coins together.

Whereas a coyote or fox is likely to charge the sound of a predator call flat-out, even across open country, bobcats prefer to utilize every smidgen of cover available during their approach, and they're masters at the art. Daytime callers regularly find a bobcat more or less in their laps before the animal is spotted. Night-hunters (where this is legal) should be able to spot a cat's eyes before he gets that close, provided

Switching tail, though stubby, is a sign this cat is wound up, ready to fight if necessary for the rabbit he believes is squealing in the clutches of another predator.

they know how to use their lights, but it isn't always easy. When a pair of eyes comes in slowly, weaving from side to side, making detours to utilize brush cover, it's probably a bobcat.

It follows from all this that a predator caller who covets Mister Bob's hide chooses different spots from which to do his calling than he might if the dog-animals were his main quarry. A stand should always be chosen where some low brush offers a cat the kind of approach routes he likes. This is true whether the hunting is to be done by day or night. Bobcats are not at all light-shy, as are coyotes, for instance, and even during the hours of darkness prefer some cover.

Another point to be kept in mind is that bobcats either do not have a very good nose, or they seem to pay little attention to scent. In any case, they'll come to a call upwind just about as readily as from any other direction, in contrast to the canines. Thus, the cat-hopeful caller must watch in all directions rather than concentrating on the up- and cross-wind sides, else he may find a big tom bobcat in his hip pocket.

Cats do have good eyesight, but they do not seem to have the powers of perception that a coyote—or a wild turkey—does, and do not interpret the form of motionless man any more readily than does a deer. Full camouflage, including headnet and gloves, is helpful, but it's neither necessary nor even desirable to conceal oneself in the brush as carefully as the coyote hunter must. The harder you are for the cat to see, the harder it may be for you to see the cat . . . and he's hard enough to see under the best of circumstances.

As in any other kind of varmint-calling, or any kind of hunting, for that matter, tootling a call here and there at random across the landscape is less productive than efforts based on intelligent scouting and pre-selection of stand locations where the sound of the call can reach into areas frequented by the game. For daytime calling, this means bedding spots, usually along rocky outcrops, broken ground along stream bottoms, or dense thickets. At night, when the bobcats are on the prowl, they'll be looking for areas infested with rats, rabbits, and the like, and so should you.

Such places are also the starting points for the other kind of bobcat hunting, which is with a pack of hounds. Any of the coon-dog breeds may be used on bobcats, but the dogs selected usually run a little heavier for the bob-tailed cat. Big Walkers, Blueticks, and Redbones are favored in my part of the country, often with a strong dash of one of the bear-dog breeds, such as Plott. Bobcat packs are specially trained, broken from running even raccoons, and include one or more fighting dogs. A big tom bobcat is more than a match for all but a very few lone hounds, even those outweighing the cat by three-to-one. I've lived

Wootters' motor-driven camera records sequence of big male bobcat approaching the predator call.

around bobcats and cat hunters all my life, but I can remember only one hound, a big Bluetick, which was capable of killing a full-grown bobcat in a one-to-one fracas. And what a fracas it will be! Fighting a bobcat is like fighting a buzz saw.

The characteristic bobcat race proceeds by spurts, if there are trees or rock formations in which the quarry can take refuge. The bobcat is fast for a short distance, but he hasn't the lungs for an endurance chase. Typically, he'll run a couple hundred yards, through the toughest, wettest, most brier-choked cover he can find and take to a tree. Then, before the hunters can come up, he'll jump out and run again, sometimes repeating the sequence for a couple miles or more until he finally holds the tree.

In some areas, hunters prefer to chase cats with only one or two experienced hounds, doggedly pushing Bob slowly and steadily until he trees for good. However it's done, a cat hunt with good dogs is a thrilling and physically demanding hunt and one which will be long remembered by the first-time participant.

As good a gun as any for hound-hunting is a reliable handgun. Shots at treed cats are at short range and at stationary targets, with plenty of time for careful shooting. A brain shot with a .22 Long Rifle does the job neatly, but most hunters would prefer a little more power. The price of good dogs being what it is these days, it makes sense to take pains to avoid dumping a wounded but not disabled bobcat into the midst of an excited pack. I'd recommend against any pistol caliber much below the .38 Special-9mm Luger level of lethality. On the other hand, if the pelt is wanted (and prime bobcat pelts have skyrocketed in value in the last few years, reaching a high of about $90 in some areas, I've heard) the big magnums are out. Probably the best all-around handgun for bobcats is a good .357 Magnum using the heavier bullets to limit hide-destroying expansion. One thing's for sure: a pistol is a helluva lot easier toting at full gallop through the swamps and brier patches in pursuit of a gang of baying hounds, especially at night.

The handgun works well in skilled hands for calling bobcats, too, although shots don't average as short as with the dogs. I've executed several bobs with the 9mm Luger and the .357, all with head, neck, or frontal chest shots at no more than 25 yards. However, those cats which come partway to the call and then sit down and watch at 100 or so

A bobcat that was bagged during a night-time hunt. (Russell Tinsley photo)

This Texas' bobcat reveals exceptionally heavy spotting, almost like an ocelot, and long hind legs typical of the breed.

yards can be frustrating for a pistolero. A good rifle does the work easily then, even at night if the shooting light is good enough.

Most rifle calibers up to and including the 6mms are suitable for bobcats. The animal isn't large, but he's remarkably tough to kill with a bad hit, no matter what he's hit with. I once saw a big tom absorb an 80-grain bullet from a 6mm Remington too far back and lead us on a tense, two-hour blood-trailing job at night. When we found him, he was still alive. All of which means that a rifle with a bit of punch is better than any of the rimfires, even the magnums, and that bullet placement is still important. The whole family of centerfire .22 cartridges is suitable for cats (fragile bullets in the higher-velocity number may damage pelts), as are most of the .24s and .25s. If I had to pick a single rifle caliber which I consider ideal for bobcats, at all ranges and under almost all circumstances, it would probably be the .250 Savage.

Wherever he's found, the bobcat adds a dimension of wildness and mystery to the countryside, a note of excitement. A close-range encounter with one in the woods, perhaps while stand-hunting whitetails, always leaves the hunter a trifle shaken, partly because of the eerie ghostliness of the animal's comings and goings, and partly because a man who looks into a bobcat's great yellow eyes will have a hard time forgetting what he sees there. He'll see an utter lack of fear, and a sort of innocent, merciless ferocity which will remind him that all cats, big and little, are still *cats*, and that the only difference between a bobcat and a saber-toothed tiger is size.

I think that's what makes the unseen presence of bobcats lend a sensation of primitiveness to any landscape, and what makes the little lynx so fascinating an animal to hunt. Country without bobcats is tame country indeed, and the hunter who hasn't encountered the short-tailed cat is missing something from his total hunting experience.

15

Woodchucks of the East

by Carlos Vinson

A WOODCHUCK REALLY STUFFS HIS POUCH from early spring until late fall. It has been said that an adult woodchuck will eat his or her weight in green every 24 hours—and the average adult chuck weighs about eight pounds.

So it is easy to see why many farmers can have woodchuck problems. The burrowing animals dig up the ground and consume a lot of alfalfa, young soybeans, clover and other farm crops, to say nothing of melon and tomato patches, and even native livestock forage.

Since the landowner usually considers the woodchuck an unwanted pest, this helps open gates to hunters and even allows gunning on some posted lands, but hunter friends and I don't treat the 'chuck with such contempt. We consider it a game animal, one deserving of the lofty title.

The animal we are discussing, of course, is the woodchuck of the eastern United States and many sections of Canada. Range of the species extends from New England westward through Minnesota, Iowa and Arkansas, southward to extreme northern Alabama and Georgia. Common nicknames are "groundhog" and "whistlepig." Although closely related,

A 'chuck cautiously looks about before emerging from its burrow. (Tennessee Wildlife Resources Agency photo)

the woodchuck is an entirely different species from its western counterpart, the yellow-bellied marmot, often called the "rockchuck."

During the past two decades the eastern woodchuck has greatly widened its range. In many areas they have scattered from the rocky limestone hilly sections where they formerly dwelled almost exclusively. The so-called permanent pasture trend accounts for this. Hundreds of thousands of acres of land have been sodded in permanent pasture mixtures of various clovers and grasses. This farm-country trend has been right up the woodchuck's alley. They thrive on green stuff and have enormous appetites during their active season. During the cold weather months they do a lot of snoozing in their underground dens. Hibernation varies considerably with the climate.

Woodchucks are found today in many areas where none existed only a few years back. Thousands of them have gradually inched their way out into the flatlands and taken up permanent abode there. It is now safe to say that considerably more woodchucks exist in most sections of their range than existed twenty years ago.

Ideas among woodchuck shooters on what is the best varmint rifle vary as widely (almost) as ideas on how our government should be run. In this piece we will try to arrive at a happy medium which will put the sport within the reach and capabilities of everyone interested.

Too many get the idea that 'chuck shooting is mainly for high-priced custom-rifle fans who fancy themselves as gnat shavers. It is true that the custom-rifle fellows do develop both rifles and handloads with almost super accuracy at long ranges. Actually they are to be envied by average 'chuck shooters. But they have quite a bundle invested in their rifles and other varminting equipment including what it takes for handloading their ammo. The average fellow who wants to get out and clobber a few woodchucks just can't peel off the required number of greenbacks for this type of shooting.

A varmint rifle does not have to be a gnat shaver to clobber 'chucks consistently up to say 250 yards. Far more woodchucks are killed at 200-yard-and-less ranges than are killed at ranges beyond 200 yards. And this includes 75 percent or more of the 'chucks bagged by the custom-rifle supershots. Up to 250 yards, most factory varmint caliber rifles if properly scoped and zeroed in will be capable of more accuracy

Long-range shooting skill paid off with this bag of Tennessee woodchucks.

than the average shooter is capable of. A factory varmint rifle can be bought as cheaply as a factory deer rifle. In some cases the same rifle can be used for both 'chuck shooting and deer hunting.

The .243 Winchester is about the best combination caliber available. This caliber was originally developed for Western States antelope hunting. The caliber caught on quickly in the East as a long-range varmint caliber and also in the more open areas of the East as a caliber for white-tail deer. Shooting 80-grain softnose bullets (factory loads), the .243 is actually good on 'chucks up to ranges of 300 yards and slightly better. Most experienced 'chuck shooters like to sight in their .243's so they will shoot 1¾ inches high at 100 yards. Using the 80-grain factory bullets, this will make the bullet strike only ½ inch low at 250 yards. The bullet would be two inches high at 150 yards and 1¼ inches high at 200 yards. An adult woodchuck sitting upright would offer a dandy target. 'Chuck shooters have to learn to judge distances fairly accurately. At 150 yards the rifle scope's crosshairs should be centered slightly below the 'chuck's shoulder area. This example of course is for the .243 caliber softpoint 80-grain bullet factory load only, but it does give a good idea of what this all-important distance and sighting-in thing is all about.

It would be too long and too confusing to run the gamut of varmint

This 'chuck shooter is using a rifle rest improvised from camera tripod.

'Chuck hunter lines up a distant 'chuck in his scope sight.

calibers. Good standard, everyday-use varmint calibers are the .243, 6mm, .222, .222 magnum, .22-250 and to a somewhat lesser extent the .225. Other calibers are often used for 'chuck shooting but the ones just specified are the leaders.

The regular .222 caliber shooting 50-grain factory bullet sighted in so it will shoot 2¼ inches high at 100 yards will be just about on the money at 225 yards. The .222 bullet falls pretty fast after 225 yards. It is not a long-range caliber like the .243, but it is very accurate within its range and highly suitable for 'chuck shooting in the more thickly settled farm areas. The .222 does not sound off as loud as the .243 when fired and has considerably less recoil. A .243 rifle has recoil comparable to a non-gas-operated 20-gauge shotgun shooting high velocity loads. The .222 magnum is actually little more than a souped-up .222 with about 20-yard gain in consistent accuracy distance.

The 6mm's capabilities are similar to those of the .243. The .225 started out as an in-between caliber in the varmint field, but has for some reason never gained the popularity of the .22-250 caliber. The .22-250 actually has as long a consistently accurate killing range as the .243, but it shoots only a 55-grain factory bullet the same as the .222 magnum. In short, more powder behind the same size bullet. But the .22-250 is a flat shooter like all the other good varmint calibers and should be sighted in at 100 yards just the same as the .243. Shooting the 55-grain factory loads, the .22-250 will be back on the money at 250 yards whereas the .243 will be ½ inch low at the same distance—not really enough difference to miss a 'chuck sitting upright if crosshaired the same way. The .22-250 has somewhat more muzzle velocity than the .243 and of course makes less shooting noise. The .22-250 is not a dual-purpose caliber, giving the .243 the advantage in this respect.

No other type of rifle seems to have the pinpoint accuracy of the bolt action. Experienced 'chuck shooters wouldn't give two hoots in a whirlwind for any other design of varmint rifle. Most prefer the medium heavy to heavy varmint barrels. Exceptions are among those who choose the .243 caliber to be used for more than one purpose. The heavy-barreled models are somewhat cumbersome in the deer woods. The combination rifle angle has been brought out for the simple reason that fully a dozen average 'chuck shooters exist to every one of the more expensive, custom-rifle type.

Best times of the day for 'chuck shooting are from about an hour after sunup until mid-morning, and then from mid-afternoon until about a

Hunting an alfalfa field paid off with this husky woodchuck.

half hour before sundown. If the weather is mild there may also be a feeding period between 11:30 A.M. and 1 P.M. If the weather is cool, the mid-day period will probably be the best of all. If it is a mild, cloudy day, 'chucks are apt to be out of their dens at almost any time.

Woodchucks normally dig dens near their main feeding grounds, in many cases well out in alfalfa, clover and other fields. 'Chuck dens can be both livestock and farm machinery hazards. Denning areas usually shift with the seasons. A grizzled old 'chuck may dwell in an alfalfa field during the spring and summer seasons and then move to some higher rocky ground nook in the immediate vicinity of the summer home and winter there.

The woodchuck may not be so smart in some ways, but in other ways he's got oodles of savvy. He learns to associate gun noise with danger pretty fast. Ditto for the bark of farm dogs. Tractor noise will not usually spook the critters. Neither will the sight of people a hundred yards or so away until Mr. or Mrs. Whistle Pig has been shot at a few times and missed. That is why 'chuck shooter clothing can play a big part in the success or failure of a 'chuck shoot. If the 'chucks in a territory (usually two or three adjoining farms) have not been shot at very much, and not chased by farm dogs, from a distance of a hundred yards or more they will not usually pay much attention to the color of a shooter's

Shooter trying an offhand shot at 'chuck which sat upright about 40 yards away.

Look for fresh den holes like this when scouting woodchuck-hunting territory.

clothing. But if they have heard the zing or thud of a few high-powered rifle bullets which failed to find their mark, they will quickly associate the potential danger of a gaily clad shooter with the rifle noise danger. So it pays in most cases to wear camouflage or other drab-colored outer garments while on 'chuck-shooting trips.

In many of the better 'chucking nooks, ground vegetation often prevents prone shooting. Many shooters buy ready-made or make up their own tripod-type rifle rests. Then they use folding dove-shooting stools which are also lightweight. They can sit on the stools, use the rifle rests,

Most woodchucks emerge from their dens cautiously as this one is doing.

When you get a 'chuck up like this, better shoot fast, for it won't remain that way long. (Tennessee Wildlife Resources Agency photo)

and not have to worry about ground vegetation interfering with their shooting. They can also shoot in more comfort this way. In the better 'chucking nooks as many as a dozen shots can often be obtained from the same stand. It is a matter of sitting and waiting for the 'chucks to emerge from their dens and start feeding. Most feeding 'chucks will sit upright to look for possible approaching danger every few minutes. In most cases they offer better targets when sitting upright.

A good rifle rest can be made from a lightweight camera tripod. Simply fashion a rifle cradle from aluminum and line it with glued-in carpeting after the cradle is fastened atop the tripod. Some of the better grade folding stools have zippered, insulated pockets for keeping drinks and lunch cool, with another container for ammo and other small items. These stools and rifle rests make it much easier for average 'chuck shooters.

A 'chucking rifle should have a sling strap. These can be purchased reasonably at most sporting goods stores.

The varmint rifle scope is almost as important as the rifle itself. Instructions for mounting come with the scopes. Practically anyone with average gun knowledge can mount a scope. Some of the scope makers also have available sighting-in guides which cost very little but are extremely valuable in sighting-in the scoped varmint rifle properly.

Power of the scope can be important. Strictly for woodchuck shooting, an 8X scope is usually sufficient on .243, 6mm and .22-250 rifles. In the case of the .243, if it is to be a dual-purpose rifle a good 6X scope might be better. A good quality 6X scope is usually sufficient on the .222 and .222 magnum rifles.

Good binoculars are also essential in 'chuck shooting. They are a big help in spotting distant feeding 'chucks. Good quality 6X to 9X binoculars are just fine. Opinions on binoculars vary among 'chuck shooters, but 9X35's are a good choice.

When scouting territory (highly important in this sport) approach the farmers cautiously. If a farm looks 'chucky but is posted, try to strike up a conversation with the farmer about the fine looks of his place, his cattle or crops, and very gradually lead up to the 'chuck question. If the farmer is approached right and is having any woodchuck problems, chances are the shooter (not more than a couple) will get 'chuck-shooting permission. Once the ice is broken and it turns out to be a good spot, keep quiet about it. A couple of 'chuck shooters can line up a half dozen or so farms and get all the shooting they want during a season. This way they will not have to shoot any one farm too often.

16

Rockchucks in the West

by Erwin A. Bauer

High in the mountains of the American West is a kind of game and of hunting which few outdoorsmen elsewhere really know about. It's a sport which carries the hunter to some of the most magnificent landscapes on top of this continent—often to the same areas where bighorn sheep and mountain goats roam. And often the target, which is much smaller than either of those trophies, is just as wary and just as exciting.

We're speaking here of the rockchuck or whistlepig, which is more properly known nowadays as the marmot. But even that is a little misleading because there are actually five related members of this family, which inhabits almost all of the United States.

Besides the well-known woodchuck or groundhog of the East, there are the yellow-bellied, hoary, Olympic and Vancouver marmots. Let's dispose of the latter two immediately by pointing out that they live (respectively) in very restricted ranges of Washington's Olympic Mountains and on Vancouver Island. Neither are widespread enough in range to be very important to hunters.

But not so with the yellow-bellied (also called the golden) marmot which ranges throughout the roughest and most mountainous portions

Yellow-bellied marmot sits upright to look for danger in meadow where it has come to feed.

of the West. Its most likely natural habitat is around rock outcrops, rimrock and rock slides, all of which must be adjacent to green ground vegetation. They also have a habit of invading high meadows and mountain pastures from Arizona and New Mexico northward to Idaho and Montana. The habitat preference of the hoary marmot is similar except that it lives farther north than the golden. Hoary marmot country includes mountainous British Columbia, Alberta, Yukon, most of Alaska north to the Brooks Range and Canada's Northwest Territories.

Yellow bellies are stocky, short-legged, light brown or cinnamon above with yellow to orange fur underneath. But the color varies greatly from region to region with some being much darker overall than others. From time to time all black yellow-bellied marmots will be seen—and these may even baffle a hunter who is expecting something else. Hoary marmots run from dark gray to dirty white and are lighter underneath than on the saddles. All (golden and hoary) have darker faces. That total coloration blends in neatly with their typical sub-Arctic rock environment and makes hunting them all the harder. But no matter what the color phase, both marmots are top targets anywhere you happen to encounter them.

Like woodchucks, all western marmots hibernate in winter. It's necessary because all available food supplies (grasses, forbs, herbs) are withered and covered up under a blanket of deep snow or ice. The animals

Rockchuck taken on bleak windswept pass on top of Montana Rockies. Rifle is a .222 Magnum.

emerge in springtime and soon grow fat on the first tender green shoots which follow receding snow. For a shorter period during the hottest weather of mid-summer yellow bellies also aestivate, which means that they rest in a semi-sleep in cool tunnels underground. This explains their temporary absence and of course the temporary difficulty in locating them. But during other periods, marmots are very active during daylight hours and may even travel far to forage from their denning areas. Both marmots thrive in elevations up to 10,000 feet, but the farther north the latitude, the much lower they're likely to be.

Marmots are colonial rather than solitary. They live in groups—or communities—probably of several families nearby. Find one and you've found a concentration of them. But figure also that vast areas of otherwise excellent marmot country will be completely and unaccountably uninhabited. Like eastern groundhogs, all marmots dig, live in and raise young in burrows which they themselves dig. In many places the main or only evidence that rockchucks live anywhere are the fresh mounds of earth around burrows. Many young ones are in evidence around the entrances from early summer onward.

Like most other game species, rockchucks are certain to be more wary where they are heavily hunted. In certain spots they become as elusive as old whitetail buck deer. The result is that some of the most intriguing sport is found in areas where marmots are heavily hunted. In other words the rifleman really works for his game—and then some.

But if hunting pressure is not too great, marmots can readily be spotted on suitable mountain slopes because they are either very active or will be conspicuous when loitering in the afternoon sun on a prominent rock overlook. They use the same resting spots day after day if undisturbed. At such times it may often seem that one marmot acts as a sentinel—a watchdog—for all. At least this sentinel gives a loud piercing whistle when a hunter (or grizzly bear, which delights in digging marmots from their dens) approaches too close. Instantly all within hearing scatter for cover and none may be seen again soon.

It's unlikely that the one-marmot sentinel system is planned in any way. More than likely one old rockchuck in a colony is just more alert and cautious than all the others. He may have heard the whine of a ricochet on rock before. Nonetheless this caution—this characteristic warning whistle—is what makes this member of the rodent family a fine game animal rather than just an ordinary target.

Most mountain animals are more vulnerable to approach from above. Goats, elk, sheep, deer and bears seem to concentrate their vigilance on what lies below. They remain alert for the approach of enemies from lower altitudes; but they seldom look up. Marmots have this same tendency. You can approach within shooting range of even the most nervous marmots by making a wide circle and climbing to get into position above them.

Some other tips to prospective marmot hunters would have to include the following: singles are easier to stalk than groups of feeding animals. Warm, sunny days are by far the best. Do not make unnecessary noise; marmots appear to have excellent hearing. I've heard them whistle an alarm at a hunter's approach when it was impossible to see him. Possibly the best tip of all is to watch constantly for those telltale fresh mounds of earth that mark the entrance to marmot dens.

One summer Joe Jackson and I prowled through several old ghost camps on both sides of Montana's Continental Divide, excellent marmot country. What we found was both surprising and exciting. In a number of old abandoned mining camps there were marmots galore, but be-

Strange as it may seem, old abandoned mine area is likely habitat for yellow-bellied marmots.

cause a few people also lived there, we couldn't even consider hunting nearby. But people or not, our search had a strange quality no other hunting ever had. We walked on old wooden sidewalks where the West had been won—or lost. Just try poking around places like Elkhorn and Granite, Southern Cross and Marysville, and see for yourself. Incidentally, you *cannot* hunt in the four places I've mentioned, because

Such as this one which peers out from beneath old miner's shack.

they are still inhabited. But nobody should have any trouble finding the varmints elsewhere in *deserted* ghost camps.

Our best find was in the vicinity of a long-deserted silver mine, name unknown, and the community of wooden shacks that had been erected all around it. Joe had heard about the spot from the local game warden. But on the damp, cloudy morning when we reached the mine, nothing much was stirring. If there were any marmots about, they were staying underground.

"Looks like a bad steer," Joe commented.

But because ghost camps are fascinating, I began to poke around some old buildings anyway. In one building I found scraps of yellowed newspapers printed before the turn of the century. In another shack I found a rusted tin sign on which "Sunnybrook, the pure food whiskey" was still distinguishable. In the third building, the wooden floor suddenly collapsed underfoot, and I was deposited onto a mound of freshly dug earth.

Hoary marmot looks out cautiously over landscape from Alaskan mountainside.

"Marmots!" I said to myself out loud. Immediately, instead of nosing into more old buildings, I started to glass the hillsides all around.

That ghost camp must have been completely undermined by marmots and by various species of gophers and ground squirrels as well. The longer we looked through the glasses, the more activity we saw. For a better view, we circled to the second floor of the only two-story building on the site. It must have been the mine office, judging from the scattered cashier's slips and similar litter. From there, Joe spotted an old grandpappy marmot grazing in complete unconcern—and that one became the first we collected. Joe used the window sill for a rifle rest. The shot sent the other marmots scurrying for their holes, but 15 or 20 minutes later at least two were out feeding again. I know because I bagged one of them.

It was during a hunting trip far from any Montana ghost camps that I learned a most important thing about marmots. Guide Charlie Abou,

At first hint of danger, hoary marmot heads below to hide in rocky burrow.

Frank Sayers and I had made a difficult climb in the Cassiar Mountains of British Columbia to reach a high and lonely basin. Strewn with huge, dark boulders, it resembled the ruins of an ancient graveyard. Although our trip was primarily for caribou, grizzlies and Stone sheep, Charlie Abou hadn't brought us here for any of these.

He knew the spot was loaded with hoary marmots—and because *he* was hungry for marmot, he had brought us there to shoot some.

I'm glad he did. Not only did we enjoy an hour or two of tricky shooting at targets that wouldn't stand still, but we also learned that marmot is amazingly delicious fare on the table. Charlie dressed and skinned the animals carefully. Back in camp, he built a fire of dead spruce, on which he occasionally tossed twigs of Arctic willow. Over this he slowly roasted the marmots whole, turning them frequently. Perhaps more than anything else, the meat tasted like tender young chicken. Now this much is certain: I haven't shot my last marmot for the table. Incidentally a rockchuck will weigh up to seven pounds when full grown. An extremely heavy one may reach 12 pounds, and that is a lot of good eating.

Perhaps the marmot is the best bet for varmint hunters anywhere in America. Eastern 'chuck hunters must always be vitally concerned with what is beyond the target. Much of the available 'chuck country is completely out of the question: safe shooting is impossible because of expanding population and growing civilization. But that's only a minor hindrance in the western mountains. There you can stalk your game or try the longest shots—however you choose to do it. If you meet anybody else in summer in marmot country, it will be another marmot hunter.

Also, any rifle is a marmot rifle, although I admit the special varmint models and calibers are vastly the most fascinating and pleasant to use. I've used a Remington Model 513-T .22 target rifle with good results, but the .22 Long Rifle bullet too seldom anchors the very tough marmot right where he is hit. My best results have been with the .222 and Remington .222 magnum. The last, particularly, has great killing power on marmots, even beyond 200 yards. At that range (200 yards) with a 55-grain factory bullet, it delivers a wallop of 670 foot-pounds, as compared with 520 foot-pounds for the .222 with a 50-grain factory bullet.

But to tell the truth, most of all my marmot hunting has been done with the same battered old standby .270 and the Remington model 700 7mm magnum with a Leupold 3X–7X scope which I prefer to hunt larger mountain game. Of course that's greatly overgunning such a small animal, but my reasons are sound. Not only do I want to drop the 'chuck exactly where it is hit, but I am also getting valuable experience for other mountain hunting. As pointed out before, marmot hunting is exactly like sheep, goat or grizzly hunting—in the very same kind of upside-down landscapes where the atmosphere is thin and the slopes steep.

When hunting marmots I am getting both my legs and lungs in shape for climbing, and the best possible advice to anyone planning a big-game hunt for the first time is to do the same. Physical condition plays an important role in success or failure. While climbing and getting the "feel" of alpine elevations, I am improving my ability to spot game at long distance, and this also is vital when stalking sheep and the like. Nor is there a better way to learn to accurately estimate range where the air is thin and the horizon may seem farther away than it really is. Pace off and analyze every shot you make at a marmot.

When you go big-game hunting in the Rockies for the first time, your rifle (no matter what it is) will seem especially heavy and awkward to handle (as you climb) until you get used to it on a sling. But marmot hunting will soon eliminate a lot of this awkwardness, and scrambling about over rimrock with the rifle slung will become second nature.

Take my word also that absolutely no amount of bench-rest shooting

Sleek young yellow-bellied marmot not only is an elusive mountain target, it also is delicious on the table.

on a rifle range will take the place of actually shooting in high altitude mountain conditions at nervous, moving game. When a hunter has reached the point that he can spot a target as small as a marmot, stalk and hit it, he will have no trouble taking a trophy sheep. At least he will have greatly bolstered his own confidence and will have learned a lot about his rifle.

No article on marmots should be concluded without a stern word about moderation and conservation. It's certainly true that the animals are fairly plentiful and widespread. In a few scattered places they even tend to be a nuisance to ranching operations. But still their numbers are not unlimited—and far, far from it. So the marmot hunter's goal should never be simply to pile up a big kill—to bag as many as he can. Whole communities have been wiped out that way in recent years. There is no justification for such practice.

Our advice therefore is to go marmot hunting and take what you want to eat. Do not discard the delicious meat which rivals that of any other mountain game. Make it a quality rather than a quantity shooting experience. And enjoy the most beautiful game country left in all America.

17

Prairie Dogs and Ground Squirrels

by Bert Popowski

A Yanktonai Sioux tale tells of an Indian named Loneliness, a Super-Chief whose tribe was foodless and starving. While hunting for meat, Loneliness was captured by a monster and imprisoned in a cave. When he escaped he took with him a magic arrow from the monster's quiver. From then on he traveled widely over the Great Plains and mountains. Wherever he found hungry Indians, he shot this magic arrow into the sky and showers of lively prairie dogs came tumbling down. They immediately gathered into tribal villages and dug new homes for themselves and their pups. When all of his people were supplied with succulent prairie dogs, Loneliness broke the magic arrow and threw away the pieces. Generations of Indian small-fry have since learned basic hunting skills by stalking prairie dogs. And no Indian needed to go hungry if he could only manage to bag a few of these portly ground squirrels.

But the Plains Indians weren't the only ones to snack off prairie dogs during critical times. The Digger Indians of the Northwest got their paleface name from a diet of any roots and rodents they could scrounge throughout the year. So did some other tribes of the western and northern Rocky Mountains when they couldn't manage larger hunks of pro-

Prairie dogs are gregarious and there will be a colony of dens. (Russell Tinsley photo)

tein. Even Lieutenant Caspar Collins—for whom Fort Collins, Colorado, was later named—was once served a casserole of what a reporter of the Indian campaigns of the late 1800s robustly described as being cooked of "a bitch and five pups." While the hungry Collins didn't much care for that description, he had little choice but to join his hungry patrol in eating of the only available food.

The prairie dog got its common name from a descriptive melding of its habits and habitat. In 1742, when France's Verendrye brothers—Louis and Francois—led an exploratory party down from geographical Canada and into present-day Montana and the twin offspring of Dakota Territory, they encountered solidly established colonies of a ground-squirrel branch of the rodent family. These sassy residents sat on their den thresholds and barked defiance at the *voyageur* invaders. The imaginative French promptly dubbed them *petit chiens*—little dogs. That provided the nether half of their names.

Even upright like this a prairie dog doesn't offer much of a target. (Russell Tinsley photo)

In 1804, three-score years later, Meriwether Lewis led his expedition through some very similar country. He noted these gregarious critters were found chiefly on the prairies. So originated the forepart of the name of the busy burrower which has been here since Loneliness first loosed the monster's magic arrow into the western skies. But, in actual fact, the prairie dog is no canine, nor does it always live only in prairie habitat; thus giving the lie to all of its common name. But it's now far too late to correct a name so firmly fixed amid many American biological baptismal boo-boos.

One of the assignments given the Lewis and Clark party was to procure and preserve specimens of the flora and fauna they encountered. So, when the expedition camped near a prairie dog town adjacent to a brawling stream, the scientists busied themselves in collecting a prairie dog—unmarred by arrows or bullets. They intended to flood its burrow and grab the air-hungry rodent when it emerged. So they poured a barrelful of water down a handy den. It vanished instantly, yielding only subterranean gurgles. They poured in four more barrelfuls and were on the point of abandoning the project when a water-logged doggie emerged to be bagged. Its pelt is now in the American Museum of Natural History in New York City and is probably the oldest existing specimen of the species.

Prairie dog burrows seldom crowd each other. They permit room enough for each family to find nearby food without extensive travel. But the species is so prolific that single towns sometimes grow to cover enormous acreages and number their residents in the millions. Some of the earliest reported dogtowns were simply unbelievable in size and population. In 1852, as starters, R. B. Marcy rode his horse through a million-acre dogtown that he estimated at 5,000,000 residents—though he allowed only the lean average of five dogs per acre. In 1853, John R. Bartlett rode three consecutive days through a continuous dogtown that straddled Brady Creek, a tributary of the Colorado River in central Texas. He reported that the dens were spaced on an average of 10 yards apart and estimated only two dogs per burrow in residence. His estimate, based on an area 10 miles wide by 50 miles long, came to a total of 30,000,000 prairie dogs in residence.

In 1900, Bureau of Biological Survey biologist C. Hart Merriam spent weeks studying a prairie dog town north of San Angelo, Texas. He allowed an average of 25 dogs to the acre, in a metropolis which was 100 miles wide and stretched 250 miles in length, to come up with 400,000,000 residents. Even as recently as 1931 a Vernon Bailey conservatively estimated 6,400,000 dogs in Grant County, New Mexico.

Of late years many towns, cities and both National Parks and Monuments, even zoos, have given the prairie dog its just due. They set aside whatever living space they can spare for dogtowns. There the busy little rodents preserve their own slice of Americana. Tourists are often entranced by prairie dogs, often fully as much as the more distant sightings of American bison and pronghorn antelope—both of which were primitive-day neighbors—all of them then happily existing cheek-by-jowl by the millions when this country was young and unspoiled.

Tulsa, Oklahoma, has a tourist-baiting prairie-dog town on its outskirts. Kadoka, South Dakota, has too, along with a 12-foot concrete replica of a portly dog standing beside Highway 16, which branches off to the Badlands and its own native prairie dog villages. But these are only three public areas with *petit chiens* on display. Hundreds of owners of arid western ranches preserve remnant villages for their nostalgia value and because the busy rodents were there while the country was still virginal and before whites arrived in America.

The two general classes of prairie dogs are separated by elevation in their choices of pet habitat. The blacktailed varieties are the most numerous and live chiefly on the flatter parts of the Great Plains. The whitetailed prefer elevations of over 6,000 feet. Aside from the tail-tip color, which gives them their segregating names, the two have quite similar habits. The whitetailed doggies yip at a higher falsetto pitch. And, when digging their dens, they don't safeguard them with as high mounds against flood water as their blacktailed cousins. But the three forms of blacktailed dogs, and four forms of whitetailed, are highly gregarious, live in "towns," and subsist almost entirely on a vegetable diet, even down to the roots of plants during droughts.

It has been variously estimated that the forage which goes through the paunches of some three dozen prairie dogs would feed a sheep to maturity, and that 250 dogs eat as much as a 1,000-pound steer. In areas of thin graze and extensive ranch holdings this is of small significance. But where good animal husbandry is matched with lush croplands any

Ground squirrels offer great sport, but they don't receive much hunting pressure. (Hal Swiggett photo)

sizable dogtown is regarded as a wasteful luxury. Its days are then generally numbered as a first line of defense against daily depredation. Ranch hands haul bushels of poisoned grain to the burrow-pitted premises, dump a spoonful of such lethal bait into each den and the village becomes a stinking ghost-town. In a week it presents a barren appearance and within a month grasses begin to seal over the evidence of what was once a bustling and thriving prairie-dog village.

Like the young of much wildlife, prairie-dog pups furnish an animated commissary for many predators. The endangered black-footed ferret could not exist without its constant prairie dog diet. And such confirmed carnivores as badgers, weasels, coyotes and occasional wandering bobcats join hawks, eagles and ravens in systematic raids on the villages. Many preposterous mentions have been made about the harmony in which rattlesnakes and burrowing owls share prairie dog burrows. But the fact remains that any pup, of a size which these "neighbors" can master, promptly goes down meat-hungry hatches at any opportunity.

Fred Turner, left, and Dr. Gerald Swiggett look over prairie dog bagged with .256 Winchester Magnum Ruger Hawkeye held by Swiggett. Turner holds a Thompson/Center Contender chambered for .22 Hornet. (Hal Swiggett photo)

The usual den consists of a hard-packed cone-shaped entrance which is a veritable funnel for easy entry. The first few feet are pitched steeply downward to augment speedy escape from grave danger. The cone-shaped threshold not only serves as an elevated lookout post but also thwarts the entry of water from spring thaws, flash floods and infrequent but usually torrential rains during the soft months of spring, summer and autumn. These protective dikes are regularly higher in the comparative flatlands occupied by blacktailed dogs, chiefly because precipitation and runoff is of flash-flood suddenness and speed.

Prairie dogs provide dream targets for the rifleman. Their build is such that, when standing vertically in their common picket-pin pose, they provide three bullseyes set atop each other. At the top is the rounded head, beneath that is the larger chest and shoulders, and at the bottom is the paunch—usually distended with grub. So, whatever the range, the marksman can hold for the head and have the two lower bullseyes on which to score if he has underestimated the range. That doesn't provide any safeguard against wind drift but that's one of the challenging charms of the exacting marksmanship prairie dogs require. On horizontal poses that windage is automatically taken care of by a sensible hold, but the range must be exactly estimated. So only when both range and wind drift are exactly figured can the marksman expect his bullets to strike within minute limits of variation.

It follows that shooting is not an efficient or inexpensive method of prairie dog control. For the targets they present are myriad, fleeting and variable. Any dogtown that has been previously hunted can be a difficult assignment for casual shooters. For the dogs delight in crouching within their cone-shaped doorways, exposing only a slice of head to keep track of the marksmen. Since the mounds are packed and baked to the consistency of concrete any bullet which touches them disintegrates or deflects. It may shower the doggie with powdered dust but it is highly improbable that even the heaviest and strongly constructed of bullets will pierce the mound dirt to get to its target.

Ideal rifles of pinpoint accuracy are often hard to come by and are highly prized. When it happens that two or three shooters have only one of such exacting qualifications at hand they can still get some competition into a prairie dog shoot. We have developed a fair method by which each shooter stays in the game according to his performance. The shooters flip coins for first shot to commence proceedings. The winner gets to keep the rifle and use it as long as he maintains a 100 percent string of kills. The nonshooting competitors use binoculars in scoring his hits and their decision is final. When he misses, the rifle passes on to the next in order on the same basis. It puts a premium on accurate holding

Kadoka, South Dakota, paid tribute to prairie dog with this 12-foot concrete statue.

and definitely eliminates the wasteful flinging of bullets with little to show for their expense.

During my days as a small sprout, barely able to carry the octagon-barreled Colt rifle which chambered only .22 Shorts, three forms of ground squirrels furnished all my hunting. My father took a dim view of feeding these ground-dwelling pests and encouraged me in hunting them after I had assigned chores out of the way. But Dad was a thrifty soul and saw to it that my supply of ammunition was closely matched by the proof of marksmanship I was required to produce.

We had a straight business deal, Dad and I. He doled out 10 cartridges with the understanding that I'd turn in 10 "scalps" in the form of gopher tails. The skin of these tails was astonishingly fragile and needed only a firm tug to break loose and strip off its central bone core. When I produced 10 tails Dad gave me 10 more loads and the cycle recommenced. It didn't leave much room for missed shots!

But, during some three years of gopher hunting, I never missed. Or, to put it another way, when I ran out of ammunition I had 10 tails to swap for more ammunition. My insurance for such a perfect performance was a coiled length of chalkline which could be speedily shaped into a snare and some steel traps which I set in proven ground squirrel haunts. If I didn't nail 'em with that Colt I could always fall back on these secondary means of collecting bounty tails.

I had two close scrapes during those three years of bounty hunting. The first came when I somehow miscounted and handed over 11 tails in one trade for my next consignment of ammo. Dad stared at that evidence of my super-marksmanship, then his eyes twinkled and he handed over the 10 loads; not 11 for 11, just 10! The second heart-stopper came when my mother didn't search my overall pockets closely enough and had them in the laundry before I noticed my precious trading stock was about to vanish. I rescued them, bedraggled but intact, and I made such a howl about that near calamity that mother never goofed again.

I hunted three species of ground squirrel when I was a boy. First was the pouch-cheeked pocket gopher, which is but rarely seen since he spends 99 percent of his time underground and behind dirt-plugged doorways. He spends his time enlarging his network of burrows and shows only when shoving out the loose dirt freed by his digging. The two-thumb-wide striped gopher was most plentiful. He is sometimes called the Federalist gopher because his camouflage pattern consists of 13 alternate light-and-dark stripes. Finally, there was the Richardson ground squirrel, the largest of the lot, which borrows some of the village-dwelling habits of the prairie dog, except for size.

These three have very different habits. Pocket gophers hew to a time-clock schedule and can be expected to open burrows to rid them of loose dirt at almost exactly 8 A.M. and 4 P.M. Unless I was posted at such moments of discard I had to return hours later to sight it in action.

Blacktailed prairie dogs, like these photographed in Colorado, generally live at lower elevations than their whitetailed cousins. (U.S. Fish & Wildlife Service photo)

The procedure was unvaried. The gopher opened the burrow from underground, sat there with its head showing for a few seconds, then backed off and rapidly shoved out armloads of loose dirt. This came out in armloads, with the gopher holding as much as he could between his forearms and, with his hind legs churning busily, was pushed out into the open. The loads came out rapidly and the last one was used to again plug the burrow entrance until the next working shift. Unless the shooter was ready within that minute or two of intense action he wouldn't be provided with another chance until the next den-cleaning session. Hence the pocket gophers were always shot in the head, the only target presented.

The striped and Richardson ground squirrels were far more sociable during daylight hours. Both were abroad from full daylight from dawn to dusk. They didn't like the dim light of early and late hours, probably because that is when diurnal and nocturnal meat-eating predators were changing hunting shifts. But such treacherous light made it difficult to see the fine sights of my boyhood Colt rifle. Scope sights were still some decades in the future for me.

The striped or Federalist gophers live in rather random fashion, usu-

These rodents are three Richardson ground squirrels, which commonly live in communities, and the non-gregarious 13-striped spermophile. All often are lumped under the term "gophers."

ally in the taller grasses of fencerows, ditches, meadows and croplands. Such a slender little rodent is best hunted before the vegetation grows high enough to hide him; or right after it is cropped short by haying and harvesting. When checking out possible danger the striper often sits upright, like a furry picket-pin. But, even when full-grown he provides little more than an inch-wide target.

The Richardson ground squirrel is substantially larger. But it mostly dwells in villages and thus has myriad eyes and ears to warn the community of danger. About 25 percent the size and weight of prairie dogs of comparable age, it digs extensive burrows and mounds the waste dirt at den entrances. But such mounds are never deliberately shaped and tamped into the prairie-dog-type circular dikes to protect the dens against flooding. The mound is frequently used as an elevated lookout post. When alarmed they emit short, shrill, almost birdlike whistles, simultaneously jerking or flickering their tail. From this they are sometimes known as "flickertail" gophers. It is from these critters that North Dakota got its popular name of the Flickertail State.

There are dozens of other forms of ground squirrels, living all the way from the Alaskan tundra, through the heartland of both Canada and the United States, and clear down to the celebrated semi-tropical

The flickertail is akin to the prairie dog in its liking for roomy dens and living in communities of dozens to the acre. Flickertail also is known as the Richardson ground squirrel.

Valley of Mexico. The Valley is actually a mesa or table—surrounded by higher ridges which give it its name—with an elevation of 7,500 feet.

When found in broken-rock mountainous areas, gophers are often called rock squirrels. But wherever they live they use up both vegetation and crops which mankind can otherwise use for human food and forage for big game or domestic livestock. None of them has any utilitarian value so they are everywhere regarded as pests. Finally, their reproductive capacity keeps them from any danger of becoming extinct.

The Richardson flickertails are joined by several other forms which like to live in communities. Included are the Belding's, Columbian, Oregon, Perry's, Snake Valley, Townsend, Uinta, Washington, Yukon, Mexican and even several Apache spotted forms. Their range varies enormously, all the way from streamside and irrigated valleys up to elevations of 10,000 feet, wherever they can find native or crop foods.

A second branch of the ground squirrel family is chiefly marked by long and well-haired tails which range from six to eight inches in length. The Ring-Tailed and Goldman's forms have tails up to 10 inches long, actually exceeding their body length. Such hirsute plumage may lead casual observers to suspect them of being some kind of tree squirrels. In actual fact, the California and Douglas forms have been observed in trees up to 60 feet off the ground. Several of these forms regularly harvest berries, nuts and seed pods from the taller shrubs and shorter trees. But they store such food caches in their underground living quarters.

In this group are the Franklin, Perote and its allied forms, and the Black-Backed, Mexican and Say's rock squirrels. These last three prefer to live in the rubble rock of canyons, where their dark coloration helps hide them in the deep shadows of crevices.

Finally we come to a group of ground squirrels which should be known as exotics, simply because their pelage is much more revealing than concealing. They are also like chipmunks in their nervous twitchings and even carry their tails aloft when on the run. Presumably this is a defense mechanism, inviting predators to grab for the plainly visible tail while the body of the squirrel evades sudden death. They climb well and often harvest food from shrubs and trees. But they live in ground dens, often rimmed by rocks to foil hungry enemies.

Ground squirrels usually pack seed, nuts and other food of good keeping qualities in their cheeks and carry them for storage in dry underground chambers for winter munching. Naturally, they have to make many trips to fill these granaries. Occasionally they'll tackle food that appeals to them but is oversized for their mouths. One striped gopher was observed gathering crab apples from an abandoned homestead and eventually cached a quart of them in its winter storehouse. The apples were too large to get into his mouth and he had to bite into each one and tilt its head upward for the carry. Another striper was seen packing in burr-oak acorns. But gophers usually confine their gleanings of winter food to weed seeds and small grains up to the size of corn.

Communal ground squirrels are generally warier than those which live as individuals thinly scattered over their habitat. Such communities often offer quantity shooting, much like prairie-dog villages. Such a concentration of targets is best handled by rifles which can accurately span 100 yards or more. The lowly .22 rimfires, even the .22 WRM and 5.56-mm, are minimal calibers for villages of such small targets.

Most prairie dog and ground squirrel hunters go to the lower ranges of centerfire cartridges, of which the .222 has established excellent reputations for accuracy. When the ranges are close to 200 yards, accurate .243 and 6mm rifles are favorites, especially when smoking up a prairie-dog village. The heavier bullets of these 6mm twins are less susceptible to wind drift than any .22 centerfires.

Of course, many centerfire calibers can be reloaded to provide cheap

John Popowski got these ground squirrels with scoped Winchester .22 rifle.

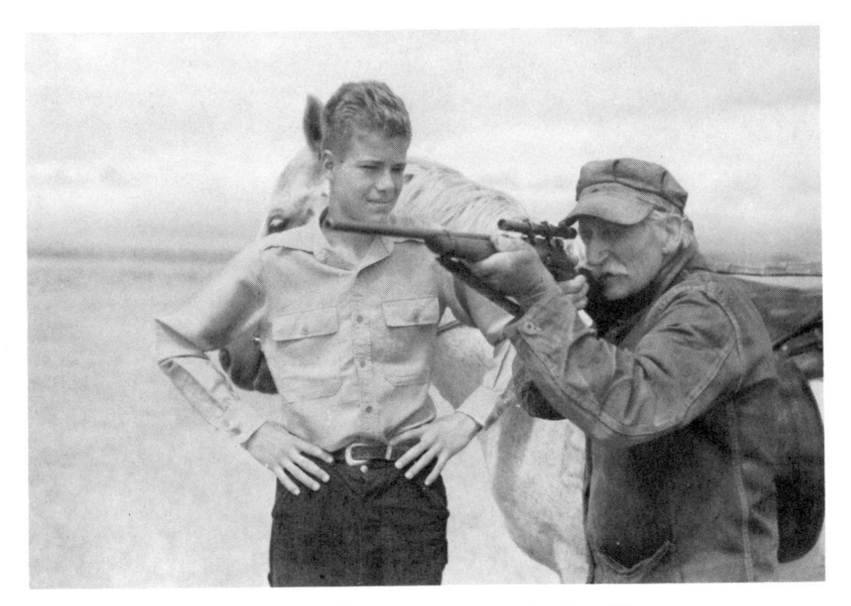

John Popowski lets a sheepherder try out his prairie-dog rifle.

shooting, something which is impossible with the one-time rimfires. Many hunters of medium-sized big game thus use these rodents as tune-up targets for off-season practice. The experience they gain in estimating range and holding off for both distance and drift helps sharpen their marksmanship for the important meet- and trophy-collecting big-game seasons.

The main difference is that reloading antelope and deer calibers for use on these small pest targets calls for lighter bullets than are best for big game. Such bullets are of more fragile construction and are often loaded to higher velocities to provide spectacular blowups on small targets. They also disintegrate readily when flesh-and-blood targets are missed, thus minimizing ricochet dangers. On big game they would create large, meat-damaging wounds. Nonetheless many a serious hunter gets valuable experience in reloading and shooting to give him enormous confidence in his performance when the chips are down.

One side benefit of such experimental loading is that it also provides efficient testing of the reduced loads which are essential to such fragile game as turkeys and the shootable forms of furbearers; to save the delicious meat of the former and the valuable midwinter pelts of such critters as foxes, coyotes, bobcats and others. With the high prices paid for long-haired furs, this is an important seasonal activity, especially in the winters of the more northerly states.

18

Offbeat Species for Year-round Sport

by Byron W. Dalrymple

On a 350-acre ranch that I own in south-central Texas we have about a mile and a half of stream with a good year-round flow. There are high rock bluffs some of the distance, and rock bottom most of it. But there are also small stretches with flat banks where floods have deposited substantial amounts of soil, and along these much heavy grass of several streamside varieties grows. It holds down the soil fairly well when there is a new flood, thus inhibiting erosion. Or it did until the nutrias came.

These South American animals, introduced originally in Louisiana marshes and elsewhere as fur animals, have long been in Texas. In fact, the game and fish department at one time tried them in streams as aquatic grazers to keep water weeds in check. They may have checked some weed growth, but they didn't check their own. They spread widely.

Now I am not one of those who believes that just because something moves you should kill it. I rather liked having a few nutria on the place. We even enjoyed one year watching a mother raise four youngsters in one of our small lakes. But when they multiplied swiftly that was too much. The nutria is a vegetarian. It looks somewhat like an outsize muskrat, except that the face is blunt or squared and the long tail is round. An adult may weigh eight to ten pounds.

These clipped the grass right down to the roots, denuding every inch of stream bank. Then, running short, they took to the hills and we actually saw them high on wooded ridges foraging around several hundred yards from the water. We started nutria hunting.

I am not going to imply that the nutria is any tremendously sporty animal. They run rather awkwardly on land, although in the water they are masterful swimmers, maneuvering adeptly, swimming often underwater just as muskrat and beaver do. They have spread their range across the South and have been introduced in a few states outside it. Although Louisiana trappers still take them for fur, they actually were a debacle in the muskrat marshes, and the fur market never has found suitable uses for the fur that would make it especially valuable. They may or may not be protected in certain states, depending on how the trappers utilize them. Where they are not protected they can furnish offbeat sport at any time of year.

We hunted them with a .22. Although the nutria forages by day, it is predominantly nocturnal. So, we prowled the creek and now and then collected one both day and night, often after quite a strenuous splashing

Nutria is a sporty small-game target, especially in the swamplands of the South. (Russell Tinsley photo)

Very few shooters try for rock squirrels. They are extremely wary.

chase around bends, trying to spot the animal underwater and then get in a quick shot when it came up. Some hunters in east Texas have from time to time made quite a sport out of hunting them from a skiff at night.

That was not quite all of the nutria story on our place. I had learned that on their home grounds in South America they had long been considered quite a delicacy. As a youngster living in Michigan I had been, like many country kids, a trapper of small animals such as muskrats, and we had commonly eaten them. To many that may sound preposterous. The fact is, muskrat is delicious, and there should be no stigma whatever about eating it. At that time, in fact, numerous places along the Great Lakes where there were marshes bought muskrat carcasses from trappers and served muskrat dinners, which were very popular. Further, for many years when the Louisiana muskrat marshes were turning out tens of thousands of hides annually, carcasses were shipped 300 to the barrel to New York City—where they were used by the better hotels as one ingredient in expensive turtle soup!

So, we tried nutria. The meat looks rather red when raw, but cooks as white as chicken. It is absolutely delicious; in fact, except for the heavier bone structure it would be difficult to tell from chicken. Thus for several years we had some unusual off-season sport and wound up with some superb meals. We'll do it again if and when the nutria population gets out of hand.

Open-sighted .22 rifle and black rock squirrel of Southwest make a good combination for learning hunting fundamentals. (Russell Tinsley photo)

Certainly not all offbeat animals that can be turned into "small game" by a hunter seeking the unusual experience will metamorphose into culinary delights. But the fact is that there are several little utilized species, most of them pests in one way or another, that can at least furnish good off-trail shooting. Much of this shooting can be pursued year-round. Or, if it is seasonal, it can fill in during those times such as mid-to late summer when there is little if any standard hunting.

One of the side values is that this is excellent practice for hunting larger game. Make no mistake, if you can stalk a ground squirrel, for example, or a prairie dog, close enough to score, let's say, with an open-sighted .22, or even with a scoped .22, you will know the rudiments to a T for doing likewise with a heavier rifle on an antelope. And, if you use a standard big-game rifle for such small targets at long range, you will either become a deadeye shot or chalk up all misses.

The reason for using the .22 on most such species, however, is that it is much more economical than buying ammo for a heavier caliber. Lately I have been using an unusually heavy .22 rifle for such shooting. It is a Remington slide action and on it I have mounted a full-size scope, a Redfield Widefield 4X. This combo without a sling weighs just one pound less than a Winchester bolt action .243 with 3X–9X Redfield and sling that I use for deer and antelope. Thus, carrying the heavy .22 and handling it and shooting it gives the "feel" of the larger caliber and makes the switch to the big-game gun an imperceptible one.

Not all of the offbeat animals are overlooked everywhere. It is a curious fact in the world of shooting that a species considered "game" or sporty in one region may be wholly overlooked by outdoorsmen in another. Although it can't be considered in this chapter on the offbeats, a good example outside that category is the woodchuck. In some eastern states this is truly a game animal to numerous hunters who avidly pursue the sport at every opportunity. In other states—as an example the Great Lakes area and southward—only an occasional or incidental potshot is taken at a 'chuck.

In my area rock squirrels are numerous. A number of shooters make quite a sport out of hunting them. Yet elsewhere in their range they draw no attention. Rock squirrels are relatives of the 'chucks and ground squirrels, more closely related to them than to the game tree squirrels. This is chiefly a species of the Southwest. It ranges from portions of Utah and Colorado southward far into Mexico. An adult may weigh up to two pounds. Although these animals occasionally climb trees, they live most of the time among rocks, in slides and canyons.

Rock squirrels are basically vegetarians. But they do eat meat, small birds, and eggs whenever possible. In my area they have a reputation—deserved or not—for ruining nests of wild turkeys, and so are not exactly revered. In this region they are black, or look so at a distance. Closer examination shows grizzled hair scattered throughout, and in old specimens the rear half of the back is distinctly reddish brown. Farther west, in New Mexico and Arizona, most rock squirrels are gray.

As a hunting project, rock squirrel shooting is sporty as they come. Whether used to human intrusion or far back in a remote canyon rock squirrels are awesomely shy, secretive and furtive. At sight of an intruder, they utter a sharp whistle. Sometimes they call to each other this way and thus can be located. Once you frighten a rock squirrel it instantly dives into a den among broken shale or other debris, and it may be a long wait for you before it again appears. On numerous occasions, however, I have scared one into hiding at perhaps 100 yards, then set up shop, taking a good rest and getting comfortable, then simply waiting it out. Presently, watching with a binocular, I see a dark head appear in the opening. The glasses are very gently and slowly let down, and the shot squeezed off.

Glassing is very definitely a part of this sport. So is listening and watching. I've tried scoped .22s for rock squirrel shooting. It makes the stalk and maneuvering more exciting. I've also tried eating rock squirrel. I'd term it at best emergency food!

A good many shooters don't feel that way about the armadillo. I recall an east Texas piney-woods dweller who spoke of this little armored

Armadillos furnish some good shooting and also good eating.

critter as "poor man's pork." Although we are no great fans of armadillo meat at my house, when well cooled out and refrigerated overnight after cleaning, it actually is quite good, white meat that is reminiscent of pork. Most people in our area barbecue it or use it in chili.

My main experiences with armadillo hunting have been to cut down the usually large population where we live. We have 24 acres at our home place, mostly woods and with a couple of ponds. Although our lawn is only of native grasses, we intermittently cut about 3½ acres—and the armadillos work hard at digging the best areas apart, looking for worms, grubs and insects upon which they mainly subsist. We have no desire to eliminate every one. They're an interesting little critter to have around.

Whether by releases made by tourists who carted small armadillos home with them, or by their own prowess, this animal has spread its range considerably over the last couple of decades. It is now found in varying numbers clear across the south even to Florida. It also ranges from Texas north to portions of Arkansas and Oklahoma, and is rather plentiful in parts of Louisiana.

There are no special techniques for armadillo hunting. If you come to know what their "diggins" look like, where they probe for insects under leaves and in soft dirt with their hard snouts, or recognize their dens, dug under a rock or a stump, you will know whether or not animals are plentiful. They may be out in daytime, but do much night foraging. The armadillo is not exactly bright. It can be approached closely, but when it does make up its mind to run, it does so with startling zigzag speed and makes a perplexing target. A .22 is all the armament needed.

The porcupine is another offbeat creature that is low in intelligence, and easy to approach to close range. Some protectionists would decry the shooting of porcupines. But tree farmers across the north, and landowners in some places where the animals do tremendous damage to desirable trees don't feel that way. In the past there have even been bounties in some places because porcupines became too numerous.

They sometimes do great damage to tree plantings, and to desirable trees especially on the fringes of their range. For example, I know of a huge ranch in far west Texas, in the Big Bend Country, that is mostly of desert-mountain and grassland terrain, but runs up to some 6,000-plus feet in elevation, and changes, as one climbs, from typical desert-type area to timber. The timber consists of oak and piñon, and at the very top madrona is intermixed.

This is a fringe range for piñon and the owners feel that the trees are valuable, not for timber but because of their uniqueness. It is stunningly beautiful high country. Such an expert colonizer is the porcupine that it seems capable of reaching out its range to any place forage trees grow. I have seen them in Wyoming way off in all-but-treeless country well away from the timbered mountains, where only scattered cottonwoods and brush grow along stream courses. In these fringe ranges they can, if plentiful, ruin an amazing number of desirable trees.

On that west Texas ranch they go so far out of hand that hardly a piñon can be found over the modest amount of range on which the tree is able to survive that has not been either girdled or marked copiously by porcupine gnawing. There is no sport whatever, of course, in shooting porcupines at the close range to which one can stalk them. But each fall during deer season guests on that big ranch get in some long-distance practice while helping control the porcupine population. Binoculars are used to locate the dark blobs at long range across canyons or on a broad

Hunting as a new control measure for prairie dogs should see future popularity.

slope. The shooting is done with standard deer calibers, often at 300 to 400 yards.

The present range of porcupines is throughout most of Alaska and Canada, over all of the western states, the Great Lakes region, New England and across New York and Pennsylvania. Although there is not likely to be a lot of hunting for them, in places as described where they are a nuisance they furnish some offtrail shooting.

It is possible, as I stated in Chapter 1, that prairie dog shooting may become popular once again over the coming years. Poisoning had the prairie dog on the ropes throughout most of its range, but since most of that has been stopped the dogs are coming back swiftly and will need control. Elsewhere in this book prairie dog shooting is covered in some detail. So I will limit my remarks about it here. Where the animal is causing range problems because of over-abundance, hunting as a control measure offers the shooter some unusual opportunities.

As an example, some years ago I shot a good many at the request of a rancher friend in Wyoming. I used a well-scoped big-game rifle and did it all long range. If you want to make the endeavor far more sporty, however, try it with a .22. You have to get much closer to be effective. If you like it super-sporty, then try it with an open-sighted .22. I spent some days one summer, in Montana, crawling around a big dog town doing just that.

I collected darned few that way because they are just too sharp and would duck into their burrows before I could get close enough. Nonetheless, I went from this undertaking to the ridiculous. I unlimbered a bow. I will say that I am not remotely in the expert archer class. It just

Hunting Columbian ground squirrels in Montana in summertime with .22 rimfire rifle.

never grabbed me. But the combination of the sharp little dogs and the awesomely awkward bow and arrow as tools to lug around totally open country while crawling was just too interesting to be ignored. I'm not going to divulge my score—arrows released to dogs collected—but I will say if you like challenges this is one.

Ground squirrels are also covered in more detail elsewhere, but I'll say a few words about them here. In my opinion these often fantastically abundant little animals, strictly pests even though all are handsome and interesting creatures, offer some of the best stalk training and .22 hunting to be had. There are many varieties, widely distributed: the Mexican ground squirrel of the Southwest, the lined "gophers" of the Great Lakes states and eastward, the big, bushy-tailed California ground squirrel of the Far West, spotted ground squirrels of the Southwest, the big, fat-looking reddish brown Columbian ground squirrel of Montana and southern Canada, and numerous species and races even scientists aren't sure about.

I have seen some of these, in sagebrush foothill country in Wyoming and Montana for example, so populous that dozens of them constantly scurried as my boys and I walked through the cover. Shooting them is often just shooting *at* them. They are shy and swift and erratic. The .22, as noted, is the best tool I believe. We even used on numerous occasions

When a winter thaw comes and a night is warm, skunks come out to wander and forage, as these tracks show. They offer hunting, if you're up to it.

single shot unscoped models. I recall years back having shot the big bushy-tailed ground squirrels in Oregon when farmers raising grain begged me to pop every one I could. They can be extremely destructive because of their prolificness.

As an example, the good-sized Columbian ground squirrel was used some years back in an experiment to ascertain just how much grain one single individual ground squirrel might destroy. (I must interject here that all ground squirrel shooting is a summer endeavor. The animals spend more time in hibernation than above ground, go down early in fall and don't come out until late in spring.) Two enclosures were built squirrel-proof in a wheat field. A single adult Columbian was placed inside one. The harvest from the one with no squirrel was 40 pounds, plus nine straw bundles of equal size. From the squirrel enclosure only four pounds and one comparable bundle of straw was present!

Possibly the offbeatest of the offbeat for hunters is the skunk. There may not be many takers for this sport. But I remember with both amusement and nostalgia that when I was a kid I trapped many a skunk. The hides were valuable then, and may be from time to time again. We also went on warmish winter nights when there had been a thaw with a friend who had a hound. Skunks move out of their burrows or wintering spots beneath old buildings at such times and wander around feeding. A fellow has to like the outdoors and the chase mightily to put up with some of the experiences that we bore, if not with grace at least with resignation.

To be frank about it, we had great fun. The runs weren't as long as for raccoons, but anyway it was exciting. We used a .22 for dispatch purposes, but in those days we also had to use an old-fashioned kerosene lantern for light. That meant getting within shooting distance of the skunk—I mean *his* shooting distance!—in order to furnish enough light for the dispatcher to do his work. There were occasions when there was no school for me next day because the smell just couldn't be subdued by any means my family could hatch so that I would be acceptable.

Skunks are of several varieties—striped, spotted, hooded, hognosed—and range over practically all of the U.S. and much of Canada. Some Indian tribes considered them delicious. I have even discussed this with a modern hunter who gave skunk a try. He claims that when uncontaminated by the musk, skunk meat is excellent. That's one of those oddments of information I'm not sure I even need to know.

Ringtail cat of the Southwest is a handsome critter with a fairly valuable hide. It makes for interesting nocturnal hunting.

Throughout its range the extremely handsome and appealing ringtail offers a different hunting experience, and most years the hides sell at least for enough to subsidize the sport. Eastern hunters and others unfamiliar with this animal should not confuse it with the raccoon, which is commonly called a "ringtail." The true ringtail, or ringtail cat (it's not a cat but distantly related to the bears and the raccoons) is a slender, large-eyed nocturnal animal tawny in color with an unbelievably long and bushy tail ringed in black and white. The rings are not whole circles, however. The black sections do not join on the bottom side of the tail.

Ringtails range from southwestern Oregon on southward, and from western Colorado throughout the Southwest and most of Texas and on down to and into South America. Not many hunters realize it, but they can be called quite readily with a predator call. They are also hunted for the hides by a scattering of enthusiasts by cruising ranch trails and watching for them at night. Shining a light on the trees, in which they forage a great deal, easily picks up the shine of their big eyes.

It is interesting that for some years a few hunters daubed red fingernail polish or paint on a flashlight lens, claiming the red mesmerized the ringtail and it would stare at the light. Now it is known of course that a red light shone upon most animals isn't really mesmerizing. It is simply

Badger is one small-game animal that is often overlooked. (U.S. Forest Service photo)

that colorblind creatures are not disturbed by it. To them there seems either to be no light, or else a hazy gray illumination. For this specialized hunting of the ringtail, a .22 is all one needs. Shots should be carefully placed so as not to ruin the hide.

If I were to select the most challenging of the offtrail species, it would be the badger. Only a very few specialists ever hunt this animal, and believe me they have their work cut out. The badger has a broad range, from the Great Lakes region and slightly below on west, into the Prairie Provinces, across the prairies and plains and most of the area west of the Mississippi River and on south into Mexico. Badgers are seldom plentiful. Their distribution is thin. Thus a hunter really has to seek them out. Even when a good territory is located, the animals are not likely to be abundant.

They are very shy, difficult to spot, and secretive. Their low profile also adds to the problem. There are a fair number on the plains of Texas, in eastern New Mexico, the arid sagebrush country of Wyoming and Montana, the area west of the Missouri in the Dakotas, and across the Prairie Provinces. Those are simply suggestions. As badger en-

Even the cactus rat offers a tiny and elusive target for the .22 rifle or handgun enthusiast. (Russell Tinsley photo)

thusiasts say, "They're where you find 'em." I have for some years noted abundant diggings in the thornbrush and cactus of southern Texas, along the Mexican border, but during scores of hunts there I have seen but one, racing for its burrow.

The way to be a successful badger hunter is to first locate "live" burrows. The animals forage both day and night. Very occasionally one will come to a call, and it is worthwhile setting up at night to call within foraging range of a burrow in use. In daytime hunting it is just about useless in plains country to attempt to stalk one seen distantly. The best way is to take a stand within whatever rifle range you can handle of a burrow. Contrive a good rest, and then patiently watch the burrow, especially early and late in the day, with a good binocular. This is a patient man's game, but it will pay off.

The badger is in my estimation a real trophy animal. They are really striking animals when well furred. Men who know hides sometimes refer to badger skins as "fur badgers" and "bristle badgers." On some the hair is very soft, on others exceedingly stiff. The soft hair is of course the most desirable. Such hides make beautiful small throw-rugs when fitted by a taxidermist with colorful felt backing.

Such are the possibilities with the offbeats, in most cases for partaking of sport year-round. Try some of them. Hunters who concentrate on the same varieties of game endlessly miss many a bright interval of unusual experience with those seldom utilized for sport.

19

Javelina—Biggest Small Game

by Byron W. Dalrymple

Over much of its range the javelina, musk hog or peccary was for a great many years strictly a loser. It could not seem to find a friend, or even be extended any respect at all from human kind. Mexicans chased it with packs of mongrel dogs which cornered several animals, and then the man killed them with clubs. This was hide hunting. During the last century and the early part of this one, hundreds of thousands of javelina hides found their way to market.

That was logical enough. The leather, though thin, is excellent, and handsomely dotted with bristle pock-markings. It is hard to work with, but is beautiful when tailored. For 20 years or more I occasionally wore a pair of javelina hide moccasins. The soles were twice gone yet the leather was still in excellent shape. By the time hide hunting had been outlawed in this country and Mexico by making hide sales in the U.S. illegal, the javelina, which once had ranged north as far as Arkansas, was close to extermination. As late as the middle fifties, however, surreptitious hide dealing was still in progress. I saw dozens of hides spread out to dry in Nuevo Laredo at that time, apparently for smuggling into the U.S., where the trade had always been centered.

Javelinas of Southwest normally run in bunches, although you might sometimes find an old boar by himself. (Russell Tinsley photo)

Numerous cattlemen instructed their hands to shoot javelina on sight. Cowboys used to like to try to ride down singles in open areas and rope them, a neat trick and not often accomplished. The peccary attracted public ire because in great droves it chased tourists and natives alike up trees and kept them there for hours or days—so said Western fiction stories of the pulp magazine days and wild-eyed newspaper reports. Others less fortunate, especially dudes roaming the desert, were surrounded and hacked to pieces by javelina tusks—these occurrences also mouth to mouth or published in fiction magazines.

The casual killing of javelinas simply to eradicate them continued, often illegally and at least with no logical reason, into very recent years. I knew a ranch manager in south Texas in the 1960s who kept big dogs for the sole purpose of running javelina bands to bay. His chore was then to wipe them all out with a rifle. The rancher considered the animals vermin. Many others did. Precisely what harm they were up to has never been proved. Although they do not eat a great deal of meat, it is certainly possible that they might kill lambs or goat kids. But they do no harm to cattle enterprises.

By the time the javelina began to get some attention from game men, it was found only in south and west Texas, southwestern New Mexico only scantily, and in southeastern Arizona. Arizona was the first state to give the javelina full game status. Curiously, the game department there was far more enlightened than others. Even as early as the 1950s the animal was protected by a closed season all but a short period of the year, and a special tag was required to hunt it. Interesting, too, is the fact that

Javelina that was bagged with bow and arrow in southern Texas. (Russell Tinsley photo)

it always has been a very popular game species in Arizona, both with tourist visitors to Tucson and Phoenix in winter, and with natives. To my best knowledge those two cities produced the first guides who offered javelina hunts.

By the time New Mexico got around to helping the desert pig, it was gone, or so close to it that there was no hunting. Animals live-trapped in Texas were released on the ancestral range in the Southwest, and today the state has a modest amount of hunting most seasons. The first hunt for the reestablished species was held in 1963. There have been hunts, by quota, ever since whenever the population has been high enough to allow them.

Texas, which has always had the largest number of animals, finally began giving some solid protection only recently. Studies had been done years ago, but only a few counties had any closed season at all, in many one could hunt year-round and with no bag limit, and bag limits or hunting were not checked to any extent anyway. Now however there are only a few counties, seldom with high populations, that offer no protection, and it is a sure bet that within a short time tags on the license will be added for attachment to the kill. Curiously, this attention has been brought about chiefly because the animal has become more popular with non-resident hunters who want to collect one, and that has led to hunting fees paid to ranchers. Thus, as a valuable resource bringing added income from the harsh land that is its prime habitat, the javelina finally demands respect.

In the meantime many of the fallacies about the javelina have been laid to rest. Javelinas do not attack hunters, or dudes! Hunters just sometimes think they do. A wounded animal approached closely, especially if it is cornered, might try to fight its way out. It is certainly capable. The so-called tusks—which aren't tusks at all—are four in number, two in each jaw. They are "dog teeth," for tearing tough vegetation apart and for protection. They grow straight, not flared out as the tusks of true swine, which the javelina is not. They intermesh, uppers and lowers, and are thus self sharpening. Some javelina hunters still think they'll hold out for an "old boar with huge tusks." This is a waste of time because the "tusks" of the next hundred adults one might measure will not vary ⅛ inch in length. An inch and a half about does it.

This is not a large animal, as many a hunter once believed. An adult with neck bristles flared may look mighty large to a tyro. But a Texas study over 25 years ago during which a large number were weighed put the average adult weight at 37 pounds. Some do weigh more, to 40 or 50 and possibly a bit over that. I collected a good specimen on a hunt in Arizona one season that weighed 52 pounds field dressed.

The old malarkey about the musk permeating the meat is also now pretty well laid to rest. The musk gland is on the rump, a simple skin gland surrounded by bristles. When startled the animal may run off with bristles flared from around the gland, and the gland itself exuding a yellow-white secretion that smells distinctively although not pleasantly. The musk is used by the animals as a means of communication, to warn of danger or simply to keep track of each other and to leave sign. After a kill, if a hunter will simply cut the skin around the gland in about a three-inch circle and slice it off, there'll be no possibility of getting musk onto the meat, which is very good, especially from younger animals.

Undoubtedly the attack business started because of the extremely poor eyesight of the javelina. They run in droves, from three or four to 40, depending upon abundance. They are low to the ground and forage much of the time in dense cover. They don't need to see very far, and they can't. I have on many occasions stalked javelina with a camera, quietly and keeping the wind right, until I was so close that with a telephoto lens I had to back up to focus. The lens in question has a minimum focus distance of 13 feet!

Thus, when a shot is fired at close range, or the pigs are otherwise disturbed, they may scatter wildly. On a still day with no distinct scent from a hunter, they may all but run over him trying to get away. I have

Author Byron Dalrymple cleans a pair of javelinas.

had one brush my pants leg as I stood immobile after a shot, and the animal never realized I was there. Their hearing is very acute, but they are not always unduly disturbed by unusual sounds, just alerted. The sense of smell, however, is extremely keen. Once a javelina gets your scent it is going to move off. Sometimes it may not race away, but instead will trot or walk. Much depends on how close you are, and how much disturbance the animals have had.

For those who may wish to collect a javelina as a trophy, and to enjoy this unusual hunting, here are the areas at which to aim. In New Mexico, Hidalgo County in the southwest is a good bet, plus portions of Grant and Luna counties. Probably the Animas Mountains and the Peloncillo Mountains of Hidalgo County will offer best opportunity. The javelina population is not large, nor are permits numerous—200 or 300 is a good guess for any year. Also, they may or may not be for residents only over coming years, and there may not be a season each year. It is

Many hunters shy from eating javelina. It is excellent. This is a roasted ham.

usually sometime after the first of the year, in February or March, and rather brief.

Arizona offers broader opportunity and undoubtedly is the state where a hunt may be set up most easily, even though Texas has a higher javelina population over a larger range. Most years permits number at least 20,000. Sometimes there are more. The Arizona season falls about as the one in New Mexico, and lasts two weeks or more. The range is confined almost entirely to the southeast. Here the pigs range over the desert floor and up the slopes of individual mountain ranges. The Santa Ritas, Grahams, Galiuros, Santa Teresas, Chiricahuas, and Rincons are some of the important small ranges. Many bands are located in desert foothills, in exceedingly rough country, most of it with few roads.

Much of the land throughout this range is public, in National Forest blocks. Thus finding a place to hunt is no problem. There are guides available also in several cities. Although the game department cannot recommend a guide, you may be able to get a list from that source. The advantage of a guide is that they usually know where the bands are, or at least what mountain slope a group may be using, or the location of a tracked-up watering place. One of the most difficult facets of this hunting is finding the animals. They are not scattered out, distributed equally over a range, as deer may be. They are gregarious group animals. You might spend a whole day, in big country like this, working one side of a mountain while every pig in the vicinity happened to be on the other side.

Two areas of Texas contain the bulk of the javelina population. One is the so-called Brush Country, a vast expanse of thornbrush and cactus

The so-called tusks, not out-flaring as in wild boar or feral swine, but tearing teeth show plainly here.

in the southern part of the state. Taking San Antonio as the northern hub, most of the better range here will be enclosed by drawing the eastern line of a triangle down U.S. 281, which winds up at McAllen on the Mexican border. The other line follows U.S. 90 to Del Rio and all of Val Verde County. Within this huge triangle there is an immense amount of quality javelina range. The other important region is the Trans-Pecos—across, or west of, the Pecos River. Within this enormous region my bet would be on the Big Bend Country south of Fort Stockton, from Marathon, Alpine, Marfa, and below. This is desert-mountain country, more like the Arizona javelina range.

In Texas the season is long, generally from October 1 to January 1, and the bag limit is at least two animals. The problem is not a lack of targets but getting a place to hunt. There is very little public land. Ranches have followed a lease or day-hunt system for years. Much of the best javelina country is leased long-term by deer hunters. There are coming to be more and more package hunts for javelina, however, though there is to date no central point for finding out who offers them. The game department is not equipped to help in this respect. The best bet is to contact chambers of commerce throughout the range. I know of a hunt out of Fort Stockton, another from Del Rio, one at Pearsall, another at Hondo, and a few ranchers out in the Big Bend have from time to time taken javelina hunters. On package hunts ordinarily guide and transport are furnished at a stipulated fee.

Hunting in the mountain country of Arizona, New Mexico and west Texas differs much from that in the southern Texas Brush Country. Food utilized by the pigs also differs, or may. It is a good idea to have some knowledge of their food habits. For example, wherever prickly

Hunting the rimrock country in the Big Bend National Park region of western Texas.

pear grows profusely it is one of the staple items of diet. Find dense pear and usually you find pigs. In some areas such as the Big Bend, although there is prickly pear, it is seldom as plentiful or dense. But here *lechuguilla* is one mainstay, although many plants are taken. You won't need long to come to recognize *lechuguilla* when it covers an open slope. Just walk through a patch carelessly and the sharp-spiked, low-growing tough leaves will remind you by shredding your ankles.

The javelina feeds early and late in the day. On overcast, cool days in winter it may move around all day. If the wind is bitter, a band may move into a protected valley or canyon and feed along, staying out of the cutting breeze. But they do not like heat. Even at 70° they will move up, in mountain country, to bed down in shade of rimrocks or else move into wash bottoms where catclaw is dense. In the flat Brush Country of south Texas they go into the so-called "creek bottoms"—dry creeks except when an infrequent rain pours down. Vegetation is dense here. Or a band may move into heavy pear for shade.

Waterholes are an important key to hunting. In the Brush Country there are numerous ranch tanks, dug for stock water. Vegetation is invariably heavy around them, and there may be mud for wallowing. The javelina is not the wallower a feral or wild hog is, but they do on occasion make small wallowing places. Any waterhole, or in west Texas a windmill location where there is a water tank and overflow, will be a hub for javelina living in the vicinity.

These places, and wash bottoms along which the animals love to travel, are the spots where abundant sign is most likely to be present. The track of a javelina is roughly the size of that of a young deer, a fawn. But the toes are blunt, rounded, and the tracks thus unmistakable. Rooting is a hot sign to look for, too. The pigs dig up roots and tubers, sometimes pock marking the desert or a slope over large areas. Fresh, moist rooting in their arid range is a sure sign animals are not far away. When pear is heavy, feeding peccaries rip it to shreds, or gouge hunks out of the pads. Freshly ripped pear, rooted up *lechuguilla* leaves or sotol roots are good indications of pigs in the immediate vicinity.

If you intend to walk and hunt, go slowly, use your binocular constantly in country where that is possible, and move always into a breeze. During midday in south Texas hunting the dry creek bottoms with their heavy vegetation, moving very slowly, or else hunting around the tanks may produce action. In fact, on occasion you may even smell a band of pigs before you flush them. I suspect a hunter who had never before sniffed javelina musk might well recognize it the first time. It is pungent and unmistakable, unlike any other smell in the range.

In mountain country midday hunting requires working the brushy

Javelinas, oblivious of the thorns, often eat prickly pear cactus like this.

draws, and the rimrocks, on the shady side, or else where caves or pockets of overhanging rock offer shade and a cool breeze. This is physically hard but interesting hunting. Shots may be close, and difficult. These creatures can run faster than one would believe, and zigzag through brush and rocks adeptly. Even up in the rims you may be able to sniff a bedded band before you jump the animals. But if they become aware first, they'll simply slip silently away.

When a drove is jumped at close range in dense cover, don't be too sure as they burst away, grunting and chuffing, that they will flee any distance at all. I've often seen them scatter in dense pear and thornbrush, then individuals would stand perfectly still, listening. Easing around, I'd jump one, then another, within mere feet. Sometimes you can spot one standing that way, eyeing you. The first time one pops its teeth at you, however, you'll be an uncommonly cool character if you don't get jittery. When excited and disturbed, javelina snap their jaws so that the big teeth whack together swiftly, *clack, clack, clack*. It's an impressive sound and more than one hunter has backed off because of it. Except in extremely rare instances, the animals are bluffing and will turn tail if you press them.

Occasionally a sow with piglets can give one pause. One fall while mule deer hunting in west Texas I was walking along a wash across a flat when I saw a javelina band at close range. I stood immobile, watch-

Famed archer Fred Bear comes up to finish the job on a downed javelina.

ing them. The piglets are cute little critters, as purblind and dumb acting at times as can be. Piglets may be born any month of the year. There are never more than two, for a very good reason: the mother has only two teats. As she runs when frightened they pursue at close range, and as a rule when she stops to listen, hackles raised, they run under her belly and stand there until she moves again.

At any rate, a pair of tiny piglets moved out of the brush within a few feet of me. Squealing, they trotted up to my boots and sniffed, continuing to squeal as if wondering if I could possibly be their mother. The mama meanwhile didn't care for this one bit. She moved into view, bristles on end, eyes malevolent, teeth clacking viciously. She strutted stiff legged until she was within no more than fifteen feet. I yelled at her. No dice. The dumb piglets continued to carry on. I will admit this was one time I was not certain about my reassurances to others that the javelina is a bluff. Finally I raised my rifle and shot into the ground several feet in front of her. Dirt flew and so did she.

I must add that when hunting it is only proper to check a band to make sure you aren't shooting at a sow with nursing young. A lone pig is invariably a safe target, and may be an old tooth-worn boar. It is not easy, however, to distinguish between the sexes at any distance. Among a band, adults all look about the same size unless there happens to be one outstanding specimen that immediately catches the eye.

If you keep the wind right and go quietly, sometimes you can get close indeed, as did Levi Packard on an Arizona hunt.

The most common and productive hunting method in the south Texas brush is to hunt the ranch trails or *senderos*. These rough, bull-dozed trails are numerous, many of them cut by oil exploration crews. Moving javelina must cross one or more if they travel any distance. Although a drove may have its residence in the general vicinity of a waterhole it will roam over a square mile or more. Taking a stand early or late where you can see both ways on a *sendero*, preferably on a low ridgetop where you can watch the ridge and both valleys, will eventually bring a pig into range—if you have checked and found abundant sign in the area.

The other common method is to cruise these same trails in a vehicle, watching far ahead. Binoculars are a must for this hunting. Long shots may be tried quite often. A band will move strung out. Thus when a pig is spotted crossing, the driver stops and the hunter gets out and takes a rest and gets ready. He may get a chance at the one in the trail. If not, others are almost certain to come tagging along.

In western Texas the country is so vast that cruising the ranch trails and glassing the slopes is the traditional method. A lot of territory can be covered thus. This is rather open country, and long shots are the rule. If you don't want to accept a 300-yard chance, then you make a stalk and take your chances. Sometimes of course pigs will be spotted close in.

Arizona and New Mexico hunting is in somewhat similar country, but most of it differs because you have to get out and walk 'em up. Roads are few on the public lands, and offroad hunting with a vehicle of course is not legal. After a day of traipsing the Arizona desert or its complementing slopes, I can assure you you'll know you've been hunting. The challenge is provocative, too, for success averages only around 20 percent without a guide. Most Texas hunts are a little more surefire, almost 100 percent when guided. You may also locate, in Texas, a guide here or there who uses dogs. It's a different and exciting experience, although the moment of truth doesn't amount to much in sport.

Arizona biologists weigh javelina during road check of hunters.

All told, javelina hunting is about what you make it. This is a fine game animal if stalked fairly, or hunted at long range. It makes an unusual trophy. It also deserves more hunter and land owner respect than it all too often has had in the past. This seems to be on its way.

You won't need any magnums for this hunting. Most sportsmen simply use whatever average deer rifle they have handy. The .243 and 6mm are favorites of mine, but such standard calibers as the .270 and .30/06 are much used. For moderate ranges the .222 makes a good arm, if you don't intend to hunt deer and javelina at the same time, as some Texas hunters do. Certainly the .222 has killed lots of deer, but it hardly can be recommended for that work in average hands.

One caution. If you intend to have your javelina mounted, avoid running shots and select point of aim with care. A mount is not at all impressive unless the collar across the shoulders is included. So avoid head and shoulder shots and try for just back of the shoulder. This also will leave hams and backstrap intact, the best of the meat.

20

Cooking Small Game

by Gerry Steindler

WHEN IT COMES TO SMALL GAME for the table, most people seem to limit their choice to rabbit and squirrel. Admittedly, these are the most popular game animals hunted and rightly deserve top billing. However, there are a number of other species, often ignored for table use, that are equally delicious when properly prepared.

During the Bicentennial we are constantly reminded of the early days of this nation. We could do well to remember, too, the table fare of the early settlers of our country. They dined well on muskrat, raccoon, woodchuck and opossum and other small mammals, in addition to deer, rabbit and squirrel. Especially in these days of ever-spiralling meat costs at the supermarket, we would do well to emulate the pioneer housewife and accept such offerings from the hunter/trapper as good sources of protein which will provide a wide variety of main dishes.

SKIN A SQUIRREL IN A JIFFY

(1) First, bend the tail back and cut through it where it joins the body. Be careful, however, and do not sever skin on the other side. You only cut through skin at top, separate tail, and to—not through—skin on opposite side of tail. This provides the "pull" to commence the skinning procedure.

(2) Next, place the tail under your foot, grasp the hind legs and pull firmly and evenly. Jerking will cause the skin to tear rather than peeling off. Pull until the skin is off the forward part and folded back over the squirrel's head.

(3) Using the same even-pull procedure, peel the remaining skin toward you, over the back legs.

(4) Sever legs and head, gut carcass, wash, and you're finished. (Photo sequence by Russell Tinsley)

In the Field

It goes without saying that the hunter has to do his part—in field dressing the game promptly, then cooling it as quickly as possible, and making sure that it arrives home unspoiled. I have always maintained that the "gaminess" people attribute to wild creatures—furred or feathered—is not the true flavor of the game, but rather tainted meat, caused in large part by ignorance or carelessness when the game is first bagged.

Remove the entrails promptly to prevent tainting the flesh with body fluids, since shot or bone fragments will often puncture internal organs. As you do so, examine the liver of the animal for signs of possible infection—this is particularly true of rabbits and 'possums. The liver from a healthy animal will be free of spots, firm, clear and dark red in color. Small white spots on the liver may be indicative of tularemia or other infection and the animal should be buried deep—right on the spot. After handling such an infected carcass, be certain to scrub your hands with soapy water and then disinfect them immediately, for the infection can enter your bloodstream through any cut or scratch on your hands. Wipe the body cavities of healthy animals with paper towels, clean cloth or grass, paying particular attention to any blood clots. Water used to rinse the body cavity tends to make the flesh soft and may speed up bacterial action.

Since it is easier to skin these small animals while they are still warm, it is best to do this job while you are still in the field. This has the added benefit of allowing the flesh to cool more quickly. Many of these critters have scent glands under the skin, usually located under the forelegs and along the spine, with the muskrat having an additional pair in the pelvic region. Proceed cautiously with your knife blade and cut *around* these kernel-like glands, taking a bit of flesh with each one. A slip of the knife into one of these glands may cause the scent to permeate the meat you are trying to bring home in good order. Of course, any animals primarily bagged for their fur should be skinned as soon as you return to home base.

The main objective of the hunter can be summed up in a few words: keep the game meat cool, clean and dry until you can get it home. All of these factors will help delay the bacterial action that means spoiled or tainted meat. Wrap each carcass loosely in paper or a cloth sack after any stray hairs from the skinning have been removed with a damp cloth. Don't dump the game in a heap in your hunting vehicle but spread it out so that air can circulate around.

As you dress and skin these animals in the field, it's a good idea to note whether the game you have bagged is young or old, since this will be a determining factor in the cooking method to be used. Younger animals are lighter in weight for the species involved, they will usually have soft pliable ears, sharp teeth and claws rather than blunt or worn-down ones.

At Home

Once back at home base, each carcass should be gone over carefully before it is stored in the refrigerator or wrapped for freezing. Cut away any bloodshot tissue, check for any additional shot pellets or fragments of bone that may have penetrated the flesh. Remove any bits of tissue that may have been left in the body cavity during evisceration, as well as any hairs that may have remained on the carcass. A quick but thorough rinse under cold running water is permissible at this point, but only if the carcass is then thoroughly dried inside and out.

Although some small-game animals, such as rabbit and squirrel, are very lean, there are others which have a considerable layer of fat. This fat should all be stripped off during this final cleaning process at home, for it is often one more source of "gaminess" that can be objectionable. Even in the freezer, this fat will permeate the flesh with its off odors.

The matter of hanging game to age it and to make it more tender is a controversial one. The enzymatic process of breaking down the tissues begins the minute game is shot and continues even when the game is held in the refrigerator. If you prefer to age your game, store it loosely wrapped in waxed paper—not one of the plastic film wraps—in the refrigerator for a day or so. But remember that game will increase in "gaminess" every day that it is held in this manner.

If the game is not to be cooked within a couple of days, your best bet is to freeze it. If the animal is to be left whole for stuffing and roasting, place crumpled waxed paper in the body cavity. This will permit less drying air to remain within the package. If you anticipate cooking the game cut into serving pieces, the time to do this is before wrapping for the freezer. This has two advantages—the game will thaw more quickly when you are ready to use it, and you can make a more compact package for the freezer by stacking the pieces with a double fold of waxed paper between each layer of game in the package.

Freezer paper with a moisture-proof barrier is recommended for freezer storage. It has been my experience, however, that this type of paper alone does not do the job. The bulk of the paper makes it difficult to exclude all air, and this air trapped within can cause freezer burn on the meat. Wrap the meat closely with Saran or other plastic film wrap, padding any protruding bones first with some crumpled waxed paper to avoid puncturing the wrappings. Exclude all possible air at this point, then overwrap with freezer paper, using the drugstore fold, and securing with freezer tape.

Mark the contents and the date on the package with a wax pencil. I

The quicker game is field dressed after it is killed, the better it will be on the dinner table. (Russell Tinsley photo)

find it helpful to add a few cryptic notes of my own to the label so that I don't have to play guessing games when I pull a package from the freezer: "Family only" might indicate that the game was badly damaged and would not be attractive for broiling or roasting, "Stew" would indicate an older animal to be cooked by any of the moist heat methods.

Fundamentals of Game Cooking

There are no hard and fast rules to guide you in game cooking, just a few basic principles. First, govern the recipe you will use to the age of the game—for older game, cook slowly with moist heat in stews, pot roasts, fricassees; for younger game, broiling, roasting or frying by dry heat methods may be used. When dry heat is used, lean game should be basted or covered with fat in some fashion during the cooking to prevent its drying out, and to keep it juicy and succulent.

You will find many game recipes which call for soaking the game overnight or up to 72 hours either in salt water or an acid marinade with vinegar as one of the main ingredients. This is a carry-over from the days when refrigeration was non-existent and was used primarily to dilute or disguise the flavor of tainted meat. If the game you are about to cook was carefully tended to in the field and at home, there is no need to complicate matters in the kitchen with this now-obsolete step in preparation.

Some game cooks maintain that a marinade tenderizes the game. While this may be partially true, you will find that most recipes calling for a marinade also indicate long slow cooking with moist heat, the marinade being used in the cooking as well. The true flavor of the game comes through in a more satisfactory manner—is enhanced rather than overpowered—when a mildly acid ingredient such as tomato, dry wine or lemon is used instead. At least that's been my experience and I've been cooking game for a number of years—many more than I care to admit in print. I have used marinades only in preparing such classic dishes as Sauerbraten and Hasenpfeffer, but I have yet to serve game that was too tough to be chewed.

You can't hurry a game dinner, especially when you are cooking older game. Low cooking temperatures have been found by controlled laboratory experiments to add greatly to the tenderness of the meat being cooked. For example, when you are cooking a stew which calls for simmering, keep the heat under the pot as low as possible, so that the surface of the liquid is, as the French say, "barely shivering." An occasional bubble may lazily emerge from the bottom and plop on the surface, but any more activity than that means that you're trying to hurry things too much, and the meat may be tough no matter how long you cook it.

Many of these game animals may be used in your favorite recipes for chicken and other domestic meats, but in adapting these recipes, keep in mind that even oven temperature should be lower—for roasts, oven casseroles or oven-fried game. About 300° to 325° instead of 350° or more, for a longer period of time, is about the best guideline I can give you—when a muscle offers little resistance as you pierce it with a fork or skewer, the meat is done. In roasting small game, more frequent basting will keep the meat from drying out and becoming tough. When the joints move easily and the leg flesh is soft when pressed with the fingers (protected with paper towels, of course) then the roast is ready to be served. Any further cooking would make the roast dry, tough, and tasteless—the very things you have tried to avoid.

The recipes which follow are intended to serve as a jumping-off point for your own culinary adventures with small game. They serve to illustrate some of the various combinations of ingredients and cooking methods suitable, and, in most cases, one species of game animal may be substituted for another in a particular recipe. Don't hesitate to use your own ingenuity and creativity to change or adapt these recipes to suit your own family's preferences or the ingredients you may have on hand. That's part of the fun in cooking game—believe me, I speak from experience!

Armadillo

This small mammal, native to South America and found in the South and Southwest, is aptly named for the small bony scales which cover its body—"armadillo" in Spanish means "small one in armor-plate." The meat is light in color and resembles pork in flavor. After the animal is drawn, the meat is removed from the bony armor, the head and tail removed and the legs skinned. Armadillo sausage seems to be the preferred recipe above all others, and in some places where these critters are hunted, you may find a smokehouse where they will prepare the meat for you from their own special recipe. If not, you might like to try the following:

ARMADILLO SAUSAGE

4 lbs. armadillo meat
1 lb. brown bread crumbs
Liberal pinch ground allspice
½ tsp. crumbled sage leaves
2 tsps. salt
2 tsps. pepper

Grind the meat and mix well with the bread crumbs and seasonings. To test for seasoning, fry a small portion until it is well done, then taste it. If you prefer a hotter sausage, you may add cayenne pepper or a dash of chili powder. The sausage may be stuffed into large casings and smoked over a low smoking fire for a week or so, or may be fried or grilled in patties as you would cook pork sausage.

Beaver

First you must find a beaver hunter or trapper. Beaver meat, with its dark color and rich flavor, has been rated on a par with venison and rabbit. A mature animal may weigh as much as 60 pounds, but the younger animals are more tender. Strip all visible fat from the beaver before storing in the refrigerator or freezing.

(Leonard Lee Rue III photo)

CHICKEN-FRIED BEAVER

Cut a young beaver into serving portions, then parboil in salted water along with an onion which has been stuck with a few cloves, until the beaver meat is nearly tender. This parboiling helps to remove additional fat which may be within the tissues. Remove the beaver pieces, pat dry, then roll in crumbs or flour seasoned with salt and pepper, a pinch of either thyme, sage, or poultry seasoning. In a heavy skillet over moderate heat, brown the beaver pieces slowly in butter or drippings. When all is well-browned and tender, remove the beaver to a heated platter and prepare gravy from the pan drippings by blending in half a package of dehydrated onion or mushroom soup. Add boiling water in small amounts, stirring constantly, until the desired consistency of gravy is reached.

ROAST BEAVER

Preheat the oven to 450°, then place a young beaver on a rack in the roasting pan, season with salt and pepper and a sprinkling of thyme. Cook at this high heat for about 20 minutes to allow fat within the tissues to drip out and to sear the outside of the roast. Lower the oven temperature to 325°, and scatter onion slices, carrot chunks and a few pieces of celery over the top of the roast. Roast for 30 minutes per pound. Although it is not necessary to baste the beaver, you may occasionally use a bit of beef bouillon spooned over the top. Do not use the liquid which collects in the bottom of the roaster, for this is primarily fat which has dripped out of the meat. The rack in the roasting pan is essential, for otherwise the roast would be in the fat that is dripping from the meat.

BEAVER STEW

3 or 4 lbs. boned beaver
3 tbsps. drippings
Boiling water or stock
Juice of ½ lemon
Liberal dash of Worcestershire sauce
1 clove garlic
2 onions, sliced
2 bay leaves
Salt and pepper
Dash of paprika *and* allspice
Carrots, cut in strips
Small whole onions
Potatoes, cubed
Turnips, cubed (optional)
Cabbage, cut in thin wedges (optional)

Cut the beaver meat in cubes, cutting away any fat that may be within the flesh. Put just a film of drippings in the bottom of a Dutch oven and when hot, brown the beaver cubes on all sides. Do not crowd the pot with all of the beaver at once, or it will not brown as readily. When a part of the meat is browned, transfer it to a plate, add more drippings as necessary and continue until all the meat is evenly browned. Return the meat to the pot, add boiling water or stock just to cover the meat and all of the herbs and seasonings as well as the onions and the clove of garlic, which is pierced with a toothpick (so that it can be easily retrieved when the meat is tender). Cover and simmer on a very low flame until the meat is almost completely tender, skimming any surplus fat that may rise to the top of the liquid. Add the vegetables after the garlic clove has been removed and continue to simmer about 30 minutes, but only until the vegetables are tender. About 15 minutes before serving, check the seasonings—you may need more salt after the addition of the vegetables. If the gravy needs thickening, blend flour or cornstarch with cold water to form a smooth paste and add it drop by drop, stirring constantly until gravy is the desired thickness. Serve in a heated bowl with biscuits to sop up the gravy.

Javelina

While no one would disagree that the javelina or collared peccary of the Southwest is a good trophy animal, there is considerable dispute over the edibility of the meat. Their diet is omnivorous, anything that is available to them, but then so is the bear's diet. I imagine that the strong smell of the musk gland is what turns so many people off. This gland, oval in shape, lies along the spine about seven–eight inches forward of the tail. As long as this gland is removed intact as soon as the animal is dropped, there should be no hint of musk on the meat. After removing this troublemaker, be sure to wash thoroughly anything that has come in contact with it—including your hands and the knife blade.

For trophy heads and fine leather, the mature animals are, of course, more desirable. For food, young javelina are preferred. In areas where these animals are hunted, there are some smokehouses which specialize in preparing javelina. If you are not a native of the area you're planning to hunt, it might be wise to ask your guide if there is such a smokehouse in the vicinity. If not, proceed to dress your trophy in the same manner as previously described, stripping off all visible fat. Javelina is cooked in basically the same manner as domestic pork and is always well done.

BARBECUED JAVELINA

Although barbecue has taken on other meanings over the years, in its original sense it means a whole animal roasted in a pit of coals, with barbecue sauce slathered over the roast before sealing the pit, and then after the pit was opened. If you haven't the place where you can dig such a pit for a whole or side of javelina, then you will have to compromise, perhaps with the ribs grilled over a moderate bed of coals in your backyard grill. Baste frequently with your favorite barbecue sauce, or try one of the ones listed below. These are from my *Game Cookbook*, published by Stoeger Publishing Co.

BARNEY'S BARBECUE SAUCE—for boar chops or ribs

1 tsp. dry mustard
1 tbsp. flour
1 tsp. celery salt
½ tsp. cayenne pepper
½ tsp. cloves
¼ cup vinegar
¼ cup water
½ cup catsup

Blend all ingredients together and simmer 10 minutes.

BARBECUE SAUCE II—for bear, boar or ribs

1 cup chili sauce
¼ cup vinegar
2 tbsps. Worcestershire sauce
1 tsp. salt
1 tsp. pepper
1 tsp. chili powder
Dash of cayenne
1½ cups water

Combine all ingredients and simmer together 10 minutes.

BARBECUE SAUCE III

¾ cup catsup
2 tsps. prepared mustard
2 tbsps. sugar
Dash of Worcestershire sauce
½ cup vinegar
2 tbsps. butter
1 green pepper, chopped
1 onion, chopped
½ cup chopped pickles
1 tsp. lemon juice

Combine the first five ingredients and simmer for 10 minutes. Brown the onion and pepper in butter, add the pickles and lemon juice and combine the two mixtures. Cook for an additional 5 minutes.

JAVELINA CHOPS

Allowing at least two javelina chops per person, brown them slowly in a small amount of butter in a heavy skillet which has a tight fitting cover. Season the chops with salt and pepper, then sprinkle over one-half package of dehydrated onion soup. Add sufficient water to come half way up the chops, cover and simmer on very low heat until the chops are tender. Depending on the age of the javelina, this may take an hour or more. Turn the chops occasionally, adding a bit more water to maintain the original level if necessary.

ROAST JAVELINA

Using either the saddle or ham from a young javelina, season the roast with salt and pepper and poultry seasoning. Place on a rack in the roasting pan in the oven preheated to 325°. Roast uncovered for the first half hour or so, then spoon over some apple juice or sweet cider and cover the roast. Cook for a total time of 35 minutes per pound, adding a few more spoons of apple juice to the top of the roast from time to time. When the meat is tender and the juices run clear when the meat is punctured deep in the heaviest part of the roast, remove the roast to a heated serving platter and garnish with pickled crab apples.

Muskrat

This is another of the "bonus" meats from a trapper, and can be most delicious if the trapper empties his traps frequently and tends to the dressing of the critters promptly. If you are presented with a muskrat which has a pronounced gamy aroma, soak the carcass in a salt solution for several hours, changing the brine once or twice. Removing all visible fat helps, too, in reducing the gaminess.

MUSKRAT SAUERBRATEN

Marinade: Boil together for five minutes and then cool the following:

3 cups water
1½ cups vinegar
2 bay leaves
12 whole peppercorns
4 cloves
1 carrot, sliced
2 onions, sliced
2 branches celery, sliced

Place two muskrat, cut in serving pieces in a glass or earthen bowl (never metal) and cover with the cooled marinade. Set the meat and any reserve marinade in a cool place for several hours or overnight, and turn the meat in the marinade once or twice.

In a Dutch oven (preferably stainless steel) brown two slices of bacon which have been cut in cubes, then remove the crisp bacon bits. Remove the meat from the marinade, pat dry with paper towels, then brown in the hot bacon fat. Season the meat with salt and add the reserved marinade along with all the vegetables and the bacon bits. Bring the liquid to a boil, then cover and reduce the heat so that the liquid is barely simmering. Cook until the meat is very tender, about two hours, adding additional liquid only if necessary. When the meat is fork-tender, remove it to a heated platter and keep it warm while you prepare the gravy.

Bring the liquid to a boil, add 12 gingersnaps broken in pieces and three tablespoons of butter kneaded together with an equal amount of flour, then stir until the gravy is thickened. Strain it through a sieve, pressing the vegetables through also. Add three tablespoons sour cream and reheat over a low flame for several minutes without allowing the mixture to come to a boil. Serve with home-made noodles, dumplings or boiled potatoes and red cabbage.

MUSKRAT IN CREAM GRAVY

Cut muskrat in serving pieces, roll in flour seasoned with salt and pepper and a pinch of thyme. In a heavy skillet with tight fitting lid, melt butter or drippings and brown the meat on all sides, adding two sliced onions part way through the browning process. Reduce the heat under the skillet and add either one cup sour cream or one can cream of mushroom soup. Cover tightly and simmer over lowest possible heat until the meat is tender. (Sour cream tends to separate if it is brought to the boiling point.) Remove the muskrat to a heated platter and, still over low heat, blend the gravy together until it is smooth. Pour over the meat and add a sprinkle of paprika or cayenne pepper.

MUSKRAT CREOLE

Creole Sauce:
¼ cup butter
2 onions, minced
2 medium green peppers, diced
1 cup sliced mushrooms
2 cups chicken broth
Salt and pepper to taste
Dash of cayenne
1 bay leaf
Pinch of thyme
¼ cup minced ham
One quart canned tomatoes or two pounds fresh tomatoes, peeled and chopped

Saute onions, peppers, and mushrooms in butter for about five minutes in the bottom of a heavy pot. Add the remaining ingredients and simmer 15 minutes, stirring occasionally to prevent sticking.

Brown muskrat cut in serving pieces in hot oil or butter in a Dutch oven. Add enough of the above Creole sauce to cover and simmer over a very low flame until the meat is tender. Stir occasionally to make certain the sauce is not sticking or scorching on the bottom of the pan. If the sauce becomes too thick before the meat is tender, add a spoon or two of hot water. Serve with rice.

NOTE: This sauce is so versatile that I usually make it in large quantities with vegetables fresh from the garden. It can be frozen successfully and is equally good with other small game, poultry, and fish.

Opossum

Br'er 'Possum is not what you would call a persnickety eater—he will devour anything available. Since this creature is able to live close to civilization, he may turn to garbage and carrion for subsistence. On the other hand, in rural areas of the South, he may feed primarily on persimmons and berries. 'Possums are frequently found on nocturnal 'coon hunts and it's easy enough to knock one out of a tree, since the 'possum would prefer to play dead rather than put up any sort of struggle. If a 'possum is taken alive and you can improvise a pen in which to hold him for a week, a diet of table scraps, bread and vegetables will eliminate any possible off flavor in the meat. If the 'possum has been clubbed or shot, eviscerate and skin promptly, remove all visible fat, then soak six to 12 hours in enough salted water to cover (about two tbsps. salt to a quart of water). This will accomplish the same purpose as penning and feeding him.

Since opossums have generous deposits of fat between the layers of muscle, it is best to cook them soon after they have been killed, or freeze them only for a short period of time and then cook as soon as they are thawed. The classic way of preparing 'possum is with sweet potatoes—but there is more than one way to proceed. The two recipes listed here achieve the same end result, both will rid the 'possum of excess fat within the flesh.

'POSSUM 'N' 'TATERS—I

In a deep kettle, parboil the 'possum in salted water to cover for about one hour. Drain and pat dry, then place in a roasting pan in a 350° oven, seasoning with salt and pepper and a liberal pinch of poultry seasoning or crumbled sage, allowing 30 to 35 minutes per pound total roasting time. During the first hour of roasting, parboil sweet potatoes in their jackets for 20 minutes, then peel and cut in thick slices. Place the sweet potatoes around the roast the last 30 minutes of cooking, baste all with the pan juices several times, and sprinkle the sweet potatoes with a bit of brown sugar after each basting.

'POSSUM 'N' 'TATERS–II

Season the 'possum inside and out with salt, pepper, and poultry seasoning, place on a rack in the roasting pan and roast for 15 to 20 minutes in an oven preheated to 450°. Lower the oven heat to 325° and roast uncovered for about an hour, draining off the fat as it accumulates in the bottom of the pan. Add the sweet potatoes as described in the above recipe about 30 minutes before the roast is done, along with thick slices of apple which have been cored but not peeled. Spoon over some apple juice if the roast appears to be getting dry.

Although most old-time recipes for 'possum do not call for it, you may stuff the critter before roasting, using your favorite bread stuffing for turkey, adding one cup of diced apples.

Porcupine

The slow-moving porky is usually left alone in the woods to provide food for the lost and hungry traveller, but at times he may become a real nuisance around a woodland cabin. His passion for anything salty may lead him to devour canoe paddles, ax handles, even cabin steps that have a trace of human perspiration. Under such circumstances, the cabin owner is fully justified in doing in ol' porky. The porcupine's diet is vegetarian, and it would be a pity to have up to 40 pounds of meat go to waste, so skin the porky after you have put on heavy gloves. Start work on the underside of the beast and you should have no problem with his quills. Eviscerate and remove all excess fat. If a porcupine has been killed in pine woods, the flesh may be somewhat resinous in flavor. To eliminate this, parboil the porky in lightly salted water. You will, at the same time, remove some of the excess fat within the tissues.

BROILED PORKY

Drain the parboiled porcupine and pat dry. If small, the whole animal may be balanced on a spit. Otherwise, cut in serving pieces, then broil over moderate coals, seasoning with salt and pepper. One of the barbecue sauces listed in the section on javelina may be used to baste the meat as it broils.

As previously mentioned, game recipes are interchangeable, so you might also try a stew for that parboiled porky. Use the recipe given for Beaver Stew, patting the meat dry before browning it. The cooking time will be shortened, of course, because the meat has been parboiled.

Rabbit

Rabbits and hares score high on the list of all game, with hunters and diners alike. Only the jack rabbits are not considered very good eating. Although the danger of tularemia is always a possibility, it can be greatly minimized if the hunter does not shoot sluggish rabbits, and follows the few precautions mentioned in the early part of this chapter concerning field dressing of game. Your favorite recipes for chicken may be used for rabbit, in addition to the ones for squirrel which follow. Rabbit, like other small game, should be cooked until well done.

(Leonard Lee Rue III photo)

OVEN-FRIED RABBIT

Cut young rabbits into serving pieces, roll in fine dry bread crumbs which have been seasoned with salt, pepper and thyme or marjoram. Place the pieces in a shallow baking pan that is coated with melted butter. Dot the rabbit with additional pieces of butter and place in a 325° oven. Using a bulb baster, baste the rabbit frequently with the butter in the bottom of the pan. In about 1 to 1½ hours the rabbit should be tender and well done, and the coating should be crisp and browned. If there is any doubt about the age, and therefore the tenderness, of the rabbit, you may cover the baking pan with aluminum foil for about 30 minutes halfway through the time allotted—just be sure to uncover the pan again so that the coating has a chance to crisp up once more. For a flavor variation in the above recipe, mix a liberal sprinkling of grated Parmesan or Romano cheese with the bread crumbs and substitute oregano for the thyme or marjoram.

RABBIT PIE

3 lbs. older rabbit (or other game)
3–4 tbsps. butter
Water or broth to cover
1 tsp. salt
Generous grinding of pepper
1 bay leaf
1 small onion, sliced
½ cup chopped celery
½ cup peas
1 cup finely diced potatoes
3 tbsps. butter
3 tbsps. flour
¼ cup light cream
Dash of cayenne pepper
Pastry or biscuit dough

In Dutch oven, brown rabbit pieces in hot butter, add water or broth to cover along with seasonings, bay leaf and onion. Cover and simmer on very low heat for 1½ to 2 hours, until meat is very tender. Remove the meat and bay leaf, then pick the meat from the bones and place in an ovenproof casserole. Cook the vegetables in the broth for about 10 minutes, then remove with a slotted spoon and scatter over the meat. In a separate saucepan, melt butter and stir in flour, cooking over low heat until bubbly and smooth. Slowly pour in 1 to 1½ cups of broth and the light cream, and cook until slightly thickened. Add a dash of cayenne pepper and check to see if additional salt and pepper are needed. Pour over the vegetables and meat. If you are using a pastry crust, roll it about ⅛ inch thick, cut gashes for steam to escape and cover the casserole. Bake at 400° about 20 minutes, until the crust is browned. If you are using biscuit dough, roll the dough about ½ inch thick and cut into rounds. Place these atop the casserole and bake at 425° about 30 minutes, or until the biscuits are browned.

HASENPFEFFER (from author's *Game Cookbook*)

Marinade:
Equal parts of wine vinegar and water to cover rabbit
4 tsps. sugar for each cup of liquid
½ tsp. salt per cup of liquid
Few peppercorns
2 onions, sliced
2 branches celery, sliced
2 carrots, sliced
2 or 3 juniper berries
1 bay leaf
2 or 3 whole cloves

Cut two older rabbits or hares into serving portions, place in a large glass bowl and cover with the above marinade. Cover and marinate in a cool place for two days, turning the rabbit pieces twice daily. Drain and dry the pieces of meat, reserving the marinade. Roll the pieces of meat in flour seasoned with salt and pepper, then brown in a Dutch oven in bacon drippings. Add the marinade, including the vegetables, bring to a boil, then lower the heat, cover the pot and simmer until the meat is tender. Remove the rabbit to a heated platter and keep warm. Strain the sauce through a sieve, pressing the vegetables through also. Blend one tbsp. flour with ¼ cup sour cream and add slowly to the strained sauce, heating it just to the boiling point. Pour some sauce over the rabbit and serve the rest in a heated sauceboat. Serve with dumplings.

BROILED RABBIT

Split young rabbits in half, season with salt and pepper. Either skewer slices of bacon around them or baste liberally with melted butter with a bit of lemon juice as you broil them over slow to moderate coals. This usually takes about 45 minutes to one hour—if the juices run clear when a knife is inserted in a thick part of the muscle, the rabbit is done.

(Leonard Lee Rue III photo)

Raccoon

The 'coon not only provides exciting sport for man and his hounds, but is good eating—especially when young. The meat is dark and tastes similar to pork when roasted. Although a 'coon's diet is omnivorous, his special preference is corn, as any farmer or gardener in the Midwest can tell you. The 'coon is not a true hibernator like a bear, but does lie dormant at times in winter and his layers of fat keep him well insulated against the cold. This fat should be trimmed off before freezing or cooking, even though it is not usually strong or gamy.

ROAST 'COON

Parboil in salted water to cover for 30 minutes or so, depending on the size and age of the 'coon. Drain and pat dry, season with salt and pepper and any herb of your choice. Roast at 300° with a bit of apple juice in the bottom of the roaster for about three to four hours, basting with the liquid that accumulates in the pan. If the 'coon is not a youngster, you may wish to cover the pan for a part of the cooking time, but be sure to remove the cover during the last 30 minutes or so. If you dust the meat with flour after each basting the crust will be crisp and crackly. Roast 'coon may also be stuffed, if you desire.

JUGGED 'COON

(This is an excellent way of dealing with any small game that you suspect may be tough.)

2 or 3 lbs. 'coon, in serving pieces
1½–2 tsps. salt
⅛ tsp. pepper
½ cup flour
4 tbsps. fat or drippings
2 branches celery, chopped
¼ cup chopped parsley
½ cup long grain rice (not the instant variety)
6 whole cloves
3 whole onions
Liberal pinch thyme
1 bay leaf
3 tbsps. catsup
½ lemon, cut in thin slices
2 tbsps. butter

Coat 'coon with seasoned flour, brown in heavy skillet in hot fat or drippings and transfer to a bean jug. Sauté celery, parsley and rice in the drippings until the rice begins to brown evenly, stirring frequently. Add two cups of water to the contents of the skillet and boil for 10 minutes. Add this mixture to the jug, along with the onions which have been stuck with the cloves. Add the other seasonings and top with the lemon slices, adding additional water, if necessary, to cover the contents of the jug. Cover tightly and bake at 300° for about three hours or until the meat is very tender. Thicken if necessary with the remaining seasoned flour, adjust the seasonings, and stir in the butter. Serve from the jug.

Squirrel

Squirrel is a close second to the rabbit in popularity, not only among hunters but among those lucky enough to eat them with some regularity. Unlike some of the small game already described, the delicately flavored meat is lean and needs butter or bacon in cooking to prevent the flesh from drying out. It is never necessary to soak or parboil squirrel.

(Leonard Lee Rue III photo)

PRIDE OF THE OZARKS—SQUIRREL AND DUMPLINGS

(Serves 4)

2 squirrels, cut in serving pieces
4 tbsps. fat (½ butter, ½ drippings)
Water to cover
1 tsp. salt for each 3 cups of water
3–4 carrots, cut in thin sticks
⅛ tsp. freshly ground black pepper
Celery tops
1 small onion, sliced
2 branches celery, sliced on diagonal

Dumplings:
1 cup flour
2 tsps. baking powder
½ tsp. salt
2 tbsps. margarine or vegetable shortening
2 tsps. minced parsley
½ cup milk

Brown the squirrel pieces in hot fat, turning with tongs so that all is evenly browned. Add water and seasonings (including celery tops) and bring to the boiling point. Cover and simmer slowly for about an hour or until the meat is tender. Remove the celery tops and add onion, celery and carrot sticks, and cook for about 10 minutes. While the vegetables are cooking, prepare dumplings by sifting the dry ingredients together, cutting in the shortening, adding parsley and milk to form a soft dough. Drop the dough by spoonfuls atop the simmering liquid, allowing space between each dumpling for them to expand. Work quickly, dipping the spoon in the hot liquid before each dumpling is added. Cover the kettle tightly and steam for 15 to 20 minutes, depending on the size of the dumplings—you should have about 10–12 dumplings. Do not lift the lid while the dumplings are cooking, or they will be heavy as lead instead of fluffy and light! Set a serving platter and plates to heat in the oven, and then prepare either a flour or cornstarch paste with cold water to thicken the gravy. Remove the dumplings, squirrel and vegetables to the serving platter and return it to the oven to keep warm. Bring the liquid to a boil and add the thickening a few drops at a time until the gravy is the desired consistency, stirring constantly with a slotted spoon. Check for proper amount of seasoning, then pour some gravy over the contents of the platter, garnish with additional parsley sprigs, and serve the remainder of the gravy in a heated bowl or sauce boat.

BREADED SQUIRREL

Cut squirrels into convenient serving pieces, dip first in flour, then in egg which has been beaten with one tbsp. water, finally in fine dry bread crumbs seasoned with salt and pepper and a pinch or two of thyme or marjoram. Set each breaded piece of squirrel on a sheet of waxed paper as you complete the breading process and allow the breading to firm up for a few minutes. Heat butter in a skillet which has a tight fitting lid, then brown the squirrel pieces over moderate heat until they are a rich brown, turning the pieces with a broad spatula so as not to disturb the brown crust. Cover the skillet and lower the flame, and continue to cook for about 45 minutes. Remove the cover the last few minutes to crisp the breading crust.

SQUIRREL CASSEROLE–SOUTHERN STYLE

(Serves 4)

2 squirrels, cut in serving pieces
Flour, seasoned with salt and pepper
3 tbsps. fat
¼ cup wild rice
2 green peppers, finely diced
1 small onion, finely chopped
1 cup diced celery
1 cup diced green apple

About an hour before preparing the casserole, cover the wild rice with hot water and set aside. Roll the squirrel pieces in seasoned flour, then brown in hot fat. Place the browned squirrel in a well-buttered casserole, drain the rice and rinse in cold water, then sprinkle the rice, chopped vegetables and apple over the squirrel. Top the casserole with boiling water (or water in which chicken bouillon cubes have been dissolved) just to cover the ingredients, cover either with the casserole lid or aluminum foil and bake at 300° for about one hour, or until the squirrel is tender.

SQUIRREL AND OYSTER GUMBO

24 oysters (reserve the liquor)
1½–2 lbs. squirrel, cut in serving pieces
Flour, seasoned with salt and pepper
6 tomatoes, peeled, seeded, then coarsely chopped
6 sprigs of parsley and 1 bay leaf, tied together

6 tbsps. fat or butter
1 cup finely chopped onions (include if possible a few scallions with part of the green tops)
¼ cup finely chopped green pepper (optional)
½ tsp. dried thyme leaves, crumbled
Salt and pepper to taste
½ tsp. cayenne pepper
2 tsps. filé powder
Freshly cooked long-grain white rice (one cup per person to be served)

Drain the oysters through a fine sieve, adding enough water to make four cups of liquid, then set both aside. Coat the squirrel pieces lightly and evenly with seasoned flour, then brown in hot fat (four tbsps.) until they are evenly colored on all sides. Remove to a plate, add the other two tbsps. of fat to the skillet and over moderate heat, cook the onions and green pepper for about five minutes, until the vegetables are soft but not browned. Add three tablespoons of the seasoned flour to the skillet, and stirring constantly, cook until all is evenly blended and bubbly. Pour in, in a thin stream, the reserved oyster-liquid, and still stirring constantly, bring to a boil over low heat.

Turn the contents of the skillet into a four–five quart Dutch oven or stovetop casserole, add the squirrel pieces, tomatoes, parsley, bay leaf, and thyme. Season to taste with and salt and pepper, and add the cayenne. Bring the mixture to a boil, then reduce the heat to low, cover the casserole or Dutch oven and simmer the contents for about 1½ hours, or until the squirrel is tender, stirring occasionally. Add the reserved oysters and continue to simmer a few minutes longer, only until the oysters plump up and the edges begin to curl. Remove the kettle from the heat, discard the parsley and bay leaf, then stir in the filé powder. Adjust the seasonings, if necessary, but do *not* return the kettle to the heat or the filé powder will turn into a mess of gluey strands.

To serve gumbo in the traditional fashion, place a mounded cupful of rice in each heated soup plate and spoon the gumbo around the rice.

BRUNSWICK STEW

Since this dish is traditionally made with squirrel as the main game ingredient, it is listed here. However, other small game—including rabbit, woodchuck, even a wily old cock pheasant that may be in your freezer—could be included with equally delicious results.

5 lbs. small game, disjointed
Bacon drippings
3 onions, sliced
Meaty ham bone, if available
1 tbsp. salt
¼ tsp. black pepper
2 quarts tomatoes, drained (reserve the liquid)
4 medium-size potatoes, peeled and diced
½ tsp. cayenne pepper
Liberal pinch of both thyme and parsley flakes
2 cups fresh lima beans
2 cups fresh corn
2 cups okra

Pat the pieces of game dry with paper towels, then brown in hot fat in a Dutch oven. Season with salt and pepper, then add onions and continue to brown for another minute or two. Add liquid from drained tomatoes and enough water or chicken bouillon to cover, adding meaty ham bone if available. Cover and simmer on low heat until the meat is tender. Remove meat from the bones and cut in pieces, return to the liquid along with the tomatoes, potatoes, cayenne, thyme and parsley. Cook for an additional 30 minutes on low heat, then add the other vegetables and continue cooking until they are tender but not mushy. If frozen vegetables must be used, shorten the cooking time after they have been added. Check the seasonings before serving, and if necessary thicken the stew either with small bits of butter kneaded with flour or with fine dry bread crumbs. Don't get carried away on the thickening, however, for Brunswick Stew should be the consistency of a thick soup and is usually served in soup plates, along with corn bread.

Woodchuck

This summertime target of the varmint shooter is seldom thought of as food for the table. More's the pity, for the 'chuck is strictly a vegetarian and gorges himself on grains and greens. 'Chucks are not as active as rabbits and squirrels and their flesh is less firm and inclined to be fat as the animal grows older. Lean, young 'chucks are the best for table use and may be prepared in most any of the recipes given in this chapter. I often freeze them, stripping off any excess fat first, then use them to extend the amount of meat required for Squirrel and Dumplings or Brunswick Stew.

Appendix: Small-Game Laws

by Russell Tinsley

JUST WHAT IS a small-game animal, with emphasis on that key word "game"?

Perhaps you call the generally hated coyote "game," but not many wildlife management people or stockmen would agree with you.

Personal likes or dislikes aside, the definition "game" is important from a legal viewpoint because it usually dictates if the animal is protected by a season and/or bag limit, plus other considerations.

Maryland law, for example, stipulates there is no closed season on fox, skunk and woodchuck. *Louisiana* defines foxes, wildcats, coyotes and armadillos as "outlaw quadrupeds" (antonym to game animals). In *Texas* the unprotected mammal list includes all rabbits, armadillos, coyotes, prairie dogs and ground squirrels. Thus in a state such as *Missouri* the cottontail is an avidly sought game animal, but in *Texas* it is looked upon as something of a pest and there is no closed season nor a bag limit. *Oklahoma* law states there is "no closed season on bobcat, coyote, skunk, civit cat, opossum or badger."

Game laws vary from state to state. If there is any standardization, it is mere coincidence. It is imperative, therefore, that every hunter do his homework, reading the game laws of his home state or the one he intends to visit, to determine what he legally can or cannot do.

A typical state has laws broken into several categories. There are general laws which apply to all hunters, then specific sections on big game, small game, upland gamebirds, etc.

Under the general heading, in *New Mexico* "it is unlawful to drive off established roads while hunting on state lands." *West Virginia* prohibits Sunday hunting, "except that raccoon hunting may be continued until 5 a.m. on Sunday morning." *Virginia* regulations note that "hunting with a dog or gun or possessing on person or in a vehicle a strung bow, or a gun which is not unloaded and cased or dismantled, in the national forests and on Virginia Game Commission owned lands and on lands managed by the Commission under cooperative agreement is prohibited except during the periods when it is lawful to hunt." This means, as one example, that if you are driving through a national forest at night with a loaded gun in your vehicle, you are in violation of the law. In *Wisconsin* it is illegal to use a mechanical calling device to hunt any animal, which dictates that only a mouth call can be used for calling predators.

Also under the general heading you find requirements as to whom needs a valid state hunting license when hunting what. In *Maine* if you are in the woods during the closed season with a loaded gun and your excuse is that you're only target practicing, that probably isn't good enough. That state's law states "the possession of firearms in the fields or forests or on the water or ice in Maine shall be prima facie evidence of hunting with burden of proof otherwise on the possessor."

In the *Wyoming* proclamations under the subhead Predator Hunting, it states: "Wyoming law classifies the bobcat, wolf, coyote, skunk, weasel, porcupine, jack rabbit, raccoon, red fox, and stray cat as predatory animals. They may be taken by nonresident hunters any time of the year in all parts of the state. No license is necessary, no shooting hours imposed, and there are no restrictions on weapons used. Any type of call, manual or electronic, may be used."

But in *Florida* you must have a license, the law demanding that "all hunters must possess valid hunting licenses, except those persons under 15 years of age, and residents 65 years of age and over." *Vermont* law says "in order to take any kind of bird or animal legally, a hunting license is required for persons of all ages." *North Carolina* has this to say about the woodchuck or so-called groundhog: "No closed season, no bag limits. Not classified by law as a game animal, but hunting license requirements apply."

Some states allow hunting at night with a light for predators and varmints; many do not. And some prohibit night hunting—period. In *Alabama*, for instance, with the exception as to raccoons and opossums, "it shall be unlawful, except as to trapping as otherwise provided by law, for any person to take, capture or kill or attempt to take, capture or kill any bird or animal protected by the laws of this State between sunset and daylight of the following day." This leaves sort of a gray area when after an unprotected animal like, say, the coyote. So in a situation such as this, to be on the safe side write your state game and fish department or contact your local game warden and find what is and what is not permitted.

Missouri law is more specific: "Wildlife may not be hunted, pursued, taken or killed by throwing or casting the rays of a spotlight, or other artificial light, on any highway, in any field, woodland or forest for the purpose of spotting or locating such wildlife (except raccoons or other fur-bearing animals when treed with the aid of dogs,) while having in possession or control, either singly, or as one of a group of persons, any firearm, bow or other implement whereby wildlife could be killed."

In *California* some public lands are open to night hunting for predators with a light while some are closed, as outlined in the California Hunting Regulations issued each year. Additionally, on most privately-owned property of that state "non-game mammals may be taken from one-half hour after sunset to one-half hour before sunrise only by the landowner or his agents, or by persons who have in their immediate possession written permission issued by the landowner or tenant that states the permittee can trespass from one-half hour after sunset to one-half hour before sunrise on property under the ownership or control of such landowners or tenants."

The type of weapons which can be legally used in small-game hunting also vary from state to state. In *Minnesota* "it is unlawful to use a pistol or revolver for taking protected animals" and that includes rabbits and tree squirrels. When hunting in *Alabama* for raccoons and opossums at night "such animals may only be legally taken with the use of a shotgun using shot no larger than number eight, and the person or persons so hunting must be accompanied by a dog or dogs." *Tennessee* law, under the sub-title "Shotguns for Small Game: Three-shell load limit, No. 2 shot or smaller." *Georgia* law, under Small Game and Varmints: "Firearms for hunting small game and non-game species shall be limited to shotguns with No. 4 shot or smaller, .22 rimfire rifles, the .30 cal. Army carbine, the .32-20, or any centerfire rifles with bore diameter of .257 or smaller, all caliber pistols, muzzleloading firearms and long bows, except on management areas."

But your state game and fish department, no matter its official title, is more than just a wily game warden hiding behind the nearest tree to grab you if you do something wrong. Other than just issuing hunting regulations, this agency is a goldmine of valuable information. You can, as one example, find where certain species are most abundant in the state, or which lands are open to public hunting. Many issue how-to booklets which can be had free or for a nominal charge. You help fund the agency and you should take advantage of what it has to offer. That is, actually, its function, to serve the public.

Listed below are the respective state game and fish departments, plus comparable agencies in Canadian provinces:

ALABAMA

Department of Conservation, Game & Fish Division, Montgomery, Alabama 36104.

ALASKA

Department of Fish and Game, Subport Building, Juneau, Alaska 99801.

ARIZONA

Game and Fish Department, 2222 West Greenway Road, Phoenix, Arizona 85023.

ARKANSAS

Game and Fish Commission, Game and Fish Building, Little Rock, Arkansas 72201.

CALIFORNIA

Department of Game and Fish, 1416 Ninth Street, Sacramento, California 95814.

COLORADO

Division of Game, Fish & Parks, 6060 Broadway, Denver, Colorado 80216.

CONNECTICUT

Board of Fisheries and Game, State Office Building, Hartford, Connecticut 06115.

DELAWARE

Department of Natural Resources & Environmental Control, Division of Fish & Wildlife, Dover, Delaware 19901.

FLORIDA

Division of Game and Fresh Water Fish, 620 South Meridian, Tallahassee, Florida 32304.

GEORGIA

Game and Fish Commission, 270 Washington Street S.W., Atlanta, Georgia 30334.

HAWAII

Division of Fish & Game, 530 Hotel Street, Honolulu, Hawaii 96813.

IDAHO

Fish and Game Department, P.O. Box 25, Boise, Idaho 83707.

ILLINOIS

Department of Conservation, State Office Building, Springfield, Illinois 62706.

INDIANA

Division of Fish and Wildlife, 607 State Office Building, Indianapolis, Indiana 46106.

IOWA

State Conservation Commission, State Office Building, 300 Fourth Street, Des Moines, Iowa 50319.

KANSAS

Forestry, Fish and Game Commission, P.O. Box 1028, Pratt, Kansas 67124.

KENTUCKY

Department of Fish & Wildlife Resources, State Office Building Annex, Frankfort, Kentucky 40601.

LOUISIANA

Wild Life & Fisheries Commission, P.O. Box 44095, Capitol Station, Baton Rouge, Louisiana 70804.

MAINE

Department of Inland Fisheries and Game, State Office Building, Augusta, Maine 04330.

MARYLAND

Department of Natural Resources, Fish & Wildlife Administration, State Office Building, Annapolis, Maryland 21401.

MASSACHUSETTS
Division of Fisheries and Game, 100 Cambridge Street, Boston, Massachusetts 02202.

MICHIGAN
Department of Natural Resources, Stevens T. Mason Building, Lansing, Michigan 48926.

MINNESOTA
Department of Conservation, 301 Centennial Building, St. Paul, Minnesota 55101.

MISSISSIPPI
Game and Fisheries Division, P.O. Box 451, Jackson, Mississippi 39205.

MISSOURI
Department of Conservation, P.O. Box 180, Jefferson City, Missouri 65101.

MONTANA
Fish and Game Department, Helena, Montana 59601.

NEBRASKA
Game and Parks Commission, State Capitol, Lincoln, Nebraska 68509.

NEVADA
Department of Fish and Game, P.O. Box 10678, Reno, Nevada 89502.

NEW HAMPSHIRE
Game and Fish Department, 34 Bridge Street, Concord, New Hampshire 03301.

NEW JERSEY
Division of Fish, Game and Shell Fisheries, P.O. Box 1809, Trenton, New Jersey 08625.

NEW MEXICO
Department of Game and Fish, State Capitol, Santa Fe, New Mexico 87501.

NEW YORK
Department of Environmental Conservation, Albany, New York 12201.

NORTH CAROLINA
Wildlife Resources Commission, P.O. Box 2919, Raleigh, North Carolina 27602.

NORTH DAKOTA
Game and Fish Department, 103½ South Third Street, Bismarck, North Dakota 58501.

OHIO
Department of Natural Resources, 1500 Dublin Road, Columbus, Ohio 43215.

OKLAHOMA
Department of Wildlife Conservation, 1801 North Lincoln, Oklahoma City, Oklahoma 73105.

OREGON
State Game Commission, P.O. Box 3503, Portland, Oregon 97208.

PENNSYLVANIA
Game Commission, P.O. Box 1567, Harrisburg, Pennsylvania 17120.

RHODE ISLAND
Division of Fish and Wildlife, 83 Park Street, Providence, Rhode Island 02903.

SOUTH CAROLINA

Wildlife Resources Department, P.O. Box 167, Columbia, South Carolina 29209.

SOUTH DAKOTA

Department of Game, Fish & Parks, State Office Building #1, Pierre, South Dakota 57501.

TENNESSEE

Game and Fish Commission, P.O. Box 9400, Nashville, Tennessee 37220.

TEXAS

Parks & Wildlife Department, John H. Reagan State Building, Austin, Texas 78701.

UTAH

Division of Fish and Game, 1596 West North Temple, Salt Lake City, Utah 84116.

VERMONT

Fish and Game Department, Montpelier, Vermont 05602.

VIRGINIA

Division of Game, P.O. Box 11104, Richmond, Virginia 23230.

WASHINGTON

Department of Game, 600 North Capitol Way, Olympia, Washington 98501.

WEST VIRGINIA

Department of Natural Resources, Wildlife Resources Division, Charleston, West Virginia 25305.

WISCONSIN

Department of Natural Resources, P.O. Box 450, Madison, Wisconsin 53701.

WYOMING

Game and Fish Commission, P.O. Box 1589, Cheyenne, Wyoming 82001.

CANADA

ALBERTA

Fish and Wildlife Division, Natural Resources Building, 109th Street & 99th Avenue, Edmonton, Alberta.

BRITISH COLUMBIA

Fishing and Wildlife Branch, Parliament Buildings, Victoria, British Columbia.

MANITOBA

Resource Management Division, Department of Mines, Res. & Env. Mgt., P.O. Box 11, Winnipeg, Manitoba.

NEW BRUNSWICK

Fish and Wildlife Branch, Department of Natural Resources, Fredericton, New Brunswick.

NEWFOUNDLAND

Wildlife Division of Tourist Development Office, Department of Mines, Agriculture & Resources, Confederation Building, St. John's, Newfoundland.

NORTHWEST TERRITORY

Department of Industry and Development, Government of Northwest Territories, Yellowknife, Northwest Territory.

NOVA SCOTIA

Department of Lands and Forest, P.O. Box 516, Kentville, Nova Scotia.

ONTARIO

Wildlife Branch, Ministry of Natural Resources, Toronto, Ontario.

QUEBEC

Quebec Wildlife Service, Department of Tourism, Fish and Game, Parliament Buildings, Quebec, Quebec.

SASKATCHEWAN

Tourist Branch, Department of Industry and Commerce, S.P.C. Building, Regina, Saskatchewan.

YUKON TERRITORY

Director of Game, Yukon Territorial Government, P.O. Box 2703, Whitehorse, Yukon Territory.

—R.T.

Index